UNREWARDING WEALTH

*The commercialization and collapse of agriculture
in a Spanish Basque town*

for
PILAR

UNREWARDING WEALTH

*The commercialization and collapse
of agriculture
in a Spanish Basque town*

DAVYDD J. GREENWOOD

Department of Anthropology, Cornell University, Ithaca, New York

CAMBRIDGE UNIVERSITY PRESS

CAMBRIDGE

LONDON · NEW YORK · MELBOURNE

Published by the Syndics of the Cambridge University Press
The Pitt Building, Trumpington Street, Cambridge CB2 1RP
Bentley House, 200 Euston Road, London NW1 2DB
32 East 57th Street, New York, NY 10022, USA
296 Beaconsfield Parade, Middle Park, Melbourne 3206, Australia

First published 1976

Typeset by Progressive Typographers, York, Pennsylvania
Printed in the United States of America by
Vail-Ballou Press, Inc., Binghamton, New York

Library of Congress Cataloging in Publication Data

Greenwood, Davydd J.

Unrewarding wealth.

Bibliography: p.

1. Agriculture – Economic aspects – Spain – Fuenterrabia
2. Fuenterrabia, Spain – Social conditions. I. Title.

HD2025.F8G7   338.1′0946′61   75-25429

ISBN 0-521-21021-6

CONTENTS

Contents

LIST OF TABLES AND FIGURES

TABLES

List of tables and figures

FIGURES

MAPS & ILLUSTRATIONS

PREFACE

My acquaintance with the Basques began with the many works of Don Julio Caro Baroja. His gentle yet firm guidance fundamentally altered my understanding of anthropology.

Fieldwork was a family affair. In addition to the usual acknowledgment of my wife and my son's forbearance under difficult conditions, I am in my wife's, Pilar Fernandez-Cañadas de Greenwood, debt for her constant appraisal of my understanding of the people of Fuenterrabia. Because she is from central Spain, she was able to define aspects of life in Fuenterrabia that were local in nature and to contrast them with practices common in other parts of Spain. To her the book is dedicated.

Many others assisted me during the research. The municipal officials in Fuenterrabia and the staff of the provincial branch of the Ministry of Finance were generous with their time and provided important information. Milagros Barcaíztegui Bidegain aided me in the provincial archives and Padre Andoni Lecuona instructed me in some of the accounting techniques I have used. Liborio Aramburu introduced me to Fuenterrabia, made the maps, and provided an immense amount of information about farm life. Padre Ladislao de Vidania was a most enthusiastic guide to Basque culture.

The various drafts of this study have been improved by the comments of L. Keith Brown, Sidney Mintz, David Penny, Julius Rubin, Harold Schneider, Arthur Tuden, Douglas White, and two anonymous readers. William Douglass read and criticized the manuscript twice and, through the Basque Studies Program of the University of Nevada at Reno, he provided support for a stay in Reno from which the study emerged much improved.

Walter H. Lippincott, Jr., Cambridge's editor, gave me excellent suggestions for improving the manuscript and provided encouragement when it was much needed.

The final typing was aptly handled by Coraleen Rooney.

Support for the study came entirely from Public Health Service

Predoctoral Grants 5-F1-MH-29, 027-03 and MH-11, 335-01 through the National Institute of Mental Health.

Finally, to the farmers of Fuenterrabia, I offer this book as a partial portrait of their struggles and achievements. Their distrust of my motives was always expressed gently and the few friendships my family and I formed with them are an enduring part of our lives.

December, 1975   D. J. Greenwood

1

The problem and the methods

That man does not live by bread alone is a maxim asserting that economic gain is not the sole object of our lives. Most of us would subscribe to the truth of this maxim, yet we forget it when the economic changes taking place in this century are analyzed and when policies to promote economic development are formulated. Partly this is a result of our attempts to simplify the complex changes we observe so that we may comprehend them better; we make an analysis "as if" economic gain were the object of most people's daily activities. Many analysts and policymakers subscribe to a philosophy of history in which the role of the economy is seen to be large and the direction of history is understood to be toward greater reliance on motives of economic gain in all areas of activity. These simplifying assumptions are convenient; however, they relegate nonprofit activities to the background, and the consideration of their importance to those we have come to call "humanists."

If they are to be useful, simplifying assumptions must facilitate rather than obstruct analysis. The argument of this book is that these assumptions are wrong, misleading both the analysts of capitalism and the development policymakers. They are wrong because they do too much violence to the complex motives underlying human behavior, a complexity that cannot be reduced to a single goal. Ways must be developed to cope better with this complexity; this book is my attempt to do so.

The Basque farmers studied here are neither non-Western nor particularly exotic; thus the study can qualify as a test of the utility of occidental ideas in an analysis of behavior of occidental people. By demonstrating that the interpretation of economic change in the West solely in terms of motives of economic gain is inadequate, I also imply that transfer of this interpretation to non-Western situations presents an even greater distortion.

The commercialization of farming and the resultant rural depopulation in a coastal Spanish Basque municipality are my subject. I follow the changes in farming as commercialization occurs in response to industrialization and international tourism, eventually resulting in rural depopulation and the closing of profitable farms. I use quantitative evidence about farming and a cultural interpretation of farm life, since only an explanation including both types of data can account for the events that took place here during this century. The farmers have considerable economic acumen and operate successful farms at high profit rates and levels, yet they are abandoning agriculture in ever-increasing numbers and moving into lower-paying and perhaps less secure urban jobs. Neither an invocation of "economic man" nor of the "traditionalist farmer" can explain this. I render an interpretation combining economic and cultural variables in a single economic anthropological framework.

Many studies of rural population movements have concentrated on the destinations of the migrants and on the problems they encounter when they arrive at their destinations, whereas my study focuses on the rural economy and society out of which the people are moving. Because of the complex mix of agricultural success followed by agricultural collapse, this study has relevance to the analysis of agricultural development, the cultural dimensions of population movements, and urbanization. Furthermore, it exposes some errors in assumptions underlying current economic policies.

From a methodological point of view, the charter of the study is that it combines, in a single framework, extensive quantitative data with a detailed cultural analysis. Though no single aspect of the farm situation is exhaustively treated, the systematic combination of quantitative and cultural analysis yields some insight into the interaction between pecuniary and nonpecuniary considerations in the evolution of modern Basque agriculture in one municipality, and raises some questions about the interpretation of agricultural development in general.

The setting and the problem

In a century of realism, the Basques of northern Spain and southern France retain an aura of mystery. In their mountainous redoubt, they have withstood the irruptions of a variety of empires and nations, and have retained their language and their unique constellation of blood group antigens. Their uniqueness long ago gave rise to an abiding interest in Basque origins and customs, ranging from popular magazine articles to a considerable accumulation of international scholarship. Such mysteries provide an impetus to scholarship but they also create some difficulties for the student. Emphasis on Basque uniqueness overlooks the fundamental reality that, in spite of language and serology, the Basques are culturally Europeans (Caro Baroja, 1967:7,10). Their technology, their social organization, and their beliefs fit comfortably into the range of variation found in Europe.

That they are Europeans does not lessen their importance. Any study of developments in the Basque country need not be limited to explaining the Basque "enigma;" it can also help to understand phenomena important throughout contemporary Europe–industrialization, international tourism, rural depopulation, and urbanization. We must also remember that the ways in which these developments occurred in the Basque country have evoked unique adaptations in the context of cultural characteristics that are peculiarly Basque. This study is, then, both an analysis of the current history of agricultural development and of the unique ways in which the Basques have dealt with it.

The specific subject is the twentieth-century evolution of agriculture in Fuenterrabia, Guipúzcoa in the Spanish Basque country. I document and interpret the shift from subsistence-oriented family farming to commercial family farming, accompanied by the present period of rural depopulation. By depicting the adaptive efforts of a number of Basque farmers in a rapidly changing world, I am able to explain how the Basque culture and the economic capabilities of the Basque farmers account for both their agricultural success and their abandonment of farming.

The Basque farmers are not dealing with a set of circumstances unique to them; they are responding to the effects of international industrialization, tourism, and agricultural commercialization as they have impinged on the Basque country. This particular case shows that the relationship between these phenomena is even more complex than is often assumed. The particular mixture of pecuniary and nonpecuniary goals suggests questions for further research which I will raise throughout the book.

Fuenterrabia itself is a coastal municipality. In 1969 it had about 10,000 inhabitants, consisting of an urban nucleus surrounded by 168 farms and some 200 villas which dot the mountainous landscape (see map on p. 4). It is a small place, the land surface being a little over 24.5 square kilometers, or about 9.5 square miles. (A conversion table for measurements and currency appears in the Appendix.)

Formed by the mountain spine of the peninsula and its sandy skirt which is flanked by the Bidasoa River, the municipality has little flat land beyond that in the river bottom area. It is a green world. Grass, alfalfa, mountain fern, pines, gardens, fruit trees in

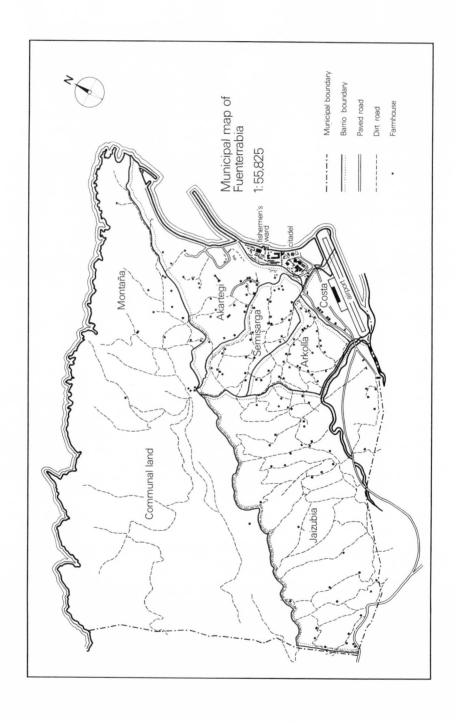

Municipal map of
Fuenterrabia

1:55,825

Municipal boundary
Barrio boundary
Paved road
Dirt road
Farmhouse

Montaña

Akartegi

fishermen's
ward

citadel

Semisarga

Costa

airport

Arkolla

Communal land

Jaizubia

N

this rainy, temperate climate, each add their own hue. With few frosts and little snow, even the winters are green. The farms are dispersed over a moderately rugged landscape, some within shouting distance and yet far apart because of the watercourses separating them. Only a few farmers are fortunate enough to have cultivatible flat land.

Mount Jaizkibel, which dominates the municipality, at one time was covered with hardwood trees. The rest of the land was covered with fruit trees, there being only an occasional open field. Now the mountain is covered with pine plantations interspersed with mountain fern—signs of human activity. The hardwood and fruit trees are practically gone from the rest of the land, having given way to the cultivated fields which are the basis of the intensive commercial agriculture presently practiced. These receding fruit trees were not the original vegetation, since moving further back into history, we see the municipality blanketed with vines which gave a sour grape to make Basque wine called *txakoli*. The only trees left are those lining the watercourses eroded in the face of the mountain.

The Basques have even changed the soil itself. Years of patient labor have transformed many hectares of clay soil into sandy loams, a change once made necessary by the climate and exigencies of subsistence, and now by the exigencies of the commercial markets. In the river bottom nearly 90 ha. of sand bars had been reclaimed and were intensively cultivated until recently. This reclamation is a silent reminder of the need for land that had gripped this municipality until about 15 years ago; the sudden abandonment disappoints the old farmers who helped to reclaim the land. Little of the landscape, then, is natural since man has intervened everywhere; this is an utterly domesticated landscape.

Overlooking the rural scene from one of the foothills of the Jaizkibel is a fortified town of impressive proportions. The old city of Fuenterrabia is enclosed by 30-foot walls, originally surrounded by moats crossed by two drawbridges. Though the exact date of first fortification is unknown, Fuenterrabia was already fortified when the reigns of Catholic kings began in the fifteenth century. They ordered the walls strengthened as part of their national defense policy.

Within the walls, narrow cobblestone streets of dark houses with carved eaves and shields of nobility wind upward toward the *plaza de armas* dominated by Charles the Fifth's fortress. Beside this is the church tower which serves the faithful with its bells, and often gave warning of French invasions.

Panoramic view of Fuenterrabia's citadel.

Once segregated into artisans', soldiers', and nobles' quarters, much of the old town was turned to rubble by sieges throughout the eighteenth and nineteenth centuries. By 1850, half the dwellings were in ruins, as were the walls.

The fishermen and farmers have always lived outside the walls. Long famous for their exploits as whalers in the Bay of Biscay, the fishermen lived in small dwellings along the beach and around the port. The location of the small, shallow port has moved more than once, but now there is a permanently established fishermen's ward at the base of the city walls. It is a colorful and lively place filled with bars, brightly painted houses, and a large variety of stores; it is the hub of Fuenterrabia's present urban life.

Fishing is a reasonably lucrative commercial endeavor, especially since the advent of tourism and rapid, refrigerated transport. An enormous variety of ocean fish is available throughout the year. The fishermen do not venture far out these days; the only remembrances of whaling days and trips to Terra Nova are an old city coat of arms depicting a whale and the annual whaleboat races, a major sports attraction in the Basque country. Much of the ward is built on reclaimed land, but in spite of its quaint appearance, its present buildings are not very old. Its straight streets, tree-lined *alameda*, and colorful houses are largely a result of planned urbanization during the last 200 years.

Blanca-enea, example of Basque farm architecture.

Beyond and behind all this lie the farms, called *caseríos* in Spanish and *baserriak* in Basque. They are family farms and are found in a variety of settlement patterns throughout the Basque country. These range from farmhouses clustered in a center with the farmland surrounding the nucleus, to single, dispersed farms on their own land (Caro Baroja, 1958:21–48; Douglass, 1967:85–115). The farmland itself may consist of a single unit or of several separate parcels. In Fuenterrabia, the 168 farms that now operate are dispersed, with each sitting on its own land. The main body of that land is located around the house. Some farms have additional small plots of land, ranging from 0.10 ha. to 1.50 ha., located in the river bottom areas of the municipality. A few have mountain lands used for lumber, firewood, and mountain fern for cattle bedding.

While the variety of farm sizes, topography, and soil types makes the presentation of a typical farm useless, there are some characteristics which most farms share. The farmhouse and stable are combined into one building, with the stable on the ground floor and the living area on the second. In some cases, the kitchen is also on the ground floor. All farm buildings are made of stone and mortar covered with lime. The floors and roof supports are wood and the roofs are tiled. The ground floor is usually packed dirt, though many farmers have put in cement floors. The second

Matute-enea, a small farmhouse overlooking a one-acre farm.

floor always has a wood balcony which is supported by the extensions of the same beams that support the floors. The balconies face south to avoid the force of the north wind. In addition, the roof peak is used as an attic granary and storage area. All but one of the farms have had electricity for many years, many as early as 1925. There is running water in the houses on 129 farms. The houses vary considerably in size and elegance. These differences will be described later.

Farm sizes range between 0.14 ha. and 31.84 ha. There are all sizes between these extremes but the majority of the farms are under 3.8 ha. The importance of farm size will be analyzed later also.

The soils range from clay through artificially-transformed sandy loams to naturally-occurring sandy loams (see soil type map, p. 27). The transformed soils were made by adding sand and humus to clay soil over many years. Finally, there are about 90 ha. of reclaimed river bottom land.

All farms have the basic hand tools of agriculture such as the hoe, *laya* (Basque hand plow), shovel, pitchfork, scythe, sickle, and wheelbarrow. There are small power tillers on 54 farms and 32 have small power reapers. There are only 4 garden tractors, but all farms own or have access to Brabant wheeled, animal traction plows.

The labor force on farms is made up of one or two married couples of adjacent generations united by kinship to form a "domestic group" (Caro Baroja, 1958:261–82; Douglass, 1967:59–84). In calling this a "domestic group" and not a "stem family," I am following a usage suggested by Douglass. He notes that "in Basque society ego's married siblings and offspring are *not* excluded from his family concept which is not to say that they are regarded as a part of his domestic grouping" (Douglass, 1969:84, emphasis his). The household is a concept including the "constellation of dwellings, furnishings, agricultural implements, landholdings . . ." (Douglass, 1969:87). Finally, the domestic group "encompasses the persons who inhabit an *echea* [farmstead] and, hence, share the same life space, or persons who, while absent, retain the right to return and take up residence. Membership in the *echekoak* [domestic group] grouping may be obtained in one of four fashions: (1) descent, (2) marriage, (3) fictive kinship ties, and (4) consent" (Douglass, 1969:90). This defines the farm domestic groups better than the amorphous "stem family" concept. Thus only the domestic group–the social grouping living on the farms, or members retaining rights to return to them–is included in this study.

According to Basque cultural ideas, the maximum domestic group permitted on a single farm consists of an elder married couple and either spouse's unmarried siblings; a younger married couple made up of the chief heir, male or female, of the elder couple, his or her spouse, and their unmarried children. A few farms have hired laborers living in.

There are many permutations of this membership due to the dynamics of each family and their point in the domestic cycle. There is one farm with three generations of married couples living on it because of the longevity of the eldest couple. There are a few farms occupied exclusively by unmarried brothers, unmarried sisters, or childless couples. There are only two cases with more than one couple of the same generation living on the same farm. In both, the couples hold separate purses, live in separate apartments, and only one couple is involved in farming.

During the developmental cycle of a farm domestic group, the population of a farm may be reduced by the death of the elder couple to a single individual or married couple with or without children. A domestic group may also be reduced in size by infertile marriages or because all of the children remained single. However, there is no farm with less than two adults. Thus the domestic group is only moderately extended and alters in size over time. This exercises a strong effect on agricultural activities.

An aging farm family.

Basque farm life is difficult to describe briefly. The characteristics of the farm and the domestic group tend to merge into a
single social personality. Living on named, independent farms,
many over 200 years old, the domestic group members receive an
enduring social identity, generally being referred to by the name
of their farm rather than their surnames. The farm is felt to be an
outward sign of the character of the people who farm it, so that
agriculture is at once an enterprise and a way of life. The richness
or sterility of the soil, the design and condition of the house, the
amount of flat land, all become part of the social personality of
these farmers. Often the family names will be unknown even to
close neighbors.

Having access to a farm is one part of being a farmer; another is
getting an heir to carry the farm and the identity of the domestic
group into the future. To achieve this, the Basques do not divide
their lands among the heirs. Rather they are free to select one
child, male or female, who will marry and will take over the farm,
a practice at variance with the Spanish Civil Code. Other children
either receive money, an education, a dowry, or may stay on the
farm as long as they do not marry and are willing to submit to the
authority of the chief heir and his or her parents.

In choosing a chief heir the parents look for a quality of mind that they render in Spanish as *apego* to the land, a concept which combines a sort of love of and competence in farming. It is an aggressive kind of love of the land, because the relationship between the farmer and the land is difficult. The farmer extracts crops through a combination of wits, will, skill, and the characteristics of the farm. His efforts must be great because the land is broken and must be heavily fertilized. It is subject to ruining rains, hailstorms, and occasionally a killing frost. Struggle is the keynote; success in farming is nearly coterminous with economic and moral success in life, an external sign of inner worth and God's favor. Thus, domestic group identity, economic reward, and religion are all played out in the yearly agricultural cycle. The work is hard, but the work is life.

In the past, communal labor, haying, the collection of fern, and religious observances brought large groups of farmers together, but at present they gather on few occasions. Communal labor has fallen off; haying is done by machine; sawdust has replaced fern; and local churches are attended by mixed groups of factory workers, summer residents, and farmers and have lost their intimacy. In the past, larger groups met and celebrated a farm marriage. Weddings now gather only immediate kinsfolk, usually siblings of the parents of the married couple and their domestic groups. Funeral observances are mainly restricted to friends and kin of the deceased, while in the past an entire ward and occasionally the whole farming community would attend the rites.

Society here was and is class-divided and stratified. In addition to the distinction between tenant and owner farmers, there are absentee landlords. Some of these held as many as 15 farms each in Fuenterrabia, though now the largest single landowner has about 5 farms.

There were also lesser noble families with residences here; many of these were members of the military orders. One major noble family has had a residence and properties in Fuenterrabia for centuries. All these families were prominent in local and national military affairs and often held positions of authority in the municipal government. They were important links with the monarchy and national government. The soldiers garrisoned there also included people of a social category superior to the farmers.

In addition, a number of religious orders are located in Fuenterrabia. The Capuchins have a centuries'-old monastery and there have been a number of convents as well. Of course, the parish priest and his assistants were and are men of high social status locally.

Finally on a plane of class equality with the farmers, there were fishermen, smiths, coopers, and millers. Together with the farmers they formed the core of the lower class.

Presently social stratification has become more complex. Many of the noble families have disappeared, and have been replaced by wealthy, and occasionally titled summer residents having a clear social superiority over the farmers, fishermen, and artisans. The individuals and corporations involved in the development of tourism, especially in house and apartment construction, have proliferated. They are wealthy, prominent, and powerful. A large corporation which bought 60 hectares of land for a country club and a housing development is perhaps the biggest political force in the municipality now. The service occupations and small stores, bars, and restaurants have multiplied rapidly as tourism has developed. These form the core of an urban middle class, along with the many bank employees, notaries, and civil servants now working in Fuenterrabia.

It is a complex, stratified community, in which the farmers have always been part of the lower class. Social deference, patronage, and dependency have always been important. However, Fuenterrabia is not a typical example of a stratified European community for two reasons. First, before the imposition of national legal codes on Guipúzcoa in the late nineteenth century, the province had its own law and government. Each community, on the basis of population, elected representatives to a provincial junta at which major governmental matters were taken up. Thus there was an element of representative government.

Perhaps more significant is the second reason, the Basque concept of "collective nobility" which will be described in detail in Chapter 4. This idea asserts that, regardless of differences in social station, all native born Guipuzcoans are of pure Christian blood and thus, by definition, "noble." This idea was widespread in the Basque country and a few other areas of the north. It does not deny differences of wealth or power, but it asserts a fundamental equality of all persons born in a particular place.

The social stratification of the community thus was mediated somewhat by representative government and by the idea of the common nobility of all community members. Some of these ideas about equality still exist and form a crucial part of my explanation of rural depopulation. They certainly are an important part of the present generation of farmers' pride in their agrarian calling. However, the young Basques, born on farms, generally do not accept their parents' view of farming, and farm abandonment is becoming a severe problem. The old farming life-style is waning.

A summary of these changes between 1920 and 1969 provides an introduction to the analysis to follow. The year 1920 was picked because there is a very detailed local census for that year, complete with data on land tenure. Municipal data from 1913 indicates this period to be the beginning of the development of tourism, a critical factor here. It is accessible through the minds of the aged, who provided a wealth of data. Finally it begins after the First World War and before the Spanish Civil War which deeply affected the local economy. What follows is a sketch of Fuenterrabia's history, emphasizing the period from 1920 to 1969.

A date for the founding of Fuenterrabia is not available, but it was probably an inhabited area in Roman times. The municipality was separated from San Sebastián and given an independent charter by Alfonso VIII in 1203, indicating the existence of an organized population.

The military importance of the city lay in its location relative to France and its dominance of the Bidasoa River. The city had been fortified and refortified. Many attempts were made to make the Bidasoa navigable far inland, but they were unsuccessful, and the river never gained a commercial importance to match its military significance. The walled citadel remained militarily important during the fifteenth, sixteenth, and seventeenth centuries in the constant diplomatic and military manipulations over the location of the French-Spanish border.

The *plaza de armas* was, at one time, under the jurisdiction of a military governor and was defended by a garrison of government troops. Subjected to many sieges, the most famous in 1638, the town was lost and won many times, earning at different times the honorific titles and privileges which today make up its full name—*Muy noble, muy leal, muy valerosa y siempre fiel Ciudad de Fuenterrabia*. At the end of the eighteenth century it began to lose importance because, surrounded by hills, it fell prey to the improved cannons of the day. By 1800 the city was a shambles, and after the Napoleonic invasion and the Carlist Wars it was reduced to rubble. So Fuenterrabia entered the twentieth century as a town of poor farmers and fishermen with little, other than the ruined citadel, to show for its military past. The soldiers and most of the rich families had left; the port had little commercial activity; and day-to-day subsistence was the main concern of the populace.

While this is a study of the commercialization of subsistence agriculture between 1920 and 1969, an important caveat must be entered. During the long era of Fuenterrabia's military importance, local farmers sold produce to the soldiers, to the fishermen, and artisans living in the urban nucleus. Cider, grapes, corn, beans, and potatoes have been cash crops for centuries. Though they did not rely fully on the market for their income, cash undoubtedly played a significant role in the farmers' lives from the fifteenth through the nineteenth centuries.

The decline of the military importance of the town, the exodus of many of the wealthy families, and the general decline of the Spanish economy pushed farmers toward greater emphasis on subsistence activities. For 1920, the archives and the old Basques I talked to present a picture of subsistence agriculture with very minor cash involvements. In a sense, this period was the worst economic depression the farmers of Fuenterrabia had suffered in 400 years.

I emphasize this since it is tempting to view commercialization as developing irreversibly out of subsistence agriculture. The pattern here is one of centuries of moderate commercial involvements, then a decline into nearly total subsistence farming, and finally the development of fully commercialized agriculture after about 1955. It is not a unidirectional movement.

Each century brought its own social and economic upheavals to Fuenterrabia, but the farm landscape has been most radically altered by events in this century. Until about 1920, the family farms worked by domestic groups were devoted to subsistence agriculture and the cultivation of apple trees. Corn and beans were raised for human consumption, along with potatoes and a few vegetables. The farmers kept one or two cows for milking and for plowing, and subsisted on a diet of corn cakes, vegetable stew, and milk. From the apple trees they made cider to drink, and for their small cash revenues, they sold apples and an occasional calf.

Although at this time the farmers' way of life fit under the general rubric of peasant agriculture, the processes that were to do away with it had already begun. Most farmers always sought ways of making cash to supplement subsistence, meet debts, save for dowries, and perhaps to buy a farm or farm equipment. The new emergence of commercialism proved to be the basis for the gradual evolution of the completely commercial farming situation found in 1969.[1]

The industrial development of the neighboring municipality of Irún began around 1920. It recently has achieved rather large proportions, and has provided a strong stimulus to agriculture in Fuenterrabia. The factories attracted people to the area and the increased population of Irún has raised the demand for milk, meat, and vegetables. By the mid-1920s some of the farmers from Fuenterrabia were taking milk to customers in Irún and sending it by train to San Sebastián. Some customers began to ask for vegetables as well and gradually the farmers increased vegetable and milk production to meet the demand.

The cash earned allowed purchase of the farms from the landlords, along with purchase of equipment. Total production increased gradually as the idea that milk and vegetables could be depended on for cash earnings spread. Gardening was important for the very small farms because it required only small parcels of land and provided a dependable cash income. Before long the small farms specialized more in gardening and were able to eliminate some of the livestock. The bigger farms tended to emphasize cattle and to depend on milk and meat production for cash income.

Other events also played a critical role. The fiscal anemia of the Spanish government in the 1920s led the provincial authorities to tax cider. Income from cider was small and the tax further reduced it. Soon the apple trees began to give way to the more profitable meadows and garden plots; by 1945 apples had ceased to be an important crop.

Another important and colorful influence on the local economy was contraband. During the 1940s and 1950s the international market conditions and tariffs made contraband the biggest enterprise along the French-Spanish border. Most farmers were deeply involved in it. Items ranging from watches to car chassis and grand pianos were moved across the border at night, producing money and a wealth of lively stories about scrapes with the border guards. This dangerous enterprise pumped capital into the farm economy, allowing people to purchase farms and machinery and to take advantage of the improving market for produce.

Both the Spanish Civil War and World War II had local effects. Though Irún was virtually destroyed in the Civil War, Fuenterrabia was hardly touched. The farmers who were not called up survived the war by returning to their subsistence mode of farming of a few years before. When the Civil War was followed by famine in Spain and the disruptions of World War II, the farmers' lot improved. Food commanded high prices in the best seller's market in living memory. This period of solid demand again increased the commercialization of farming and increased production volume.

The final and most decisive influence on the local economy has been national and international tourism (see Greenwood, 1972). Fuenterrabia has had two distinct types of tourism. In the nineteenth century Guipúzcoa was the summer playground for Spain's royalty and hence for the aristocracy and high-level functionaries as well. By 1913 there were over 30 large summer villas built on what had been farmland. Though the royalty was subsequently eclipsed, the association of this area with upper-class ways has continued, and the desire of the rich to summer here is seen in their steady demand for land for summer homes. Not a few upwardly mobile Spaniards also summer here to enhance their prestige, sometimes living beyond their means to do so.

The second kind of tourism is mainly the post-World War II phenomenon of mass tourism. Large numbers of middle-class Spanish and French tourists flock to the Basque country during the summer, quadrupling the population of Fuenterrabia. This tourism has created a sharp seasonal demand for meat, milk, and vegetables, resulting in high prices and large sales volumes. The farmers, already commercialized, began to regard this seasonal demand as a major income source. Gardening, particularly, can be exploited to produce large amounts of vegetables at specific times, though of course considerable farming skill is required to get the crop to market at the right time. Since about 1955, farmers have planted larger plots of vegetables and have aimed for the months of July and August. With high returns nearly a certainty, they have been willing to invest heavily in machinery and in chemical fertilizers. They are alert to new ways to increase productivity.

Mass tourism has also created an enormous demand for summer vacation apartments. This has stimulated Fuenterrabia's construction industry, created new jobs for artisans, and has resulted in the proliferation of bars, clubs, shops, and service occupations of every kind. In short, the growth of industry and population created an expanded market for farm produce which was met by increasing devotion of resources to production for cash.

Recently the increasing demand for foodstuffs has raised the price of local produce to the point that large-scale truck farmers from outside the local market area have been attracted into the market, causing a slight downward adjustment of profits. The ultimate effect of this on local agriculture is not yet clear. Industrialization and tourism, which stimulated agriculture by increasing the demand for produce, have also bid up the value of farmland to extremely high levels. Local industry provides an alternative source of employment, and rapid movement of farm labor into these relatively low-paying jobs has created an acute scarcity of wage labor in farming. The profitability of farming has not kept people on the farms.

At present farming is fully commercialized. Dairying and the raising of beef are carried on with the aid of power equipment, factory feeds, and selective breeding. Gardening makes use of machinery, improved seeds, constant application of chemicals, and careful attention to consumer preferences. The farms are businesses, deeply involved in local, national, and even international markets.

In 1969, 84 of the 168 farms relied on dairying and/or beef raising entirely for their income, 9 relied solely on gardening, and 67 combined cattle and gardening. All but 5 farms produced enough vegetables for home consumption and all but 9 produced at least the milk they consume. These farms are a far cry from the subsistence farms of only 50 years earlier.

Another trend developed in farming along with this commercialization. In 1920 there were 256 farms, but only 168 in 1969. Since about 1946, farms have been closing down and there has been a general rural depopulation; this process has speeded up greatly since 1960. Yet an economic analysis of farming between 1950 and 1969 and my detailed quantitative study from September, 1968 to August, 1969 demonstrate beyond doubt, that agricultural profit rates and levels are high, and that the farmer's standard of living is generally superior to that of the urban factory worker. Still, the farmers are leaving and the time when farming will disappear entirely seems to be drawing close.

Clearly, while Fuenterrabia has a farm economy, it is not and has never been an exclusively agrarian town. Even during the period of subsistence farming, only 35 percent of the municipal population lived on farms. The commercialization of agriculture and the present rural exodus have occurred in the immediate context of the local fishing economy, industrialization, and the development of tourism. It is specifically the interactions between industrialization, tourism, and agriculture that interest me here as they occur within this municipality. Other studies (Douglass, 1971, 1975) deal with the responses of more completely agrarian communities to these conditions.

In Fuenterrabia then, peasant farmers have commercialized their farms successfully and now earn high profits, allowing them an excellent standard of living, yet they are abandoning agriculture for lower-paying urban jobs. This apparent paradox neatly raises the problem of the relationship between economic maximization and other cultural goals, and argues that the latter cannot be ignored in our thinking about economic development.

How is the Basques' decision to abandon farming for factory work to be explained? This book is my attempt to answer that question and to show some of the implications of my answer for research related to economic development.

In the following chapters I contend that the successful commercialization of agriculture shows that the Basques have the ability to perceive avenues of economic gain and to exploit them profitably. In demonstrating that they are leaving agriculture when profits are high, I eliminate a common explanation of rural exodus. I devote much space to proving this point with quantitative evidence, because my analysis revolves around their leaving high profits behind. To explain this apparent paradox, I point to farm abandonment's nonpecuniary side. I argue that the farmers are abandoning agriculture because it no longer satisfies their ideals of dignity in work. These ideals have a long history in the Basque country, and the Basques are willing to sacrifice known economic rewards to retain them. In addition, the increased value of land and other pressures created by commercial involvement have exacerbated latent conflicts in the Basque systems of inheritance of land and succession to authority. These conflicts make the urban alternative attractive to many young people. In the general context of minimal governmental support for farming, the burgeoning tourist industry, and the idealization of urban living, farming would seem to have no future in Fuenterrabia.

This case shows that a rethinking of the complex interactions between agricultural development and rural depopulation is needed; the changes in Fuenterrabia have taken directions not at all predictable from the pecuniary viewpoint. By establishing that farmers with a capacity for economic maximization suspend the pecuniary motives in favor of other considerations, I contend that any model of the commercialization of peasant agriculture must be a reasoned blend of economic and cultural elements. Total reliance on a pecuniary interpretation renders this example of rural depopulation unintelligible; exclusive emphasis on cultural elements disguises the capabilities of the farmers as economic maximizers. Thus the most general implication of this work is that the Basque farmers' behavior can only be comprehended if we add more dimensions to our models of commercializing peasant agriculture. The complex behavior of these farmers, the people "on the ground," so often overlooked by grand theories of development or of culture, does not yield up meaning to unidimensional models.

Having recognized that this complex behavior cannot be understood through a monocausal model, we arrive at a theoretical debate in the study of economic anthropology–the controversy between the "formalists" and the "substantivists." The nub of this debate is a differing understanding of human nature. The formalists hold that most important aspects of human behavior can be analyzed in terms of maximization of gains. Hence, they argue that many of the tools of formal economic analysis, clearly a highly developed form of maximization theory, are applicable to all societies.

The substantivists counter this with a vision of human nature in which the maximization of economic gains is the exception rather than the rule. In the extreme form, they argue that only when market systems coerce people into maximizing economically, will they do so. From this, they insist that the tools of formal economic analysis are only applicable to market-integrated societies and that entirely different tools must be developed to analyze behavior in societies that are not market-integrated. Because of the polemical tone of this debate, many students of economic anthropology feel constrained to choose between the formalist tools with their emphasis on maximization and the substantivist ones with their focus on the institutional and cultural contexts that organize economic activity.[2]

In studying a Western case I face a peculiar dilemma. Both camps agree that formal economic analysis is capable of explaining human behavior in market-integrated societies such as Fuenterrabia. However, neither side is clear about the relevance of the substantivist tools to this kind of case. Yet , as will be demonstrated in this study, the behavior of Fuenterrabia's farmers cannot be understood by relying solely on formalist analysis. By taking this argument into the context of a society fully integrated into the capitalist market system, I hope to show some of the advantages and limitations of both formalist and substantivist tools and to repudiate, as a gross oversimplification of the human condition in all societies, the polemically enforced choice between two complementary approaches. As far as I know, this study is the only attempt to apply systematically both formal and substantive approaches to the same data and to compare and combine the interpretations each is capable of generating.

This combined approach is not generated by a concern with the elaboration of theories; my interest is in explaining what has happened in Fuenterrabia. I could have dealt with the farmers' new preference for urban living by simply asserting that they value urban living more highly; hence they maximize what they value most. However, I limit maximization to pecuniary matters, seeing little value in broadening it to include the pursuit of all goals. To say that the farmers leave because they value urban living more highly is patently true, but because I am interested in portraying the exact reasons why they have come to value the urban alternative more highly, I render my interpretation in specific institutional and cultural terms. I deem it more important to attend to the specifics of Basque culture and social organization than to decide whether or not to bracket them all away under maximization.

It would have been equally possible to analyze these changes in institutional and cultural terms alone, ignoring the questions of economic maximization or at least relegating them to a secondary position. But this would have required me to overlook the strength of their pecuniary motivations and their remarkable economic acumen. This too would have resulted in an inadequate analysis.

Bearing this combined approach in mind, let us turn to the plan of this study which is as follows. The first part provides a detailed formal analysis of the economics of agriculture in Fuenterrabia in 1968–1969, compared with a reconstructed version of agriculture in 1920. Included is a general economic accounting of agriculture for 1968–1969 showing profit rates and levels and comparing them in dairying, beef raising, and gardening. An analysis of variance of the distribution of the factors of production by specialization is made in relation to the accounting. The rest of the book discusses those aspects of Fuenterrabia's agricultural history not explicable in formal economic terms alone. A substantive analysis of the economy, including the cultural goals of the farmers and other conditions affecting their economic activity, is elaborated to account for rural depopulation in the context of high profits. Finally, I make the conclusions more concrete by providing the histories and accounts for six farms to support and expand my basic argument.

It is necessary to point out that the sequence of the analysis does not reflect increasing causal importance. That is to say, the substantive analysis does not appear at the end because it explains more of what is happening in Fuenterrabia. All of the elements in the argument are equally important and deserve equal attention.

For the many nonanthropologists interested in the subject of agricultural commercialization, I should provide a brief statement of the general position from which this analysis has been made.

Two major themes have dominated the study of peasant economics in the last 30 years or so. One variety specifically deemphasizes economic maximization in peasant society and examines the constraints that noneconomic factors impose. The other, dealing with the flexibility and success of peasant economies, has stressed peasants' ability to maximize economically, in spite of the constraints imposed by noneconomic factors.[3] As noted above, the general tendency has been to adopt either one or the other of these views, though some important exceptions are works by Firth (1966) and Salisbury (1970). I have tried to carry on in their tradition.

This study also relates to the anthropological literature on peasants. Cultural anthropologists have been concerned with describing and defining the peasantry and analyzing their various internal and external institutional relationships (Potter, Diaz, and Foster, 1967; Wolf, 1966). The anthropologists who are interested in peasants can be divided into two major groups, one seeing the peasant as a traditionalist, and the other seeing him as a sly economic, social, and political man, usually oppressed by the state.[4] The Basque case suggests that peasants are neither traditionalists nor perfect strategists, but that they are a little of both. Such polar stereotypes do violence to the fundamental complexity of peasant behavior in particular and human behavior in general. In fact, peasants are best understood as elaborating an adaptation to their situation that contains a variety of elements (see also Greenwood, 1974).

For European agrarian history, this study suggests that a reinterpretation of rural depopulation may be needed. In contrast to the ideas of most economic development theories, depopulation in Fuenterrabia is caused neither by a change in values nor by low profits. The people of Fuenterrabia shift from rural to urban employment in order to retain basic cultural values that are centuries old. Rural depopulation here does not imply the modernization of values, but rather that rural life's ability to satisfy basic values has rapidly eroded. This could mean that keeping a segment of a national population in farming through reliance on market incentives might fail, for high profit levels fail to keep the Basques on the farms.

For rural development, this study supports a rising tide of opinion against the interpretation of the problems of underdeveloped agriculture as primarily technical bottlenecks, to be solved simply by better technology and administration. The ultimate failure of agricultural development in Fuenterrabia does not arise from technical difficulties, but from the little understood cultural implications of the developmental process itself.

Thus the efforts and adaptations of a few Basque farmers can have implications extending beyond the boundaries of the Basque country. The Basques can be both an enigma and a lesson.

Methods and definitions

While I do not wish to make a detailed elaboration of theory and methodology, I do intend, for a number of reasons, to be quite explicit about the framework I am employing. In the first place, the climate created by debates within economic anthropology itself requires explicit statements of theoretical orientation. Further, the primary, recognized need in economic anthropology now is for the operationalization of theory and the creation of "frame of reference" that others may employ usefully in their own work, on the model provided by Edward LeClair (1962). Due to the lack of operational approaches to follow, the present study is built around an approach developed in the fieldwork process itself. I do not claim it is in any way perfect, but it is systematic and parts may be of use to others.

Because my goal is to derive lessons about the world process of agricultural development from the history of Fuenterrabia, I present this theoretical and methodological digression so that my approach will be readily intelligible and its validity fairly judged across the gulfs of disciplinary independence. In all this, I have been guided by a desire to use only as much theory as is necessary and no more, the point being to understand Fuenterrabia and its potential significance.

Five basic suppositions underlie the study. First, reality, as far as social science is concerned, does not exist independently of knowledge of it. Second, social scientists perceive reality by means of various types of models, as do all human beings. Third, while it is possible to learn about native models of reality (as in the field of ethnoscience), I believe that native models cannot be reproduced exactly; all models in social science are the investigator's. Fourth, among the economic processes of production, distribution, and consumption, I place most emphasis on production. This emphasis is largely a result of the problem I have chosen, because I show that it is not the technical problems in production that are driving the farmers out, and because the producing unit is the basic social unit in which the decision to abandon farming is made. Attitudes toward work and the effect of commercial involvement on these farmers also loom large in my explanation of farm abandonment.

Finally, I think that models differ basically depending on the scale and type of data with which the investigator is working. Thus models of the behavior of small social units are quite different from models of statistical aggregations of behavioral outcomes. I will explain this below in detail.

I do not treat farming as a separate social system because neither the farms nor the aggregate studied constitute a bounded social system. I deal with one occupational specialization within one municipality, and the municipality itself is not a bounded social system either. Thus I am examining a particular aspect of the regional and national economy which impinges directly on the farms of this town and the farmers' responses to the resultant conditions. Consequently, while strong correlations do appear in the aggregate analysis, they are not the results of the equilibrating processes of a closed system.

This kind of approach is often called "social field" analysis, and in my case, is derived from a version taught to me by Emrys Peters.[5] It hinges on an analytical separation between the elements in a social field (such as the factors of production) and the means of access to them. The aim is to make behavior, in domestic groups and in the aggregate, intelligible in terms of the variety of elements and means of access to them. I describe the social field as an aggregate of the factors of production, the various means of access to them, and the distributions of factors having resulted from past activities. The analysis of individual farms explores the specific convergence of the elements and means of access, tracing the exact behavioral logic that links them together in the activities of each farm.

This approach is particularly useful to me because the temporal dimension fits in easily in the form of changes in the elements, in the means of access, and in the behaviors linking the elements in particular cases. The past itself is part of the social field because the distribution of the elements in the field is a product of past behavior.

Earlier I mentioned that the models used to analyze statistical aggregates are different from models used to analyze the operation of small social units. This is relevant here because I deal with profits and ideas and believe it is wrong to infer peoples' motives directly from the analysis of quantitative results of their behavior. It is equally wrong to study their motives in the absence of data about the aggregate results of their behavior.

In this case, looking at the data on aggregate production, one finds high profit levels and rural depopulation occurring together. Faced with this, it is tempting to explain it in terms of some commonsense behavior assumption, such as the "traditionality" of the farmers which impedes their perception of the high profits. Or one can simply make an educated guess. Perhaps the profits are caused by the depopulation or are somehow conditioned by it. As inadequate as the commonsense approaches are, they often form the basis of agricultural policy. Thus, we must go beyond the aggregate results of behavior and examine the situation as it appears to the people who live in it. In this case, only through an analysis of the institutions and ideas of the farmers does the relationship between high profits and rural depopulation make sense.

This creates a problem for economic development theorists and policy makers who tend to respond to national and international level problems with large-scale solutions. That agricultural policy must be built on detailed cultural analysis as well as on the analysis of aggregate statistics and national and regional institutions makes a hard job even harder.[6] But the record of failures in agricultural development indicates that too many dimensions of human behavior have been overlooked.

The approach I use is represented in Table 1.1. The study begins with formal-aggregate analysis including a socioeconomic census. This is followed by an analysis of the distribution of the factors of production among alternative enterprises, and a formal accounting for 1968–1969 which will be compared with data from 1920. From the distribution of the factors of production, inferences about changes in agriculture and the profitability of the present adaptation will be made, and the anomaly of farm abandonment during a period of high profits will be shown to exist.

Following this is a substantive-aggregate analysis using data about the jural rules and dominant cultural conceptions affecting production, the institutional problems surrounding inheritance and succession, and the Basque ideas about the dignity of work. In comparing these for 1920 and 1969, I will show changes in the

Table 1.1. *The dimensions of analysis*

	Unit of analysis	
Type of analysis	*Statistical aggregate*	*Domestic group*
Formal	distribution of factors of production among alternative uses, formal accounts	distribution of factors of production among alternative uses, formal accounts
Substantive	jural rules, legal codes, means of access to the factors of production, Basque ideas about work	family history, aspirations, idiosyncrasies

availability of various factors of production and changes in the operation of jural rules and other cultural ideas related to farm activities. Finally, a formal-domestic group and substantive-domestic group analysis will be combined in six farm case histories. The formal analysis includes detailed accounts for each farm and the substantive analysis discusses family history, aspirations, and idiosyncrasies. These cases serve to confirm the interpretations presented in more abstract form, and to provide a sense of the variety of paths ultimately leading to rural depopulation.

While this apparatus is not perfect, it permits me to combine a quantitative analysis of agricultural profitability with a cultural interpretation of farm abandonment and to show that the farmers know how to maximize economically but choose not to do so when this no longer satisfies their larger goals as Basques. To explain the abandonment of profitable farms, I do not need to brand them entrepreneurial incompetents or perfect economic men; I am free to reproduce a small part of the diverse motivations that guide their actions. It is this diversity that I want to emphasize. Methodology cannot be as complex as human behavior itself, but there is no reason why it should deny the existence of that complexity.

2

The agrarian history of Fuenterrabia from 1920 to 1969

THE FORMAL-AGGREGATE VIEW, PART I

The pattern of commercialization as it developed and the profit-responsive distribution of the factors of production among commercial specializations in Fuenterrabia are the subject. An analysis of covariance in the socio-economic census is presented as a test of the relationships I describe and is further summarized in a factor analysis. The following chapter details the techniques and costs of production and provides an accounting for farming in 1968–1969. This accounting serves to point out profit rates and levels and to describe more concretely the specializations.

Though it is not exhaustive, this analysis includes a great deal of specific information. This information is included to describe the situation better, to allow the reader to check my reasoning, and to provide data about Basque agriculture that can be compared with other cases. The utility of having extensive statistical data has been demonstrated by Tax (1953), Pospisil (1963), Salisbury (1962), and classically by Chayanov (1966), but we still have very little data to support or to challenge anthropological views on farm economies.

Factors of production in the twentieth century

Land

The peninsula on which Fuenterrabia is located points north-northeast (see map on p. 27). The populated area, with the exception of eight farms, is on the inland face and is flanked by the river delta through which the Bidasoa opens into the sea. This valley between Mount Jaizkibel and the Bidasoa is the largest in the province of Guipúzcoa.

The seaward side of the peninsula was originally sea floor and the spine was the point at which the sea floor faulted and rose. Thus the seaward side of the peninsula is unstratified soil of similar sandy composition throughout, while the inland side is stratified, including both clay and sandy loams (see Fig. 2.1). The peninsula

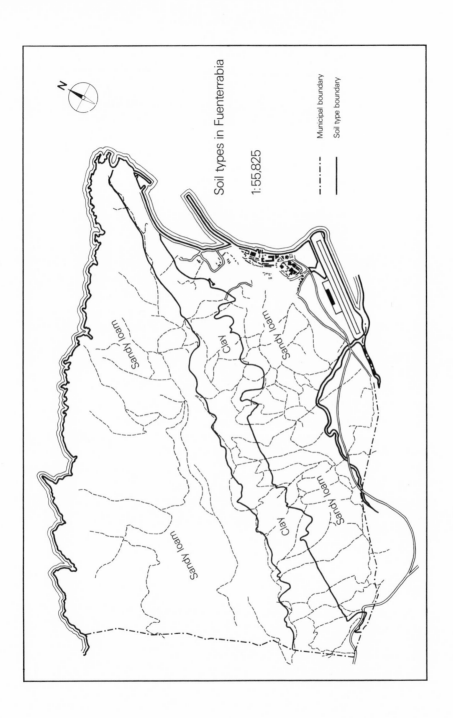

Soil types in Fuenterrabia

1:55,825

Municipal boundary

Soil type boundary

Sandy loam

Clay

Sandy loam

Sandy loam

Sandy loam

Clay

Sandy loam

N

protects the inland side from the force of the winter storms, while giving rise to the differing soil types.

Basically the soil types derived from this formation are two: clay and sandy loams. In discussing them I will move from right to left across Figure 2.1. (Note that this figure is merely a sketch, and is not drawn to scale.) The sandy loam is easily cultivatable even with hand tools. However, plants dry out rapidly and regular rainfall is a necessity for agriculture. This soil is important on about 20 farms. There are 1,125.50 ha. of it in the municipality.

The clay soil is hard to break with hand tools, though the Brabant plow can easily work it. It holds moisture well, but once saturated by continued rain, it requires from five to ten days to dry to a workable consistency, the exact time depending on the slope. Upon drying, it often forms a crust which impedes the development of plants. It is a poor soil to farm in this climate; there are 484.20 ha., all located in the inhabited area of the inland face.

Another band of sandy loam, derived from erosion of the higher sandy soil and clay bands, covers 658.70 ha.; the last type, with a very high sand content, arises from river deposits and land reclamation. Together there are 178.20 ha. of river-deposited soil and reclaimed land (see soil type map, p. 27).

To reclaim land the farmers brought in large stones by barge and laid them in the river bed. Sand and river silt were then piled on top of this until the land was above the water level at high tide. Small dikes and water runoff channels were built and then more soil was laid on top. Its real liability is during torrential inland rains when the river floods. There is great variation in the market value of this land. I will discuss this in detail later.

Fuenterrabia has abundant natural water supplies, even at high altitudes. All but a few farms are conveniently located with regard to drinking water.

Figure 2.1   The geology of Fuenterrabia (after Adán de Yarza, n.d.)

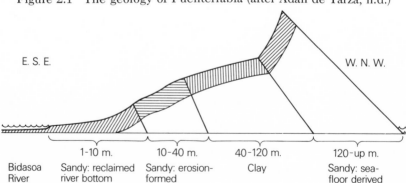

1-10 m.	10-40 m.	40-120 m.	120-up m.
Bidasoa River	Sandy: reclaimed river bottom	Sandy: erosion-formed	Clay	Sandy: sea-floor derived

The climate is temperate-humid. I have data provided by the weather station at the San Sebastian airport in Fuenterrabia[7] for 1961–1966. The average yearly temperature for the period is 13° centigrade and the average rainfall is 1,723 mm. There are from 17 to 26 freezes a year, though the intensity of each one and the number of days of successive freezes would matter more than the exact number. Hailstorms vary from 0 to 7 a year; there are clearly good and bad years in this regard, although not all farms suffer equal damage.

The predictability by month of the weather is important. The warm and cold seasons are fairly predictable, as are the dates when freezes and hailstorms can be expected. But the distribution of the driest and wettest months over the year is chaotic. For example, August, 1962 was the driest month of that year and August, 1963, was the wettest month of 1963. Under soil conditions that require continuous, light rainfall, these variations create difficulties. Any ten-day period without a good rain is a drought for the farmer, because the sandy soils dry out so rapidly.

This lack of predictability is tied to a weather phenomenon typical here, *estancamiento* (stagnation). A given weather situation, either rain or drought, often becomes stabilized and may last continuously for three to five weeks. Thus rainfall is constant in amount over the years but unpredictable in its distribution within the individual year.

Summarizing, there are two soil types having different productive characteristics. The topography is rough so that some farms have a considerable amount of land with slopes and others have little. The weather is rather unpredictable during the year. Since gardening can only be carried out on sandy loams and land with sharp slopes can only be used for production of some grass, a little fruit, and mountain fern, it is clear that the land factor does not favor all farms equally and sets clear limits on production alternatives (see p. 43).

Capital

Capital is the factor that has undergone the greatest change in recent history here. The concept capital, defined as produced goods utilized in further production, could well apply to artificially-transformed and reclaimed land, but I restrict my attention to house-stables, tools and machinery of production, and the money invested in present production costs.

The house and barn building is part of the capital of the farms. The lower floor of the house is the stable and toolshed and the attic is used for storage of seed, drying of various crops, and making cider. Because these buildings combine the functions of production with the living area, it is difficult to separate the value of the part of the building entering directly into the productive process from the part that serves as living quarters. These are also hard to cost because they are often received via inheritance. After the heir has indemnified the siblings and paid taxes in the manner to be described later, he or she may have paid much or little for the building. The form of the building has not radically changed for hundreds of years.

All farms have the full range of hand tools: wheelbarrows, hoes, pitchforks, scythes, sickles, wooden rakes, shovels, axes, buckets, a variety of baskets, hammers, and some Basque hand plows (*layak*). These tools have an average productive life of about five years and are not a costly investment.

Since 1956, a variety of machinery and vehicles has appeared: power tillers and reapers, garden and farm tractors, cars, trucks, scooters, and motorbikes. Only the Brabant type steel plows and the cow cart were available before.

Purchase of cows, calves, seeds, feeds, chemicals, and other production costs are considered to be capital which varies with the yearly production decisions. The calculation of magnitudes here is complex and will be explained in the formal accounts. Seed, factory feeds, and chemicals all appeared after 1920. Previously, the farms were nearly self-sufficient in these items, and raised their own milk cows and calves.

Labor

The labor force has almost always been constituted exclusively by the farm domestic group. Wage labor and permanent live-in laborers were present in small numbers in 1920 but have largely disappeared in recent years. For purposes of my own census, a laboring adult was considered to be a person of 18 years or over, since this seems to be the age at which a full day's work is expected.

The division of labor is not rigid on these farms; it is always molded around practical needs. There is no farm task I have not seen both men and women perform, including cooking, plowing, milking, and the operation of motor vehicles. For purposes of formal economic accounting, male and female labor must be assigned equal value. I did not include the labor of children in my analysis because I had no way of estimating its worth. Children do not participate much in farming at present, although older children who babysit have always been important in freeing adult labor for farm work.

Summary

Together the possible variations in the factors of production relate directly to farm production possibilities. Farms may differ in soil type and topography, farm size, land value, building and machinery value and state of repair, variable capital employed in production, and the amount of labor employed in farming. These variations are not random; they form characterizable complexes which are the basic knowledge for an understanding of agriculture in Fuenterrabia.

Factors of production in 1920 and in 1969

By describing the factors of production and their distributions in 1920 and 1969, I can point out the changes in agriculture over time while also describing the character of farming in more detail.

Fuenterrabia in 1920

The land factor was quite similar to the situation I described earlier. Reclamation of the river bottom land had nearly ceased and limited transformation of soil was converting some clay into sandy loam. The major feature that was different was the vegetation. Much of the inhabited rural area was blanketed with apple, pear, and plum trees, the major source of cash during this time of heavy involvement in subsistence. The communal lands on the mountain still had a number of species of hardwood trees, and very few pines. Meteorological changes, if any, cannot be determined because there were no local observations made at that time.

Farm buildings were nearly the same as now; farms in use then are occupied, though many have been converted into villas. The major internal difference was the lack of running water and electricity in most houses.

The inventory of hand tools was as I have described it. The tool of most importance then was the hand plow (*laya*). It was used instead of animal traction plows in most of Fuenterrabia in 1920. The *laya* was widely used until at least 1945. The backbreaking labor involved in plowing a 0.20 ha. field with a *laya* is subject matter for many old peoples' conversations. Usually four men and women worked in a team, each person with two *layak*. The old people brag about having been able to plow 0.20 ha. in about seven hours! That means it took four adults with eight *layak* seven hours to plow about a half acre of land.

At this time there was a small animal traction plow in use, but apparently it was hard to control on the slopes. The introduction of the Brabant plow around 1920 began a minor revolution in agriculture. The Brabant plow is a heavy wheeled steel plow which has to be drawn by a team. Two people are required to operate it, one to guide the team and the other to control the plow. It cuts deeply and rapidly, and can reverse directions easily. Though in 1920 there were only a few, by 1945 nearly every farm had one Brabant plow, and many of the team labor arrangements lapsed.

The livestock inventory was different from the present one. Since milk production in 1920 was for home consumption, the calves were raised for meat and sold for cash, most farms only keeping one or two cows. The cows were nearly all Swiss, with a few Pyrenean cows still to be found. Holsteins did not appear until after World War II. The Swiss was well adapted to local needs because it gave a good deal of milk and could also pull a Brabant plow and the cow cart, the major means of transport at the time.

The feed given the animals was almost entirely grass and hay, with occasional small rations of corn and bran. Apparently the cows thrived on this diet and were a reliable source of milk.

Farmers began selling milk commercially around this time. Farmer-milkmen are now a major feature of the contemporary landscape.

The main source of cash, besides the sale of calves, was apples. Although now there are only about 300 apple trees, the area was covered with them as late as 1945. Around 1920 there were 37 large cider presses on farms and six in the town. Only two still operate. In the town alone there were 366 cider vats, each with a capacity of about 6,250 liters for a total of about 2,287,500 liters of cider. Cider was everyone's drink as wine was too expensive. There were nine cider bars in the urban area and the potbelly of the cider drinker of the time has become incorporated into the popular image of the Basque male. Now it is a despised drink and is difficult to find in Fuenterrabia, having been supplanted by wine.

Generally, then, a calf or two and a few bags of apples were the limit of a farmer's involvement in the cash economy at the time. It was largely subsistence agriculture. Since most of the farmers lacked cash, they had to substitute labor for it as far as possible. From the farmers' point of view there was never a surplus of labor and though wage and live-in labor were available, most farmers could not afford them.

All bedding for the stalls was made from mountain fern; daily trips up to the commons were necessary to cut it, and an intensive fall cutting was needed to provide a store for winter. All transport was by cow cart or on the farmers' shoulders. One man, who used this fern until about five years ago, said that to supply his 12 cows and 10 calves with fern for the winter, the labor of three men for at least two months was needed. Thus, merely to take care of the cattle the farmer might spend four or five hours a day traveling in his cow cart, if he had one. Then he would cultivate the forage crops, feed and milk the cows, and with the other chores, the day would be over. The women worked beside their husbands. This did not produce sufficient cash to pay rents, to meet dowry, and other cash obligations, and so apples had to be sold yearly. If ends still did not meet, odd jobs were done for cash. However, there were few jobs outside agriculture. The fishermen and bargemen did not receive much cash; often oddjobbing was an act of desperation.

The distribution of the agricultural factors of production in 1920 was as follows: There were 256 farms, utilizing over 90 percent of the arable land in the municipality. This compares with 168 farms and only 38 percent of the land under cultivation in 1969. In 1920 only 59 farms were owner-operated while 197, or 77 percent, were tenant-operated. As demonstrated in Table 2.1, there is little

Table 2.1. *Comparison of factor distributions: 1920 and 1969*

1920	1969
Land factor	
256 farms	168 farms
59 owner farms	94 owner farms*
197 tenant famrs	66 tenant farms*
Farms by soil type and altitude:	
0–40 m. sandy	
41% of total farms	37% of total farms
41–110 m. clay	
47% of total farms	53% of total farms
111–up sandy	
12% of total farms	10% of total farms
Average farm size:	
5.8 ha.	3.9 ha.
Capital factor	
hand tools, cow carts, Brabant plows; evenly distributed	hand tools, cow carts, Brabant plows, power machinery, chemicals, feeds; unevenly distributed among farms
Labor factor	
7.5 persons per farm (average)	5.5 persons per farm (average)
35% total municipal population living on farms	9% total municipal population living on farms

* Although there are 168 farms, I have accurate information on only 160.

change in the distribution of farms among soil types. This is important because it shows that the farms abandoned between 1920 and 1969 have not merely been marginal farms on poor soils. Farms have disappeared from good as well as from poor soils.

Data on farm size are not readily available but generally indicate that on the average, farms were larger in 1920 than now. While there has been a decrease of 34 percent in the total number of farms since 1920, there has been a decrease from 90 percent of the arable land in the municipality under cultivation to 38 percent in 1969. The 88 farms which abandoned agriculture took 52 percent of the land out of production.

Thus farms which had abandoned agriculture since 1920 were not those with the poor soils, nor were they the smallest farms. This indicates clearly that farm abandonment is not simply the dropping out of marginal farms, while the really good ones continue. Large farms with good soils have also been abandoned, and a more complex explanation of the process is needed.

For the capital factor I have very little information. The major variations in 1920 were between those farms having the cow carts and those that did not. This was important because the carts greatly facilitated collection of hay, firewood, and fern, and the transport of people to the fields. The general impression is that the tenant farmers had less productive capital than the owner farmers, but that the differences between owner and tenant farms were smaller than they are now because the total stock of capital on any farm was so limited. The cash reserves so common now were uncommon in the past.

Farming, fishing, and small-scale service and artisan occupations were the prime alternatives. There was little factory work. Of the various occupations, farming was perhaps the best because subsistence was generally assured even though the working hours were long. Farm labor was drawn mainly from the domestic group with all farm earnings going directly into the family purse to be doled out by the family head.

The work was demanding. Daily trips were made up the mountain for firewood and fern, along with field work, gardening, and trips to the market for the few goods to be exchanged or bought. But this labor did assure a fairly steady though inelegant diet, a relatively low cost of living, and a minimal degree of material security.

The 1,932 persons who in 1920 lived on the 256 farms made up 35 percent of the total municipal population. The urban population (65 percent) fished or ran small stores, shops, and bars. As far as I can tell from archival documents, this is the highest agricultural population that Fuenterrabia ever supported. As indicated, about 90 percent of the land was under cultivation. The farming adults numbered 1,208 (97 percent) of the total adult population living on the farms. This shows the farm population to have had a low degree of involvement in the economy outside of agriculture. The average number of persons per farm was 7.5.

In 1920 every farm needed two cows, plus whatever calves they could raise. The animals produced milk and manure for the corn, beans, squash, grass, and the kitchen garden upon which the survival of both the cattle and the family depended.

Methods for raising cattle were much the same then as now. Inputs corresponded to those I describe for exploitation level three diets, and the outputs of meat and milk were similar (see pp. 64–8, 84). The major differences were absence of chemical fertilizers for the forage crops, the necessity of hand plowing and cultivating, and the absence of factory feeds. Crops were less productive and the labor requirements of forage production were greater. The maintenance of two cows required a good deal of labor.

The major cash sources were the sale of fattened calves and of apples or cider. Production of the apples required knowledge of arboriculture, but was done without the benefit of the wide range of chemical pesticides for trees. The farmer had to know how to choose the best apple varieties for cider, to graft, prune, and fertilize the trees. Generally there was a good crop every two years, a good crop being about 120 kilos of apples per tree. In 1920, a farm with 60 trees covering perhaps 0.20 ha., produced about 200 pesetas in cash, a great help in covering rent, dowry, and other expenses. Details of apple cultivation have been provided by Laffitte (n.d.).

The other component in the farm economy was the kitchen garden. The main crops were onion, leek, cabbage, garlic, navy bean, squash, potato, and some tomatoes and green peas.

Together with the raising of one or two pigs each year, this constituted the farm economy. Farmers still short of cash after selling calves and apples, had to involve themselves in odd jobs. Many did barge work in the river, hauling sand and stones for construction projects.

Great changes have occurred since then. A market for milk and vegetables developed, replacing the reliance upon subsistence and occasional market transactions with total involvement in the cash economy. Physical labor is eased by the use of machinery and crops are improved by fertilizers.

Fuenterrabia in 1969

In 1969, there were 168 farms in operation, encompassing 38 percent of the farmable land, a marked decline in farms and amount of land under cultivation.

Closing down of farms has been most intense on the outskirts of the urban nucleus. The present 633 ha. of farmed land are worth 713,646,655 pesetas or a little over 10 million dollars. The price of land is very high, caused by the influx of urban developers.

With the aid of an agricultural engineer, I set up criteria for classifying the buildings in Fuenterrabia. They range in size from about 100–200 m² of floor area and in value from 30,000 to 600,000 pesetas. The worth of each farm building was then assessed by this scale. The total value for farm buildings is 41,935,290 pesetas or about $587,000.[8]

The actual cost of the hand tools used is quite small, about 3,000 pesetas. They have a productive life of approximately five years and represent for all the farms a total investment of only 495,000 pesetas or about $7,000. Machinery and vehicles are much more expensive and are unevenly distributed over the municipality. The machinery and vehicles used include Brabant plows, power tillers, power reapers, garden or farm tractors, automobiles, motorscooters, and motorcycles.

The motor vehicles are included as part of farm capital because they are instruments used in the productive process. Cars are used for hauling feeds, grass, milk, and vegetables and are important in all stages of production. Scooters and motorcycles are often used to carry small loads of vegetables or cans of milk. Without them the amount of production and/or revenues would be lowered significantly. This form of capital has a total value of 9,476,028 pesetas or about $133,000.

Taking farm buildings, tools, vehicles, and machinery together, fixed capital totals 51,906,318 pesetas or $727,000.

Cows, calves, seeds, soil treatments, and other costs of production fall within the category of capital whose amount varies with the yearly productive decisions.

Circulating cost is an accounting concept referring to the capital that a producer must have on hand to finance the production during a one-year period between initial investment and the receipt of revenues. It includes one half of the total feed, bedding, veterinary, and upkeep costs for cattle and the total seed, fertilizer, chemical, and other production costs in gardening. It does not include labor costs or the cost of fixed capital goods. The calculation of this figure is complex and will be explained in the next chapter. Here the quantity serves to give some idea of the magnitude of investment involved. It is 39,019,299 pesetas or about $546,000.

The total value of agricultural capital in Fuenterrabia used in 1969 is thus 90,925,617 pesetas or about $1,273,000.

The value of the labor factor is arrived at by a circuitous route because the farmers do not pay themselves or members of the domestic group for their work. They evaluate the profitability of farm labor as compared with fishing or factory work in terms of the general standard of living and the social and physical qualities of the work. In order to place a value on the labor I had to utilize the concept of "opportunity cost." The *opportunity cost* of labor is the revenue from alternative applications that are foregone in order to utilize the labor in a specific way;[9] in this case the most common alternative application for farm labor is factory work. The wages paid a man for factory labor are about 1,500 pesetas a week for a six-day week at eight hours a day, plus an additional 15.90 percent of this paid into the worker's social security account by the employer. This yields a yearly total salary of 90,402 pesetas, or an average of about 38 pesetas per hour. For this study, 90,000 pesetas per year will be taken to be the value of each farm-employed individual's labor.

Some elaboration is required before urban and rural labor can be compared. The urban laborer pays out from 20 to 40 percent of his salary in rent and must buy his food. The farmer pays only his siblings' shares in rent, in the case of an inherited farm up to about 8 percent of his income, and gets vegetables and milk at cost. Even if taxes on production are added, the cost of rent does not increase much. The farmer is eligible for social security benefits as long as he pays the social security tax himself. The benefits do not provide even half the income needed to support a retired person, either in the city or on the farm. Urban workers also get health and hospital insurance for the whole family as part of the job, while the farmer must pay for them. The urban worker usually has an eight- to ten-hour workday and tries to put in as much overtime as possible. The rural laborer works a seven-day week of ten hours a day on weekdays and two or three hours on Sunday.

Overall, the farmers' low rents and small food costs put them in a better economic position than the factory workers. Though factory workers get social security and hospitalization insurance, these benefits do not offset the costs of urban living. Certainly the difference in working hours is more apparent than real since many urban laborers work overtime or moonlight in order to make ends meet.

My census shows 438 adults engaged in agricultural pursuits. Though the exact division of this population is somewhat arbitrary, the estimates that emerge from my accounts show the total value of the labor in agriculture is 21,931,875 pesetas or about $307,000.

The complexity of my treatment of labor is a result of the accounting procedure I used. Because I separated the value of labor employed in cattle raising and in gardening for accounting purposes, and because I could not observe the actual allocations of time to each activity on 168 farms, I approached it indirectly. I found out the time it takes to cultivate a given amount of garden and sell the products and the time required to care for a given number of cows and sell the milk and calves. Then, turning to the census in which the amount of garden and number of cows and calves on each farm were available, I calculated the amount of labor employed on that farm on the basis of the above information on labor time. It is a crude technique, but is the best approximation I could achieve.

This is the bloodless outline of the economic magnitudes in farming. Much has changed in the 49-year period under consideration and Table 2.1 summarizes the changes. Referring to it, we can see that in 1969, as compared with 1920, there were fewer farms; farms tended to be smaller; there were more owners and fewer tenants; the variety and amount of capital increased; and the labor force and farm population dropped considerably, as had the agriculturally-active population.

Thus 1969 was clearly not a period of increasing involvement in agriculture; it represents instead a phase of rural depopulation. The poor prognosis for agriculture might be changed if the decline could be shown to apply to marginal farms, but as I have indicated, this is not the case. The rural population had dropped to less than half of the 1920 level and the farm residents were more involved in nonfarm occupations than before. The only hedge against this general decline has been the increase in the number of owner farmers and the increased use of capital which makes exploitation with less land and labor more productive. High productivity and careful husbanding of resources have made many of the farms that remain extremely profitable.

A statistical analysis of the factors
of production in 1969

This section is an analysis of the distribution of the factors of production derived from my farm census. Each factor of production will be analyzed separately and then concatenations of the factors will be presented. The point is to provide a picture of the use of resources in farming that is detailed, specific, and can serve as the basis for the economic analysis to follow. To say that there are "many," "few," a "tendency," and so on, as is often the case in anthropological descriptions of farming, is not enough. I am attempting to show that the present distribution of the factors of production among alternative specializations represents a sensitive response to the profit differentials and that, within the limits set by soil type and market organization, they are presently distributed so as to maximize factor use in the highest profit specialty. Demonstration of this constitutes my evidence that these farmers are aware of the profits in farming, capable of exploiting them, and in no way fit the model of the "traditional" farmer who cannot see his own economic self-interest. The abandonment of agriculture has to be explained some other way. Because this evidence is crucial to the entire argument it is presented in detail. This statistical picture of factor distribution is followed, in the next chapter, by a full accounting for the year from September, 1968 to August, 1969. Together these constitute the statistical support for my argument.

For purposes of this aggregate analysis, distribution will mean the allocations of the factors of production among the production alternatives present and the covariance between the factors.

The data in this section are presented in three ways. The census is analyzed by means of correlations, but also considerable description is provided to set the data in an intelligible context and to prepare for the analysis in the following chapter. Finally, the correlation matrix is subjected to a factor analysis, a procedure allowing both descriptive and analytical summary of this part.

My census was worked into 12 variables for purposes of intercorrelation and factor analysis. The resulting correlations appear in Table 2.2. The variables requiring definition are "capital value in pesetas" and "labor value in pesetas." These are classifications I constructed to take into account the alternative methods of production existing within each specialization, i.e., the factor proportions decisions in LeClair's terms (LeClair, 1962:1193–6). In brief, the factor easily varied is capital, and thus high levels of exploitation, represented by farms classified as 1 on a three-point

Table 2.2. Correlations from the 1969 census of farms (n = 160)*

	Soil type	Special- ization	Cattle- exploitation level	Cows (heads)	Beeves (heads)	Garden- exploitation level	Garden (m²)	Farm size (ha.)	Land value (pesetas)	Capital value (pesetas)	Labor value (pesetas)
Land tenure	.03	-.17	.02	-.07	-.12	.16	-.02	-.11	-.13	-.34	-.13
Soil type		-.30	-.16	.18	.18	.28	-.07	.15	.10	-.08	.01
Specialization			.26	-.23	-.10	-.77	.19	-.20	-.08	.24	.002
Cattle-exploi- tation level				-.53	-.17	-.07	.01	-.36	-.19	-.30	-.30
Cows (heads)					.24	.10	-.02	.65	.36	.27	.53
Beeves (heads)						.05	-.03	.30	.40	.32	.14
Garden-exploi- tation level							-.23	.11	.07	-.29	-.12
Garden (m²)								-.01	.01	.16	-.01
Farm size (ha.)									.67	.25	.40
Land value (pesetas)										.23	.25
Capital value (pesetas)											.25
Labor value (pesetas)											

* Significance levels:

	r	p
r	>.16	<.05
	>.20	<.01
	>.27	<.001

scale, are those using a high degree of capitalization in the production process. The exact meaning of high capitalization will be made clear in the following chapter when production techniques are discussed.

There are 168 farms but because I could not get accurate data for 8, n is 160.

It will be noted that in much of my discussion, I draw contrasts between cattle raising and gardening as specializations, and yet I have pointed out that there are three specializations: dairying, beef raising, and gardening, each with a different profit structure. When I refer to cattle raising as compared with gardening, I am combining the two types of cattle raising. There are two reasons for this ambiguity. First, no farm raises milk cows or beeves exclusively; all have some of both. This made it impossible for me to separate the factors of production devoted to each type in the census, a difficulty that will be reflected later in my accounts. Second, the prime contrast in Fuenterrabia is between cattle raising and gardening and the major decision made by farmers is which of these to emphasize. If a farmer decides to devote some portion of the factors of production to cattle, then a further decision is made about the relative number of milk and beef animals to be kept. The relative profitability of the choice between milk and beef will be seen in the six case studies found in Chapter 5, because for the farms I studied in detail, I was able to separate the factor allocations in dairying and beef raising.

The presentation of the land factor will concentrate on three main dimensions: farm size, land value, and soil type. Data sources are various. The data on soil type were obtained through interviews and by the superimposition of the interview results on the municipal map showing the approximate location of different soil types. There may be some inaccuracies but these data give a fair idea of soil type by farm. Total sizes of farms were determined by a cartographer's measurement of the municipal map. The individual farm sizes were taken from the Ministry of Finance archives and are based on Ministry measurements of air photographs of Fuenterrabia upon which farms are drawn for the purpose of taxation. The derivation of the land value is from the municipal "plus valía" index discussed in Chapter 4 where its meaning will be explained.

The municipality has a total of 2,447 ha. of land. Of this, 82 ha. are occupied by urban housing and streets and 706 ha. of the seaward face of Mount Jaizkibel are held in communal tenure by the municipality. This leaves a total of 1,659 ha. of potentially usable land. Of this, not all is equally good and in a few areas, steep slopes and rock outcroppings nearly rule out agriculture. Farming is presently carried out on 633 ha. or 38 percent of the cultivatable land, about one-fourth of the total municipal surface. The present market value of this land is 713,646,655 pesetas. The remaining 1,026 ha. of cultivatable land not in use for farming is occupied by summer homes. A number of farm buildings are occupied as residences by people who have abandoned farming, and there are ten empty farms whose landlords are awaiting approval of an urban development plan to sell the land or build villas on it. Thus the entire study deals with only a little over one-fourth of the municipal land. While this should be kept in mind, one cannot immediately conclude that agriculture has died, for the advent of intensive gardening has resulted in much less land being used more intensively. The overall outlook for agriculture will only become clear later.

The first aspect of the land factor to be considered is farm size, with which several of the variables correlated significantly. The value of the factors of production all correlate positively with farm size–larger farms strongly tend to have high total land values. This relationship is important because the number of nonagricultural land speculators in the land market led me to expect some anomalies in the relationship. Poor farmland is often highly valued for construction sites, especially if the land has a good view of the bay. Still, the value of land correlates strongly with farm size.

Capital and labor value both correlate positively with farm size, meaning that larger farms tend to have more capital and labor than smaller farms. Thus the importance of land-intensive gardening does not erase the fact that larger farms still tend to employ more capital and labor than do smaller ones.

The number of cows and beef animals on the farms is correlated with farm size, at the .001 level, both an expected and important relationship which describes a prime determinant of the cattle industry here. A farm can only support as many cattle as can be fed from the produce of its land. The exact dimensions of this relationship will be described later but it is clear that the larger farms tend to have more cattle, and yet do not have larger gardens. This can be read in a number of ways but my research suggests one conclusion. Under present technical conditions and practices, about 0.70 ha. of garden is all a farm family can reasonably handle. Once that limit is approached, most farms stop short of the maximum garden in order to employ the remaining land and capital in cattle raising. The returns to the factors of production are lower. The limits are set by marketing organization in the gardening specialty (see p. 74–79). Thus I take these correlations to show a tendency toward full employment of the factors of production through cattle raising, even though a majority of the farms are involved in the more profitable gardening specialty.

The cattle-exploitation level also correlates with farm size, showing that larger farms tend to carry on production in a more highly capitalized fashion. As will be seen later, this is a response to the profits to be earned as well as being due to the inexpansible supply of labor that dictates substitution of capital for labor on larger farms.

Finally the choice of specialization correlates with farm size at the .01 level, meaning that larger farms tend to rely more on cattle raising and smaller farms more on gardening. This is important because, historically, gardening was the salvation of many small farms that had been very hard pressed to maintain even two cows.

I separated land value from farm size, because I was concerned with the effects of speculation on the land prices. This turned out to be unnecessary, since the only variable correlated with land value and not with farm size is that of agricultural specialization. That this correlation is not found in the case of land value as well is very puzzling to me; I have not been able to come up with an explanation for this fact.

To handle soil type and topographical data, I developed a classification of farms which is described below. It combines the two main soil types with a three-part classification of topography and results in a set of six types. These types, and the distribution of the 160 farms among them are described in Table 2.3. Admittedly,

Table 2.3. *General land types*

Abbreviation	Description*	Number of farms	Percent of total farms
SUS	smooth and undulating sandy loam	52	33
BAS	broken and abrupt sandy loam	5	3
SUM	smooth and undulating mixed clay and sandy loam	30	19
BAM	broken and abrupt mixed clay and sandy loam	12	7
SUC	smooth and undulating clay	39	24
BAC	broken and abrupt clay	22	14

* The idea of topography as divided into smooth, undulating, broken, and abrupt was suggested by the cartographer who prepared the maps.

this is a very primitive way to handle a complex matter, but it suffices for the general relationships I am examining.

Before presenting the correlations with these types, I will explain their agricultural importance. SUS land is suitable for both gardening and cattle raising, and can be freely shifted between the two. It is easy to work and machinery can be used without difficulty. BAS land has favorable soil qualities but the broken topography makes water runoff rapid and the use of machinery difficult. SUM land can be used for cattle raising in the clay parts and for gardening and cattle in the parts where the sand content is high. The freedom of choice depends on the exact soil composition in each individual case. This area of soil runs along the border between the clay band and the lower sandy loam. BAM soils have characteristics similar to those of SUM soils, except that machinery cannot be used and water runoff is rapid. SUC soils are good only for cattle raising. Gardening on clay is impossible because the accurate market timing involved is thrown off when clay becomes saturated by heavy rains. Machinery can be used and cattle raising is successful here. BAC soils have the same limitations as SUC soils to which the impossibility of using machinery must be added, this being the worst farmland of all.

About one-third of the farms have the most favorable SUS type and another 19 percent have the SUM type. Thus 52 percent of the farms can be exploited nearly as the farmer sees fit and can be made productive through the use of machinery. The SUC lands account for almost one-fourth of the farms and are restricted to cattle raising. Unfavorable land types constitute a total of 24 percent of the farms, all of which are restricted in the use of machinery and are difficult to work. Combined with the SUC figure, this gives a total of 48 percent of the farms which offer only restricted agricultural choices to the farmer. Practically speaking, a problem in the milk or meat markets would put 48 percent of the farms in grave danger while the other 52 percent could choose to stress gardening more.

Sixteen percent of the farms combine gardening and cattle raising on the broken and abrupt topographies. Here the existence of hand-transformed garden patches allows gardening, most of the transformations dating back to the beginning of the century and being little expanded since then.

This land classification (called soil type) correlated with other variables in the census in important ways. However, an error in my scaling technique washed out the correlations with topography and thus the correlations discussed below refer to soil type only.

The correlation of −.30 with specialization indicates the cardinal fact of agriculture in Fuenterrabia – gardening can only be carried on where the soil is sandy. Cattle can be raised anywhere, clay soil being no obstacle to the production of forage. Thus the amount of a particular soil type on a given farm sets limits on the farmer's choice of production alternatives. All other production decisions are based on this and the high correlation between soil type and specialization reflects it.

The correlation with garden-exploitation level partly measures the same relationship but it adds the information that the most capital-intensive, high-yield garden farms tend to be found on the sandy soil. Within the general constraint of soil type, there also appear, then, adjustments in which farmers exploit at a high level only those soils showing optimal characteristics. This relationship is found throughout farming. A correlation of −.16 with the cattle-exploitation level shows the other end of the same relationship in which the most highly capitalized cattle operations are carried out on the clay soils.

In all, these correlations show that the use of soil type gives a fair prediction of the kind of specializations found on any particular farm and the capital intensity with which they are carried out.

Numbers of cows and beeves also correlate with the soil type, which shows that the more clay soil there is, the more cattle will be raised on it.

The final correlation related to the land factor is between the variable of garden size and the level of garden exploitation, a correlation of −.23 significant at the .01 level. The relationship is not tautological. It shows that the size of a garden is a good predictor of the level of capitalization employed, large gardens (from .20 ha. to .70 ha.) being exploited at a high level of capital intensity. There is no technical reason for this, but once a farmer comes to rely heavily on gardening, he makes every attempt to increase the productivity of the garden through applications of capital. Where gardens are small, labor is being expended elsewhere, often in cattle raising.

To summarize the various correlations centering on the land factor, nearly half of the correlations found in the analysis of the census are accounted for by land-related variables. Size, value, and soil type set the limits within which the farmer must work; the correlations with other factor values, specialization, and exploitation levels show that the farmers have responded to these situational constraints by working out a consistent set of adaptations, the profitability of which will be shown in the next chapter.

The capital factor is dealt with descriptively, but for the statistical analysis the capital is transformed into its peseta values. I did this because the variety of capital items is great and a more descriptive and precise mode of comparison would have been very difficult.

There are two problems in the calculation of capital values. Calculation of house values has been described, and those figures include depreciation and condition of the house-stables. Machinery values are based on the Agria farm machinery company's 1969 price list. However, the values do not include depreciation because the mechanization of agriculture began only in 1957 with the introduction of the reaping machine. There were sporadic purchases after that, but the real burst began around 1965. The effect is that a used machinery market has not yet become established locally. Moreover, I was not able to get precise information about the dates of purchase of all machinery, and this made the fabrication of a depreciation scale even more difficult. Not accounting for depreciation inflates the value of the capital, but as I treat machinery as a unit in the analysis, the inflation of value is consistent throughout and, hopefully, does not invalidate the correlations I am using. This type of capital accounts for 18 percent of the total value of fixed capital on the farms. Another type of capital, personal savings of the farmers, could not be quantified nor estimated by any means and is not included.

The total value of fixed capital is 51,906,318 pesetas. Of this, 81 percent are accounted for by farm buildings, 18 percent by machinery, and 1 percent by hand tools. Thus machinery and tools account for only about one-fifth of the fixed capital value in farming. The buildings are both living quarters and farm buildings and I could not make a separation for purposes of calculation. Thus the figure of 41,935,000 is higher than the actual value entering directly into production. But without a residence of this sort, there is no farming. Only one family in the entire municipality does not live on the farm it works. Since, in 1969, machinery had only a 12-year history here, the 18 percent figure represents a very rapid proliferation. This type of capital is a helpful indicator of farmers' intentions because only those who intend to farm for some time will purchase the machines.

I have left out the actual value of the livestock, seeds, and fertilizers. Their addition would change the picture, adding over 25 million pesetas to the cattle specialization and nearly 8 million to gardening. I omit them because their inclusion here would erase the information about fixed capital which shows important differences between the specializations. In addition, the amount of variable capital employed in production is a result of decisions about the techniques to be employed and the volume of production. This is the core of the discussion in the following chapter on techniques of farming and its implications are made clear in the accounts.

Within the census itself, the variables considered part of the capital factor are capital value, number of cows, and number of beeves. With capital so defined, six new correlations appear, plus two already discussed in the land factor section above: I am referring to the .25 correlation with farm size and the .23 correlation with land value discussed above.

The relation between capital value and cattle-exploitation level suggests that farms that raise cattle with a high degree of capital intensity have high capital values, a result which is rather tautologous. However, the capital tied up in buildings is such a large part of the total that conceivably it could erase this relationship.

Numbers of cows and beeves correlate with capital value at the .001 level. This is not tautologous because the animals themselves are only a small part of the total capital value. The correlation shows that the higher the number, the higher the total capital value. This relationship is important in that each animal requires a stall in which it lives all year. Since the stalls are on the lower floor of the farm building, expansion of these facilities requires major, expensive remodeling. Thus the building itself often sets a sort of limit on the number of animals, although the cattle-carrying capacity of the farms under present technical conditions and the number of stalls are remarkably well adjusted. In any case, the practice of year-long stabling of cattle means that the decision to add cattle often is a decision to modify the existing farm building, whereas building size does not limit expansion of garden exploitations.

The correlation between garden-exploitation level and capital value is somewhat tautologous since both measure amounts of capital value. As in the previous case, however, the predominance of the building value could have erased this relationship.

Both of the other factors of production correlate significantly with the capital value variable at the .01 level. Land value and labor value increase with increases in capital value, but the reasons for this differ in the two specializations. In cattle raising it is due to the stabling of cattle year round – each animal must be fed and the stall must be cleaned. These operations are not mechanized and any addition of capital that increases the number of animals increases the labor requirements. In most cases, the upper limit of cattle production is set not by land or capital but by the limits of the family labor force. Mechanization of these operations would require total refurbishing of stables and major outlays of capital. This is not likely, given market conditions.

In gardening, additions of capital increase production. This could result in a decreased amount of labor, but it does not. The present market organization forces each farm to sell its own produce in small units either wholesale or retail, so that half of each workday is spent in sales and in preparing vegetables for sale. The result is that each increase in capitalization gives an increase in production which in turn increases the amount of time spent in selling. Market organization thus keeps capital from being a labor-saving device. The upper limits on production ultimately are set by the size of the family labor force, a labor force that is easily capable of producing more than it can sell.

A relationship also appears between specialization and capital value in which gardening tends to be associated with a higher total capital value. This is quite important because, although there is a greater variety of capital items at the disposal of the gardener, the cattle-related capital is much more costly. That gardening tends to be more highly capitalized derives directly from the much higher profit rates in gardening, rates to be shown in the formal accounts. The gardener is able to invest in any and all suitable capital items and improve the condition of his buildings because of the profits earned in gardening. Thus the correlation is not simply a technical result imposed by the requirement of gardening as compared with cattle raising, rather it is a result of the differential profitability of the specializations. This will be documented later.

The number of cows correlates with several variables, including farm size, land value, and soil type, all discussed in earlier sections. The extremely high correlation between heads of cows and labor value supports my contention that under present conditions any increase in number of cows requires an increase in labor. The $-.53$ correlation between heads of cows and the cattle-exploitation level means that the more cows on a farm, the greater the capital intensity of the productive process, including the stalls and enrichment of the diet with factory feeds. Having more cattle limits the possibility of exploiting gardening intensively, so that farms with large numbers of cattle are committed to maximizing milk and beef production. This is problematic, for as the accounts will show, the actual productivity of capital here limits the profitability of additional investment, given present technical and marketing conditions.

The correlation between specialization and number of cows is tautologous since both variables measure commitment to cattle raising. There is a .24 correlation between the number of heads of cows and of beeves. This is a result of the general tendency of the farmers to fatten calves to one year of age and then to sell them for slaughter. Farmers claim that this is more profitable than selling the calf at eight days. My accounts generally belie this, but the practice is widespread. Practically all animals raised for beef are born on the farm and are considered to be a bonus or supplement to the prime income source, dairying. The idea of raising beef animals only is felt to be unprofitable, and here my accounts bear out the farmers' view, taking as given present technical and market conditions. In any event, because of this practice, the correlation shows that a farm with more cows will also tend to have more calves.

The number of beef animals correlates with farm size, land value, capital value, soil type, and number of cows, all of which have been discussed before. It also correlates with the cattle-exploitation level at −.17 which means that the more calves kept, the greater the capital intensity. This is the same relationship seen with heads of cows and the cattle-exploitation level.

In summary, the capital factor, divided into a number of variables, shows correlations which generally argue that the higher the capital value, the greater the other values as well. Perhaps the most important lesson here is that capital is not a substitute for labor under present technical conditions in cattle raising and under present market organization in gardening. The result is that production is ultimately restricted by the size of the available farm labor force, presently almost completely restricted to the farm domestic group itself.

Though the data on labor create complications of their own, the same format is employed in the presentation of the labor factor. The data on age, sex, and occupation of people on the farms were elaborated by combining my census with informant testimony and checking results against the municipal and parish records. These public records are complete because of the Basques' desire to baptize children soon after their birth.

I divided the population into two parts, the agriculturally active and the nonagriculturally active. To be classified as active a person has to be 18 years of age or more, an age I picked on the basis of observation. The nonagriculturally active group is made up of people over 18 who work outside agriculture but continue to reside on the farms, those who are too old to work, or invalids. This classification applies equally to males and females as both contribute equally to earning power in and out of agriculture. The segment of the population considered as children reaches up to 18 years of age, introducing a distortion since some children do help in farming. I could not quantify or even estimate this, but my observation is that their aid is negligible overall.

A further problem is that labor is divisible and many people divide their time between urban jobs and farm work. Thus the labor value in pesetas is often different from the number of people employed in agriculture, multiplied by 90,000 pesetas. In the census there are 39 people combining occupations and thus increasing their labor value. Also I valued farm labor at 90,000 pesetas per year (opportunity cost) and because the figures used in labor calculation refer to these labor units and not always to people, there are 438 of these 90,000 peseta units in agriculture, in spite of the fact that 477 individuals actually work on the farms.

The total population on the 160 farms is 878 persons. Thus in farming I am dealing with 9 percent of the municipal population, living on 25 percent of the municipal land. I emphasize this again to show that this study deals with a segment of a population separated out according to economic specialization. This is not a society or a social system.

The 878 total is divided into 450 males (51 percent) and 428 females (49 percent). Of these 200 (23 percent) are under 18 and 678 (77 percent) are over 18. Of the males 29 percent are under 18, of the females, 36 percent.

Of the adult 364 males, 11 are too old to work or are invalids. Of the 353 active males, 168 (48 percent) are agriculturally active and 185 (52 percent) are employed outside agriculture. Of the 314 women, 3 are too old to work or are invalids, leaving 311 active. These are divided into 270 (87 percent) actively engaged in agriculture and 41 (13 percent) employed outside agriculture. Taken together, the figures show a total of 438 (66 percent) agriculturally active and 226 (34 percent) employed outside agriculture.

These figures immediately indicate a number of things. About one-third of the active population is employed outside agriculture, yet lives on the farm. This shows both the marginality of some farms which support their standard of living by adding to income from outside, and it also represents the effects of the process of urban migration of unselected heirs and/or the gradual migration of entire domestic groups out of farming.

Migration rarely takes the form of a family closing a farm and leaving. The data show that children, as they grow up, take urban jobs and eventually move into the urban setting, leaving only the parents to farm. The parents try for some time to attract one of the children back to the farm as the chief heir. The outcome is in doubt for a long time. If they fail, which they usually do, they retire when they no longer can work and are supported by their children or live on their own savings. Often they sell the farm and use that money for their retirement.

This gradual migration process should not be confused with the movement of unselected children off the farms in order to make an independent life for themselves. The impartible inheritance which requires unselected siblings who wish to marry, to leave the farm is necessary to the survival of farming. Thus in the investigation of the movement of people out of farming, great care must be used to determine whether or not the closing down of a farm as an agricultural enterprise is involved, since the mere movement of people off farms is not indicative of the abandonment of agriculture.

Over half the males are employed outside agriculture while only 13 percent of the females are. Partly this indicates that the nonagricultural labor market is better for men than for women. But it is easier for males to move in and out of farming activities than for women. Often, the heavy physical work is done in the early morning and late afternoon when the men, who work outside, are home. The rest of the day the women take care of the place. Men left at home to take care of the farm, house, laundry, and cooking are exceptional, though two cases are known to me. There is a real sense in which the woman's role in agriculture is more demanding and difficult than is the man's. In a number of cases a group of women runs a farm alone, but there is only one case of two men doing it and the farm in question is extremely poor. The importance of the woman's role is the basis for assigning at least equal monetary value to the labor of both sexes.

The pattern of male involvement in outside occupations has a long history. Previously it was due to economic necessity on farms that could not provide enough cash for rents and taxes. While this may be a motive now on very poor farms, the desire to take urban jobs exercises the strongest influence. I will discuss this in Chapter 4. Even the high percentage of males working outside agriculture cannot be taken as a sign that agriculture is dead, because farm profits are at an all-time high.

One data problem I could not resolve is that exact time devoted to each specialization by each person could not be determined. Thus the figures in the following section deal with the actual number of agricultural and nonagricultural laborers on each farm, this being correlated with the farm's specialization, land tenure, size, and soil type. But in the following chapter giving the formal accounts, a lower total number of laborers is used. The lower number is calculated by the number of cattle a person can take care of and the size of garden that an individual can cultivate. Labor figures derived this way do not include 173 persons classified as agricultural labor in this section. These other people are involved in house chores, caring for the pigs, chickens, and rabbits, and taking care of general chores not directly related to either specialty. This is lamentable since it adds an ambiguity to the analysis.

Since labor value is the only dimension I gave the labor factor in my census, and because of the problems described above, the analysis of the labor factor is less differentiated than in the case of the other factors. Yet the correlations are important because of the limits the labor force imposes on production.

Of these, all have been seen before, except the cattle-exploitation level correlation. It shows that with all increases in the capital intensity of cattle production, there tend to be increases in the amount of labor employed. This shows the relationship described in various guises before, in which increase in capital necessitates increase in labor under present technical and market conditions.

The other correlations show that larger farms tend to employ more labor; the larger the number of cows, the more labor is required; the greater the value of the land, the greater the value of the labor employed; and the greater the value of the capital, the greater the value of the labor used. It cannot be over emphasized that all increases in the scale of the other factors require increases in the scale of the labor factor. The effective limits on production are set by the labor force, and these limits are imposed by the size of the domestic group and the point in the domestic cycle. Wage labor is practically not available because the laborers prefer to work in urban jobs for the same reasons that are leading the farmers to abandon farming. This will be taken as given here and I will develop a cultural explanation for it in Chapter 4.

One piece of evidence that shows the limits of the labor force is found in Table 2.4. It can be seen that from 0–399,999 pesetas in capital value, the labor factor percentages are relatively larger than the capital value percentages. Beyond the 400,000 peseta point, the capital value continues to increase while the labor force does not. Looking at the second and fourth columns, it becomes clear that the percent of labor force is simply a reflection of the percent of total farms. The average domestic group size is now 5.5 persons and once the limits of that labor force have been reached, no further expansion of the labor force is possible.

Table 2.4. *Labor value and fixed capital value**

Fixed capital value (1,000s pesetas)	Percent of total farms	Percent of fixed capital value	Percent of total agricultural labor force
0–1.9	32	10	28
2–3.9	37	33	36
4–5.9	14	21	16
6–7.9	14	30	17
8–10.9	3	6	3

* n = 160

In this farm system of independent domestic groups, the problem of manning the farm through the domestic cycle and getting an heir who will marry and carry on the farm becomes the core issue. Capital goods can be bought and land can be inherited, but labor must be obtained through marriage and reproduction. Thus "labor" is the crucial factor, and all cultural changes related to the availability of labor must be considered crucial in Fuenterrabia. The present period of rural depopulation and farm abandonment is more a failure to keep a sufficient supply of labor on the farm than anything else.

Finally, two other variables were used in the census and these provided significant correlations. They are specialization in gardening or cattle raising and land tenure. Of these correlations, the soil type, capital value, number of cows, and farm size correlations have already been discussed. The correlation of m² of garden and garden-exploitation level with specialization in gardening is not surprising. Gardening-specialized farms have more garden and exploit it more intensively, just as the cattle-exploitation level relationship shows that cattle-specialized farms tend to exploit cattle more intensively.

The important correlation is that between land tenure and specialization significant at the .05 level. There is a slight tendency for garden farms to be owner-operated and for cattle farms to be tenant-operated. The farmers themselves attribute all kinds of differences to tenant and owner-operated farms including higher capitalization. Why this relationship should appear is hard to pin down. It is possible that the greater prosperity of the garden farmers allowed them to buy their own farms during the period when landlords were selling farms to tenants. In the case studies detailed in Chapter 5, it will be seen that the tenant farmer is in an advantageous economic position, over the short run, because of the extremely low farm rents; over the long run, however, the tenant's relationship to the land is chancy.

The land tenure variable itself correlated with two others in addition to specialization: capital value and garden-exploitation level. The correlation with capital value is −.34 which means that owner-operated farms tend to be more highly capitalized. The Basques attribute this to the greater security of the owner, reflected in his willingness to make long-term investments in buildings and machinery.

Land tenure correlates with the garden-exploitation level at .16, showing that the owner farmers tend to garden more intensively. I assume that this simply reflects the more general relationship between land tenure and capital value.

Perhaps the most important finding is that landownership is importantly correlated with capitalization. Because of this and because since 1955 the landlords have ceased selling farms to tenants as they had been doing between 1940 and 1955, 1955 turns out to have been a critical year. All farms that had been bought by the farmers were then in a position to capitalize intensively and take maximum advantage of the market conditions that had developed. The tenants apparently did not feel secure enough to do this and an increasing economic differential came to exist between the two. Now many tenants are under pressure to move off the farms so that the land can be sold for urban development. Only the owner-operated farms are likely to survive this period. Tenancy in 1969 was economically a tenuous position, though not an unprofitable one, as will be shown in Chapter 5.

In summary, the correlations I presented form a basic description of the factors of production and their interrelationships. It can be seen that the commercial specializations have different characteristics, that the limited labor force is a significant problem in agriculture, and that land tenure has a decisive influence on capitalization and future farming possibilities. Before discussing these points, I will pull the threads of this section together by means of a factor analysis.

Quantification and the analysis of the resulting data often become transformed from a "means" of analysis to its "end." Those who share my persuasion that what is needed is something more concrete than generalizations are particularly liable to this failing for nothing is so comforting as a set of neatly ordered numbers. The usefulness of any statistical technique depends much on the intentions of the user. At this point I am going to introduce the results of a "factor analysis" of my census data for a specific reason.

Factor analysis is a different way of treating the same matrix of correlations already discussed.

> . . . *factor analysis* aims to express covariation in terms of k underlying factors that explain a large part of the variance and covariance of the original variables. The number of factors is much less than that of the number of variables in the study. (Sokal and Rohlf, 1969, 542, emphasis theirs)

In this case, it shows much that of the covariation in the matrix can be comprehended as the result of three factors. Once identified, these factors can be described and the loadings of each of the original variables on the factors can be discussed.

I am not at all convinced of the validity of factor analysis as a means of discovering previously unknown relationships in the data. The assumptions required, the imperfections in scaling, differences in types of scales, and the interrelatedness of the variables make it unreliable for me. But I find it very useful as a descriptive device. Factor analysis is an additional way to show the existence of separable agricultural specializations with different characteristics and a way to summarize my findings. It is worth mentioning that nonfarmers do not recognize the existence of these specializations; they treat Basque farming as a single kind of enterprise. The demonstration that three separable specializations exist sets the framework for the rest of my quantitative analysis. In analyzing the nature of different agricultural specialties, I must provide a sense of each separately and of the ways in which they can be combined. This analysis also provides a brief summary of the relationships discussed in the previous section and serves as a prologue to the discussion of techniques of production and the formal accounting for each specialty. Finally, these data show the existing distribution of the factors of production among alternatives; they are the results of production decisions made by the farmers. When I show later that the factors are distributed in order to maximize involvement in the highest profit specialties, given soil conditions, my argument that the farmers perceive avenues of economic gain and can exploit them successfully will be supported.

The factor analysis of the 12 variables in the census produced three factors which can be named dairying, gardening, and beef raising (see Table 2.5). There are no surprises here in that these are the three specialties that began to emerge from the analysis of the correlations. Their relative independence and different structure correspond to the different economic and technical conditions to which they are a response. These three factors account for

Table 2.5. *A factor analysis of the 1969 census of farms*

	Factor		
Variable	Dairying	Gardening	Beef raising
Land tenure	−.20	−.42	−.37
Soil type	.28	−.43	.21
Specialization	−.31	.81	.02
Cattle-exploitation level	.62	.06	.39
Cows (heads)	.81	−.01	−.34
Beeves (heads)	.51	.06	.58
Garden-exploitation level	.16	−.85	.12
Garden land (m²)	−.02	.38	−.14
Farm size (ha.)	.82	.01	.01
Land value	.67	.78	.35
Capital value	.44	.58	.13
Labor value	.58	.23	−.42

55.5 percent of the total variance in the matrix of covariation created by the cross-tabulation of the 12 variables.

A description of the factors is in order here. The dairying factor can be characterized as follows: a tendency toward tenant farms; more clay soil, high cattle-exploitation levels, more cows and beeves, small gardens, large farms, and relatively high land, capital, and labor values. The gardening factor shows a tendency toward owner farms, sandy soils, high garden-exploitation level, large gardens, and very high land and capital values. The beef-raising factor is rather different: a greater tendency toward ownership than in the case of dairying, clay soil, and moderately high cattle-exploitation level. Two relationships that appear are surprising, the −.34 on the heads of cows variable and the −.42 on the labor value variable. This is problematic because, as I have indicated, beef raising never appears independently of dairying on any farm. The inverse relationship to labor value is actually born out by observation in that the labor requirements of beef animals are much smaller than those of dairy cattle.

The important point is that the census data fall rather neatly into these three specializations, suggesting that the decision as to which product is to be emphasized on a farm is the prime decision upon which all other production decisions are based. It also is clear, unfortunately, that the impossibility of separating dairying and beef raising in the general accounts found in the next chapter is a weakness of the study. Confirmation for the economic differences between dairying and beef raising will be found in the six case studies in Chapter 5. Clearly, any analysis of Fuenterrabia's agriculture must take into account the differences between these three specializations and relate them to the actual distribution of the factors of production in response to local economic conditions.

This chapter has presented the distribution of the factors of production, with special emphasis on the existence of three specialties designated as dairying, beef raising, and gardening. Why, then, are the factors of production distributed in this way? Does this distribution represent an effective use of resources? My argument is that this distribution of the factors of production represents a successful response to market conditions and the limited access to certain factors of production. To support this contention, the costs and profits of production must be examined; this will be done in the following chapter.

3

The agrarian history of Fuenterrabia from 1920 to 1969

THE FORMAL-AGGREGATE VIEW, PART II

This chapter presents an effort at quantification of costs and profits in agriculture. The data on the alternative techniques of production, their costs, and the combinations used are laid out in detail. With this done, a cost-profit accounting for agriculture from September, 1968 to August, 1969 is presented and shows the differing cost-profit relationships existing during that period. From these accounts it is possible to argue that agriculture is profitable and also that the farmers allocate the factors of production to maximize profits, given the limits imposed by soil conditions and the shortage of labor. On the basis of these data, I assert that the Basques are indeed abandoning highly profitable farms.

I begin with a discussion of the techniques, exploitation levels, and costs of production, a section that perhaps represents the most difficult and costly portion of my field research and yet has the least impressive appearance. In Spain, and specifically in the Basque country, even with the aid of all officials involved in agriculture, there is no reliable information on production costs, outputs, alternative techniques, or even market prices. This situation is not particularly unusual, as the impressionistic quality of many studies of peasant economics attests. As Polly Hill has aptly pointed out, the culprit is not the simplicity of the economies in question, but their complexity (Hill, 1970). All economic activities are made up of a multiplicity of transactions and decisions enmeshed in everyday social life, and quantification taxes the investigator's patience. I point this out in order to ask the reader's indulgence for the imperfections of my data and also to suggest that one reason for the lack of good quantitative evidence in economic anthropology is the difficulty involved in collecting it.

Here, then, in full awareness of gaps and defects in the data, I present the results of an effort to define carefully the technical and quantitative context within which the farmers operate.

Techniques, exploitation levels, and costs

There are many techniques for carrying out each farming operation, and each has its own costs and benefits. These must be considered because the farmers are subtle and resourceful, having many means to achieve similar goals.

These are the rudiments of farming, the things that all farmers know, although their knowledge is phrased in rules of thumb rather than in charts and numbers. The data are time and place specific and they show the costs and profits in the specializations. Were I a trained agricultural economist or an agronomist, I am sure this part of the analysis would be more sophisticated and orderly. As I am not, it is choppy and unorthodox, but the data support my points.

What follows is an analysis of the factor proportions decisions open to the farmers, descriptive data on each technique, and a presentation of production costs.

Cattle raising

The techniques, exploitation levels, and costs involved in cattle raising will be presented first. Milk cows are stabled year round and are not allowed to range freely at all. The farmers give two reasons for this practice. First, they consider the humid, cold weather to be unhealthy for the animals, tuberculosis in particular being a problem, and second, they claim that the farms are so small that all grass must be used. Free-ranging animals trample nearly as much grass as they eat. I was unable to prove or disprove these assertions locally. Taking them as given, the implication is that the farmer must service the animals in place. He must bring the feed, carry away the waste, and provide a surface for animals to stand and sleep on that is clean and dry. As cows are stabled all year, there is no respite. The farmer must also get the grass, or hay, and produce the corn, beets, turnips, and alfalfa needed.

There are two popular breeds of cows, the Swiss and the Holstein. The Swiss dates back to about 1900 in this area and enjoys great popularity because not only does it produce milk and a fair amount of meat at slaughtering time, but it also can be used to pull the plow. The Holstein is more recent and is rapidly becoming the most popular breed. Its milk production is very good and it gives a good slaughter weight, though it cannot be used for plowing.

The rule of thumb here is that two cows can be supported with grass and forage crops on 1 hectare of land. After studying the matter, I found that this was a reasonably accurate representation of the actual situation, given the local technical conditions.

Milk production requires a range of capital items. The stable must be suitable for the animals to live in all year. There are a variety of stall designs, some with dirt floors, some with cement. In some cases, the manger is raised off the ground and in others, it is on the ground. In all cases, the animal is generally allowed about 1.9 m² space and is tied in place with a neck rope or a simple collar attached to a chain. To combat humidity in the stall, to keep the animal clean, and to improve the quality of the manure, the farmer covers the stall with mountain fern or rough sawdust once a day, and takes it out in the evening. Because the animal has been trampling it, the dung is well mixed with the fern or sawdust and is simply piled on the compost heap to be used in further crop production.

Another outlay is for the cow itself and this is a major investment. Most farmers consider the productive life of a cow to be about eight years. Feeding the animal is another major expense, and the costs here vary widely depending on the exploitation level chosen. This will be detailed below. Other outlays are for upkeep of the capital, including repair of the stable, medicine, and veterinary care.

Labor requirements in dairying depend on the number of cows on the farm. As a general rule, farmers calculate that one man can take care of eight producing cows in a full day of work. This includes cleaning, feeding, milking, cultivating the feed crops, and selling the milk.

The only major source of technical variation in dairying, aside from machinery, is the diet. The different ways of feeding cows make for differences in costs and result in different levels of milk production and a variety of slaughter weights. These diets are the basis for my classification of farms by exploitation levels and will be described here in detail. There are, of course, a host of minor variations in technique that I ignore, feeling that they do not translate themselves into major differences in the costs and profits.

In the following, production costs will be given in detail since this information is the basis of my accounts. All costs apply to the period from September, 1968 to August, 1969. In all that follows, the reader will see peseta values carried out to the last céntimo. Some peseta values are not as accurate as they appear, but I decided to include them in order to avoid any further distortion of the values through rounding off.

The value of stables has already been given in detail above. Rather than set up typical costs, I have taken these costs directly from the census data and will not reproduce them here.

A good quality Holstein in the first year of milk production costs 35,000 pesetas. Though their value decreases with each year of production, I am forced to use the initial value in my calculations because I could not get detailed information on the ages of all the cows in Fuenterrabia.

Mountain fern or sawdust for the stable has a cost, or if mountain fern is collected by the farmer, an opportunity cost. It is calculated as follows: The stall is 1.9 m² and 1 kilo of fern or sawdust is needed per m². Thus 1.9 kilos × 365 days = 693.50 kilos per year; 693.50 kilos × 0.25 pesetas per kilo = 173.38 pesetas per year per cow for fern or sawdust.[10]

Veterinary care for the animals is estimated on the average to be about 1,200 pesetas per cow per year. Building upkeep and maintenance of machinery are figured as 5 percent of the total value of these items per year.

The establishment of feed costs requires considerable detail. I include the entire cost calculations here because it is important to see exactly how the cost has been calculated. The accuracy of the accounts depends on these figures. The elements in the cost calculation also serve to introduce the reader to the techniques of production in an empirical way. It will be noted that the costs do not include the value of the land or of the labor used. These elements are added in the later accounts.

Table 3.1 discusses farm-produced feed crops. Other important feed costs have to do with feed items brought from outside the farm. Factory feeds for cattle cost 7.15 pesetas per kilo. Hay costs 2.50 per kilo, if bought outside. Straw costs 2.50 per kilo and must be bought since grain crops are not locally grown.

In calculating the diets, I employed the 0.47 pesetas cost of hay assuming that it produces a little under one-third the weight of meadow grass.[11] There is also added labor cost, resulting from the drying, hauling, and stacking of the hay. Labor costs are added to the accounting at a different point and are not reflected here. Also, I used the 0.14 peseta figure for uncultivated meadows rather than the figure for cultivated meadows. This is done because the cultivated meadow only recently began to appear in Fuenterrabia. Few farms cultivate meadows. I used the 0.05 peseta figure calculated here for the farm-produced corn, turnip, clover complex rather than the 0.07 peseta figure for forage beets in calculating the cost of forage crops. This represents the predominance of the former in the cattle diets I studied.

With these data it is now possible to work out the costs of feeding cows at each level of exploitation. The form of working up the data was supplied by the Zabalegui Rural School, but the data are my own, as is the separation of techniques into levels of exploitation.

The levels of exploitation refer to the type of diet given the cows. A balanced, rich diet produces the most milk and the highest slaughter weight. A poor diet lowers milk production and

Table 3.1. *Farm-produced feed crop costs*

		Costs (pesetas)	
	Kgs.	@	Total
1. Uncultivated meadow grass			
– 10,000 m² of land			
Manure (it lasts 3 years, thus	30,000	.25	
10,000 kgs. @ .25 pesetas)			2,500
Escorias Thomas (superphosphate)	500	2.00	1,000
Potassium sulphate	200	3.50	700
Nitroamoniacal	300	4.00	1,200
Total cost			5,400
Production: 40,000 kgs. of grass			
Unit cost: 5,400 pesetas ÷ 40,000 kgs. = .14 pesetas/kg.			
2. Cultivated meadow – 10,000 m² of land			
A. Initial costs			
Manure	30,000	.25	7,500
Escorias Thomas (superphosphate)	1,000	2.00	2,000
Potassium sulphate	300	3.50	1,050
Seed			2,400
B. Annual fertilizing – 1st year			
Nitrate	400	4.00	1,600
C. Annual fertilizing – 2nd & 3rd years			
Escorias Thomas (×2 years)	600	2.00	2,400
Potassium sulphate	250	3.50	875
Nitroamoniacal (×2 years)	400	4.00	3,200
Total cost			21,025
Production: 240,000 kgs. of grass, alfalfa, clover over 3 years			
Unit cost: 21,025 pesetas ÷ 240,000 kgs. = .09 pesetas/kg.			
3. Corn, turnip, white bean, clover complex			
– 3,000 m² of land*			
Manure	2,250	.25	562.50
Unspecified chemical fertilizer†			1,494.00
Seed: corn			262.50
turnip			600.00
bean‡			–
clover			262.50
Total cost			3,181.50
Production (kgs.)			
corn	18,000		
turnip	30,000		
clover	21,000		
Total production	69,000		
Unit cost: 3,181.50 pesetas ÷ 69,000 kgs. = .05 pesetas/kg.			

Table 3.1 (*Cont.*)

		Costs (pesetas)	
	Kgs.	@	Total
4. Forage beets = 3,000 m² of land*			
Manure (because crop occupies land			
only 1/3 year, manure is used also			
for other crops) thus 1/3 of 14,400 kgs.		.25	1,200
Unspecified chemical fertilizer†			259
Seed			600
Total cost			2,059
Production: 30,000 kgs.			
Unit cost: 2,059 pesetas ÷ 30,000 kgs. = .07 pesetas/kg.			

* These data are drawn from my own observations.
† An error in my copying left out the type and weight of the fertilizer.
‡ Beans, which are for human consumption, fit into the complex with impeding development of other plants. The profit from the beans is enough to pay for the other feed crops. Here I do not calculate it as part of the feed costs, as it is dealt with in the section on gardening.

slaughter weight. These levels represent the farmers' way of classifying producers–the most important single dimension of technical variation in cattle production.

For feed calculation the year is divided into 245 days during which grass and forage crops can be grown and brought in directly from the fields, and 120 days of winter when the cows must live on what has been stored by the farmer during the other 245 days.

The diets of levels 2 and 3 are supplemented occasionally with stale bread. In this humid climate the hard loaves eaten by the people become gummy in 24 hours and farmers collect them to use as free feed.

The labor cost, as I mentioned before, is figured on the basis that a man's labor is worth 90,000 pesetas per year and one man can care for eight cows. This means that the labor cost per cow is about 11,250 pesetas per year (Table 3.2).

Actually the cost of labor per cow is not fully accurate, because, as in most enterprises, the cost of the first cow is greater than the cost of an additional cow. However, I had no meaningful way of handling this. I took the farmers' word that one man could care for eight cows and merely divided the value of the labor by eight. Included in the cost of caring for a cow, is the sale of the milk. With eight cows, about three to four hours a day are needed for sales to clients.

Table 3.2. *Costs of feeding cows by exploitation level*

	Kgs.	@	Total
			Costs (pesetas)
1. Exploitation level 1			
A. Forage production period			
grass	50	.14	7.00
factory feed	2	7.15	14.30
Daily cost			21.30
Total cost (×245 days)			5,218.50
B. Winter			
hay	1.5	.47	.70
stored forage	25.0	.05	1.25
factory feed	3.5	7.15	25.03
Daily cost			26.98
Total cost (×120 days)			3,237.60
C. Total yearly feed costs for 1 cow at level 1:			
5,218.50 + 3,237.60 = 8,456.10 pesetas			
2. Exploitation level 2			
A. Forage production period			
grass	52	.14	7.28
Daily cost			7.28
Total cost (×245 days)			1,783.60
B. Winter			
straw	5.0	2.50	12.50
stored forage	28.5	.05	1.43
Daily cost			13.93
Total cost (×120 days)			1,671.60
C. Milk production feed			
1. factory feed (per day) for 60 days after calving to establish milk production (×60 days)	1	7.15	429.00
D. Total yearly feed costs for 1 cow at level 2:			
1,783.60 + 1,671.60 + 429.00 = 3,884.20 pesetas			
3. Exploitation level 3			
A. Forage production period			
grass	52	.14	7.28
Daily cost			7.28
Total cost (×245 days)			1,783.60
B. Winter			
straw	2.5	2.50	6.25
stored feed	28.5	.05	1.43
Daily cost			7.68
Total cost (×120 days)			921.60
C. Total yearly feed costs for 1 cow at level 3:			
1,783.60 + 921.60 = 2,705.20 pesetas			

As I indicated, these different exploitation levels result in different production levels of milk. At level 1 the cow produces about 15 liters of milk a day for a period of 300 days. The other 65 days apply equally to all levels, as that is the time in which milk ceases during the last months of gestation. At level 1, the total milk production is 4,500 liters per year at the sale price of approximately 9 pesetas per liter. This results in 40,500 pesetas per year in milk. At level 2, the production is 12 liters per day for 300 days or 3,600 liters at 9 pesetas each, giving a total of 32,400 pesetas of milk per year. Level 3 production is 10 liters a day for 300 days resulting in 3,000 liters. Multiplied by 9 pesetas this gives a total milk production of 27,000 pesetas per year.

The next product is calves. At all levels the rate of successful calving seemed to be similar and after interviewing farmers and talking with Zabalegui School, I set the calf production at 0.8 calves per year. The basis for this figure is that of ten cows, about two will fail to calve in a given year due either to failure to inseminate or to an abnormal birth. As a calf at eight days of age is worth 4,000 pesetas, this means $0.8 \times 4,000 = 3,200$ pesetas production of calves per cow per year.

Cows also provide manure which is used in the production of forage crops and in gardening. Zabalegui School estimates that annual manure production is about 13,000 kilos per cow. At a value of 0.25 pesetas per kilo this results in 3,250 pesetas worth of manure produced by each cow each year.

The final product to consider is the slaughter value of an eight-year-old cow. For each exploitation level I have established slaughter weights that are fairly accurate. A cow which produced at level 1 gives a weight of about 279 kilos which, at 62 pesetas/kilo, which is the going price paid for meat by butchers, is worth 17,298 pesetas.

A level 2 cow gives a weight of about 242 kilos which, multiplied by 62 pesetas/kilo, results in a total value of 15,004 pesetas. The general weight for level 3 animals is 213 kilos and this, multiplied by 62 pesetas/kilo, gives a total value of 13,206 pesetas.

This, then, is the basic cost and production information that makes the accounting for dairying possible.

The techniques in beef production are essentially similar to those described for milk production, but the costs are different. Calves stay in the stable all year; they are raised for beef in about one year and sold for slaughter. Occasionally a farmer will buy calves, but usually those raised for beef are simply kept from the offspring of the farmer's cows. The calves are usually a mixed breed. There has been a general lack of interest in the breeding of calves, the only concern being in assuring milk production. Also, as most cows are purchased from outside, little emphasis is placed on raising good quality milk cows on the farm.

The rule of thumb in beef raising is that three beeves can be supported on 1 ha. of land.

The stable conditions are identical to those for cows except that the stall space is smaller, being about 1.6 m². The initial investment in calves is 4,000 pesetas at eight days of age and this is the cost of purchase or cost of not selling one calf born on the farm. The labor requirements for calves are half those for cows because the jobs of milking, selling milk, arranging for the services of bulls, and taking care of the cow during calving are removed. Thus one man can take care of about 16 calves for a cost of 5,625 pesetas per calf per year for labor.

In this section I will present only the costs that differ from those given in the section on milk production. The smaller size of the stalls results in a lower cost for fern or sawdust. This is figured as follows: 1.6 m² × 1 kilo of fern or sawdust per m² = 1.6 kilos. Thus 1.6 kilos × 365 days = 584 kilos per year; 584 kilos × 0.25 pesetas per kilo = 146 pesetas per year total cost of fern or sawdust. Veterinary care is also less costly than for cows, averaging only about 250 pesetas per animal per year.

The feed costs are the same, but the composition of the diet is different and there are three dietary periods rather than two. The first is the 75 days after birth which require a special diet. The rest of the year is divided proportionally between summer and winter diets and the exact percentage of each depends on the date of the calf's birth. Lacking exact knowledge of each case, I divided the remaining 290 days of the year proportionally into two-thirds summer and one-third winter, 193 and 97 days respectively.

The exploitation levels here again refer to the diet given the animals. The differences in diet result in different slaughter weights and different profit margins. This is also the most significant variable technique in beef production (see Table 3.3). As in the case of the cows, the dietary exploitation levels result in different production figures. A calf raised at level 1 will give a slaughter weight of about 250 kilos which, at the going price of 90 pesetas per kilo, results in a total value of 22,500 pesetas. A level 2 calf weighs in at about 225 kilos which gives a value of 20,250 pesetas. The average weight of level 3 calves is 200 kilos and at 90 pesetas per kilo this comes to a value of 18,000 pesetas.

Table 3.3. *Costs of feeding beeves by exploitation level*

		Costs (pesetas)	
	Quantity	@	Total
1. Exploitation level 1			
A. First 75 days			
artificial milk	6 liters	3.20	19.20
granulated factory feed	.5 kg.	10.50	5.25
hay	.67 kg.	.47	.32
Daily cost			24.77
Total cost (×75 days)			1,857.75
B. Forage production period			
grass	23 kgs.	.14	3.22
hay	.5	.47	.24
factory feed	1.5	7.15	10.73
Daily cost			14.19
Total cost (×193 days)			2,738.67
C. Winter			
hay	2.5 kgs.	.47	1.18
stored forage	12	.05	.60
factory feed	2.5	7.15	17.88
Daily cost			19.66
Total cost (×97 days)			1,907.02

D. Total yearly feed costs for one calf at level 1:
1,857.75 + 2,738.67 + 1,907.02 = 6,503.44 pesetas

	Quantity	@	Total
2. Exploitation level 2			
A. First 75 days			
artificial milk	6 liters	3.20	19.20
hay	.67 kg.	.47	.32
stale bread and leftover food	.80	gratis	–
Daily cost			19.52
Total cost (×75 days)			1,464.00
B. Forage production period			
grass	25 kgs.	.14	3.50
Daily cost			3.50
Total cost (×193 days)			675.50
C. Winter			
hay	2.5 kgs.	.47	1.18
stored forage	14.5 kgs.	.05	.73
Daily cost			1.91
Total cost (×97 days)			185.27

D. Total yearly feed costs for one calf at level 2:
1,464.00 + 675.50 + 185.27 = 2,324.77 pesetas

Table 3.3 (*Cont.*)

	Quantity	Costs (pesetas) @	Total
3. Exploitation level 3			
A. First 75 days			
artificial milk	6 liters	3.20	19.20
hay	.33 kg.	.47	.15
stale bread and leftover food	.80 kg.	gratis	–
Daily cost			19.35
Total cost (×75 days)			1,451.25
B. Forage production period			
grass	25 kgs.	.14	3.50
Daily cost			3.50
Total cost (×193 days)			675.50
C. Winter			
stored forage	17 kgs.	.05	.85
Daily cost			.85
Total cost (×97 days)			82.45
D. Total yearly feed costs for one calf at level 3:			
1,451.25 + 675.50 + 82.45 = 2,209.20 pesetas			

Using Zabalegui School estimates again, the amount of manure produced by a calf in a year is about 5,000 kilos which, multiplied by 0.25 pesetas (the price farmers pay for a kilo of manure), gives a total value of 1,250 pesetas. This, then, is the basic technique and cost picture. The only information lacking now is the nature of the markets affecting cattle raising.

There is no marketplace for milk sales or the sale of beef animals; all milk is sold directly to customers and nearly all farmers act as their own milkmen. Occasionally, a farm woman going to the vegetable market, will take the milk along and sell it on the street. The retail butchers, to whom all farmers sell, come personally to the farms to carry out the bargaining.

In regional terms Fuenterrabia's milk goes entirely to Fuenterrabia and Irún for consumption. The beef is consumed within this same area, except that the nearby French towns also buy meat in Irún on the weekends.

Fuenterrabia is not alone in this regional market. Aside from Irún's dairy and livestock production, there is another, different type of competition. In the milk market the major influence is Gurelesa, a huge semicooperative company that has a large number of farms all over the province acting as its suppliers. These farms sell raw milk to Gurelesa at 5.25 pesetas a liter plus a

0.75 peseta credit, if the farmers are members of the Gurelesa organization. In return for selling at this price, the farmers are assured of sales of milk in any amount they produce and are freed from the job of retailing the milk themselves. The company sells the milk in various forms from fresh milk, to 2 percent milk, yogurt, cream, butter, and cheese. Gurelesa has widespread support and sells retail milk for 9.50 pesetas per liter.

In analytical terms this market gives a stable price all year. For the last two and one-half years the price has been 9 pesetas per liter for raw milk retailed by farmers or 0.50 less than Gurelesa's price. During the year the volume of sales is fairly constant because here the large milk-drinking season is winter; but during the summer, although per capita consumption is much lower, the tourist population increases the demand at least to winter levels.

It is difficult for local farmers to raise prices because the market tends to be highly competitive and farmers will undercut each other. The difference in quality between Gurelesa's boiled and bottled milk is a matter of question, but local preference is still for fresh farm milk. The farmers know that they could get 10 pesetas per liter if enough of them charged it, and they have been meeting to forge a consensus about a price increase.

Gurelesa's presence is a double-edge sword. Fuenterrabia's farmers make little profit at 6 pesetas per liter because of the high costs they face. The factors of production are considerably more expensive in this coastal area than in the upland zone where most of Gurelesa's suppliers are located. On the other hand, it is claimed and appears to be true that the province of Guipúzcoa has a surplus of milk which Gurelesa markets as dairy products in forms other than milk. Gurelesa also sells milk outside the province. Thus Gurelesa's presence tends to hold the price of milk at this level. The problem is that the 6 peseta price relates to farming conditions not applicable in the coastal area. Unless some means of bringing local prices into line with costs is found, more and more farmers will be driven out of dairying.

In the beef market there is a great deal of competition from large industrial meat packers that ship beef in and out of Guipúzcoa, operating on a national basis. Also all animals sold for slaughter to the local retail butchers must be registered and slaughtered at the municipal slaughterhouse. The government sets the retail price ceiling for beef and requires that the price list be displayed in all butcher shops. Under these conditions the farmer has full knowledge of the market price for beef and can hold his own in bargaining.

The prices for slaughtered cows and young beeves have risen gradually over the last ten years but tend to be stable for long periods. In any case, the combination of outside competition and government intervention sets the prices and these prices generally reflect farm costs in other parts of Spain where labor and land are cheaper.

One striking feature of this marketing situation is the lack of any form of local marketing cooperative, and/or the development of a group of middlemen to handle milk. The sporadic nature of beef animal sales and the low level of production make the informal, face-to-face marketing to butchers possible, but there is sufficient milk production to support a cooperative venture. In fact, cooperative marketing of milk would seem to be an ideal solution in this situation since the dairyman must spend three to four hours a day selling milk, time that could be employed otherwise.

These farmers could become members of Gurelesa, but they would have to accept 6 pesetas a liter for milk instead of 9. This has a negative outcome for them, as the following example will show. A farmer with 12 cows has about 180 liters of milk to sell, which will yield 1,620 pesetas a day if sold at 9 pesetas per liter. If sold to Gurelesa at 6 pesetas per liter, the farmer will make 1,080 pesetas a day for a difference of −540 pesetas. If the farmer were to stay home instead and use the eight man-hours that are required to market 180 liters of milk for more production, about six cows could be added to the stable and production increased to 270 liters per day. Selling this to Gurelesa would earn 1,620 pesetas. Thus by working hard and keeping six more cows, the farmer gets only the same gross revenues as he or she does by selling the milk directly and keeping fewer cows. In net profits the picture is worse, for the additional feed costs and other expenses would have to be added, while personal marketing of milk only costs the price of gasoline, auto maintenance, and labor. Unquestionably the farmer is better off selling his milk personally. Of course, the key to this situation is that dairy farmers are close enough to the market to be able to do this, whereas the inland farmers have no choice but to sell to Gurelesa.

This does not explain why the dairymen do not form their own cooperative. This is a complex matter and would mean that they would enter into direct competition with an established business of imposing size. Recently there was an attempt to form a local cooperative. The stimulus came because the provincial government decided to enforce a law requiring all retail milk to be pasteurized. The farmers, who sell it fresh, met and talked about buying a pasteurizer together and selling the milk cooperatively at a good price. The meeting failed to produce results because the small farmers felt that the larger ones would dominate the organization and cheat them. This lack of mutual confidence in time of need is a prime characteristic of farm life in Fuenterrabia. It seems to show that each farmer believes that he can defend his own interests better without the assets or liabilities of cooperative action. For the moment, everyone has adopted a wait-and-see attitude in order to find out if the law will be enforced or not. The expectation is that it will not. Should the law be put into effect, there would be another attempt to form the cooperative and if it failed, many farmers would be forced out of business.

Thus I have presented the cost, technique, and marketing picture for cattle raising. With these data I will construct the accounting for cattle raising, as soon as the gardening data are presented.

Gardening

Gardening can be described here as dry farming of garden vegetables, legumes, and potatoes with no fallowing of land. To retain soil fertility, the earth is treated with heavy applications of manure which is mixed with a considerable amount of vegetable material (usually fern and sawdust). Chemicals are used to rid the soil of pests and to add nutrients. Plowing is done by Brabant plows or with power machinery. There is still a great deal of hand work, all planting and harvesting being done by hand. The humid climate, weeds, pests, and fungi are a major threat. The only special structures used in gardening are a few cement-walled seedbeds and a few portable seedbeds made of plastic sheeting tied over metal frames.

One major difference between farms is the means of plowing and cultivating, which range from hand plowing of tiny plots to machine plowing. This seems to depend partly on the size of the plots and partly on the topography. A large, relatively flat garden is likely to use power machinery, though even here it is limited because only single plots are plowed—never the whole garden at once. At present, the method of plowing and cultivating considered ideal by the farmers is a deep Brabant plowing once a year with a heavy application of fertilizer both before and after, and then cultivation with a power tiller. Most farms approximate this goal except where the topography is too steep. Failure to deep-plow for a period of years is said to cause infestation of the soil with many pests and the general decline of fertility.

Certain well-known gardening techniques are not used here;

they are machine planting, weeding, and harvesting. These machine techniques require a much wider spacing between plants than do the manual methods, but farmers have placed a premium on intensive use of their plots. Farmers do not feel that the gain in efficiency would pay for itself. They prefer to apply their labor to greater output per m^2 and not to sacrifice more land to greater efficiency in the employment of time. Also, as will be seen, one of the principal problems is that the large gardens, for example 0.70 ha., require that two people work for at least four hours a day to sell the produce, greater production only increasing the selling time. Thus farmers can already produce beyond their capacity to sell under present market organization.

No botanical identification of the main cultigens is given because I lack the necessary expertise. The main source of quality competition between farms is not the species but the varieties within the species. Not being an expert I could get no useful information beyond the fact that competition takes this form.

Each garden is divided into plots, each containing different vegetables. During one year a farm's garden produces at least 24 species of crops and the maximum under cultivation at any moment is about 15. This means that there are about 15 plots in each garden and one to three crops per plot successively per year. Since each one has its season, growth characteristics, market price structure, and costs, the successions must be planned so that one is finished when the next is ready to begin. Add to this the variation in the size of crop per m^2 of the different species, the farmers' desire to have more of vegetables that sell well and less of those that do not, and the variable hardiness of crops, and suddenly a bewildering labyrinth of entrepreneurial decisions appears. Of course, the farmer's problem here is also the investigator's for it was necessary to develop a means of accounting for the production of gardens with all the variety of crops taken into account.

After observation and questioning, I determined that the most significant technical difference between gardens was in the level of exploitation. Here, level of exploitation is taken as the success with which crops were combined to make the largest profits from the use of the land. To determine this, the first problem was to establish the techniques employed in the cultivation of each crop and quantify costs. This was done by intensive interviewing and observation in two garden operations, one without machinery and one with a plow and power tiller. The amounts of animal fertilizers, chemicals, seed, herbicides, pesticides, and fungicides were recorded for each plot. The output per plot was then measured, either by weighing, measuring, or counting a section of the plot's produce. The output was then divided into the costs, giving the unit cost. In the final total accounting, the entire product was lowered by 30 percent which seemed to be a good average loss figure, including loss due to failure of the plant to grow, as well as to hail, freezes, and unmarketable quality.

It is important to note that the accounting procedure used here is based on classifying farms by exploitation level. The characteristic cost and production figures for each level were worked out, and with these figures I returned to my census data. Farms were allocated to exploitation levels by combined observation, interviewing, and local reputation. There was a high degree of agreement among farmers about how most farms were to be classified. For example, finding a farm operating at exploitation level 2 and having four cows and three calves, I would then multiply the costs by the number of animals. The same is true for the garden accounting, where the exploitation level is multiplied by the size of the garden plots. Beyond this, I consulted the census for the value of other capital on the farm.

Therefore, the accounting I will present for cattle raising is "representative" rather than "actual" accounting. I did not measure all the costs incurred by every farmer in cattle raising or gardening. This representative accounting is perhaps less accurate than one would wish; however, it is a compromise between my ability to obtain the data and the amount of time at my disposal. I believe the results are sufficiently accurate to lend strong support to my argument regarding the profitability of agriculture.

First, the average price for the produce had to be determined. Unfortunately, the Irún market which is the main outlet for Fuenterrabia and also the regional price-making market, never publishes its prices. To determine average prices, once a week, for 52 weeks, I got the daily prices for all garden produce from a farm woman who sold produce every day. I also corroborated these figures and spent weeks in the marketplace myself. I then made up averages of the price for each crop. Though more volume of vegetables is sold in summer I had no systematic means of weighing the averages to account for them, the effect being that the average price is slightly lower than reflected here.

With this information, a basis for calculation was laid. It was impossible to determine the total square meters of land devoted to each vegetable in the municipality, and thus I had to approach it differently. I took three cases, which to me and to the farmers represented good, fair, and poor gardens and made a detailed study of each. I mapped the gardens and with the farmers' help, listed the crops from September, 1968 to August, 1969 for every plot. Using the information derived from this, I did a full accounting of profits for the year for each and divided the profit figure by the square meters of garden in each case. As a result I obtained three different levels of exploitation per m²; these form the basis of my analysis.

The three exploitation levels refer to timing, succession, and quality and quantity of produce. Farms are reasonably easy to classify in these terms. All the gardens were classified by these exploitation levels through observation, reputation, and questioning. Finally, to calculate the annual production in Fuenterrabia, each exploitation level was multiplied by the number of square meters of garden in the municipality that are exploited at that level, and the results were incorporated into the formal accounting presented later.

The reader may have doubts about such data and the operations that can be performed with them. While I recognize the limitations, I nevertheless find the data useful. Besides, the exact magnitude of municipal production of each vegetable is not the object of this study. The point is to provide a general idea of the scale of gardening, the contributions of the different factors of production to it, and its profitability. The contrast with cattle raising is quite stark.

Garden produce is sold in four ways: directly to consumers, in the Irún market, to retail food stores in Fuenterrabia and Irún, and to permanent market women in the Irún market. The marketplace in Irún is about 1.5–2 km. from most of the Fuenterrabia farms. The sellers transport produce there in their own cars, by donkeys, or if they live along the highway, they can have the baskets picked up and returned by a trucking service.

The market building itself has three floors and four sections. The basement, which was originally intended to be a warehouse, is used by the farm women for direct sales. The second floor has a section of permanent stands for specialized market women who are professional dealers. There is also a section of butcher shops and a fish market. The building was constructed in 1957 by the Irún municipal government, has no parking or unloading facilities, and is in poor repair.

Farm women sell in a rectangular area of about 0.10 ha., divided into three rows of back-to-back benches that run the length of the rectangle. In front of the benches are low stands upon which the women lay out the produce. The women rent a 1-meter section of bench and stand by paying the municipal government on either a daily or monthly basis. There is space for 150 stands.

This section is dingy and has a second-rate air about it compared to the upstairs area. The lighting is poor and there is no heat. Off the main room there are smaller rooms for washing vegetables and for storing unsold produce. The number of women selling varies between 70 in summer and 45 in winter; almost all are from Fuenterrabia, as Irún's farms produce mainly cattle and pigs. The market week is from Monday to Saturday with Monday being the slowest day and Saturday the best. Sales begin at about 8:00 A.M. and end by 12:30 P.M. when the women go home to cut and prepare the next day's vegetables.

Irún's municipal government administers the market and has an inspector on duty full time. The rules are that the upstairs market women are forbidden to come down and buy from the farm women until after 10:30 A.M., so that the farm women have a chance to sell retail first. In fact this rule is little observed and the farm women encourage the market women to come and buy at any time.

No men sell vegetables in the Irún market, though there is no legal prohibition. The women generally have permanent locations within the market which they pay for on a monthly basis and around these locations small groups form which try to hold up the prices. Thus at any given moment there is a slight variation in price for the same vegetables at different locations within the market.

Sales are often to personal clients and every effort is made to form these long-term relationships, though the actual sale, even with clients, is carried out by price bargaining. The ability to form client relations is considered to be a very important skill for the saleswoman. She must be able to establish and maintain a quasi-personal link with clients by means of conversational grace and what the women call *simpatía*. The farm woman refers to her clients as her parish as if she were the pastor providing for the group. These relationships are also important during the summer tourist trade. Although most tourists stay only two weeks or a month, during that time they will buy from the same woman if they like her and are satisfied with the produce.

A number of problems are reducing the importance of this marketplace. First, with Irún's population increasing, apartment house developments are proliferating. The first floor of these apartment houses always has food stores. Many people choose to buy at a higher price close to home rather than to make the trip to the market. Second, buying food and anything else in Spain has long been a bargain for the French. Recently the inflationary trend of the Spanish economy coupled with France's restrictions on foreign exchange has decreased the number of people willing to shop across the border. Third, the Irún municipal government, apparently for reasons of its own, is following a policy prejudicial to the farm women. It has ordered the basement vacated and tried to send the women to a newly-furnished third floor. The women, knowing that clients would not go up there and would buy from the middle women on the second floor, have refused to move, and the situation was a standoff when I left.

These facts diminish the importance of the marketplace and increase the emphasis on wholesaling to small stores. To do this the farmer or his wife needs a vehicle; and this would eliminate a number of poorer farmers unless they have a very small amount of vegetables and can take them to town on a donkey. About ten years ago the first farmer began to make the rounds of the stores selling a little in each. Before then a few farmers supplied some stores directly without making the rounds. Now many go from store to store, together servicing the nearly 200 stores in the local area.

Here again the client relationship is important. The farmer would like the store to become a client on a permanent basis. Price bargaining takes place by writing the prices on slips of paper in order to keep the wholesale price from being overheard by the store's customers. Payment is usually immediate, as credit is not used as a means of holding clients. The guide in pricing is the Irún marketplace price and on successive days the price agreed to by the farmer and store owner is rebargained only if the Irún price changes.

Wholesale selling favors the larger garden producers because store owners want an assured supply of a variety of produce at once in order to carry on relations with as few suppliers as possible. The politics of the relationship are complex, for in winter the farmer is lucky to sell anything, whereas in summer the store owner may be forced to come out to the farm seeking two dozen heads of lettuce.

Though men do not sell in the Irún marketplace, they do a good deal of this wholesaling. There are a number of large garden farms whose women sell retail in the marketplace while the men make the rounds of the stores selling wholesale. Selling to the Irún market middle-women is carried on in the same way as wholesaling in the stores, and client relations are established between the farmers and the middle-women.

The farmers are not alone in this market because industrial-scale truck farmers from the plains of Navarra regularly ship their produce to Irún and sell in bulk at the marketplace and in the stores. The prices for these vegetables are lower both because the cost of labor is lower in Navarra and because of the economies of large-scale, irrigation production. They also have the advantage of selling graded products so that the buyer can get the sizes or weights desired and nothing else. On the other hand, the local farmers' produce is fresher and the vegetables are generally more tender due to the local soil and climatic conditions. Vegetables from Fuenterrabia are sold in Fuenterrabia, Irún, Rentería, and the French border towns.

From an analytical point of view this regional market has characteristics typical of garden produce markets generally. Seasonal crops come in at high prices which rapidly drop as the supply increases and finally rise again as the last of the crop is sold, unless it has begun to spoil. Crops available for long periods show less of this variation, tending to stabilize around a particular price for much of the season.

The market is small enough to be glutted very easily. A single large truck of leeks from Navarra, for example, can drop the market price by half in one day. Even without the complications created by the outside truck farmers, local farmers with an exceptional crop of seasonal vegetables can glut the market. As a rule, every year sees gluts of two or three main crops, though the particular vegetables involved change from year to year. Even so, a crop that makes a great profit one year will almost inevitably be subject to an oversupply in the following year.

An illustration of the workings of the market will help. Recently the Spanish government held a campaign to decrease potato planting nationwide in order to hold the price steady. Each farmer, assuming that others would plant less, planted more in order to make a larger profit at the higher price. The result locally was a glut so severe that tons of potatoes had to be plowed under without being dug.

Thus the market tends toward atomistic competition, with the complicating factors of government intervention and the outside truck farmers. The government's interventions are usually unfavorable to local agriculture. In 1969 the potato crop was late and small and prices started up. The government immediately bought hundreds of thousands of tons of Dutch potatoes and flooded the markets, sending the prices down.

The influence of the truck farmers is different. Operating on a large scale, using irrigation, large machinery, and wage laborers, they began to enter the market here when local demand outstripped local farm production, responding to the lower costs of production in Navarra and the higher prices in Guipúzcoa. The effect of their presence, besides taking away some customers, is mainly felt in the prices because the Navarra vegetables come in earlier than the local ones. Their presence thus tends to level prices out somewhat.

All in all, the tendency of the governmental intervention and the truck farmers is to eliminate the high prices for early vegetables and to make it more profitable to produce larger quantities of each crop. The picture is hardly negative for the local farmers because their produce is still preferred by the consumers. The trucker must also sell at a certain price in accord with instructions given by the farm owner who sees the Irún situation in terms of acceptable profit margins. The local farmers can actually sell at a loss for a couple of weeks to drive the Navarros out of the market temporarily. How long such measures will work is impossible to predict.

The question of cooperative marketing must be raised with respect to gardening. The single most limiting factor in the expansion of gardening is that a farm can easily produce more than it can sell. All farmers know that they could produce more if they did not have to worry about marketing. Why then do cooperatives or middlemen not take over all sales?

It is a matter of the farmers' choice. All are aware of these possibilities but all are firmly convinced that the time spent personally marketing vegetables is economically justified. All farm men and women pride themselves on bargaining ability, an ability valued as one of their most important sources of profits. It is not enough to produce, one must also sell at a good price. In the atomistic market, salesmanship and clients are the small frictions against perfect competition that allow a peseta more to be charged for a head of lettuce than the middleman would pay. Of course, in the summer when the demand is strong, the seller dominates the market and can make very high profits. Thus because they are close enough to the market to go daily, and because personal sales, especially in summer, increase the profits greatly, they feel that the time spent in sales more than pays for itself. They feel that cooperative sales and middlemen would take these profits away and they opt to fend for themselves.

Both in the cases of milk and vegetables, the farmers apparently fail to pursue their mutual self-interest because they are unable to cooperate. In a way, this is a typical problem of agriculture. However, elaborate reciprocal cooperative ties used to exist between farms (these will be discussed in Chapter 4). These ties lapsed over the last 20 years to the present point where cooperation is not possible. It is partly an indication of the collapse of the rural social milieu and partly a result of the high value placed on independent action by the farmers, who very much want to act independently and privately.

Agricultural accounts: 1968–1969

It is now possible to present the formal accounting for total production in cattle raising and gardening in Fuenterrabia. In this accounting the product mix and profit margins will be seen and compared.

Besides providing information on the magnitude of production and profits, the point of doing a formal accounting is to clarify and emphasize the cost-profit characteristics of the specializations in a framework within which they can be compared and combined. The accounts provide the basis for evaluating the profits of each specialization and help to show the degree to which the factors are allocated to each, and the exploitation level giving the highest profits. Given local conditions and techniques available here, I believe that these accounts show this to be a viable, commercial agricultural system.

This argument is not the immediate product of a philosophical stance, but rather the outcome of an analysis that could have shown the opposite. As such it is not an invocation of economic man, but simply a portrait of an adjustment to certain economic conditions. Its merit is its specificity which allows me to discount economic conditions in agriculture as the prime causes of farm abandonment. Through economics I reach the conclusion that pecuniary aims cannot explain rural depopulation in Fuenterrabia, thereby giving the lie to those who see quantitative analysis as the destruction of the view of man as an intrinsically cultural animal. Here, the economic data require a noneconomic explanation.

Finding a suitable accounting system did not appear easy. It was my good fortune to meet Padre Andoni Lecuona who teaches agricultural accounting at the Zabalegui Rural School. As it turned out, he had an accounting system learned as part of his studies in rural sociology at the Ecole Pratique des Hautes Etudes in Paris. Because of his generosity and concern for agriculture in Guipúzcoa, he gave me access to a manuscript in which the accounting system is employed and permission to use it. I have used it for this study with only minor modifications.

Table 3.4. *Formal accounting of cattle raising and gardening,*
9/68–8/69 (in pesetas)

A. Land		
A1. Cattle	671,904,885.00*	
A2. Gardening	41,741,770.00	
Total		41,741,770.00
B. Capital		
B1. Cattle	66,454,755.73	
B2. Gardening	24,470,861.00	
Total		90,925,616.73†
C. Production		
C1. Cattle	31,568,225.75	
C2. Gardening	50,614,620.00	
Total		82,182,845.75
D. Costs		
D1. Cattle	11,966,961.48	
D2. Gardening	7,984,820.00	
Total		19,951,781.48
E. Gross profits		
E1. Cattle	19,601,264.27	
E2. Gardening	42,629,800.00	
Total		62,231,064.27
F. Interest		
F1. Cattle	3,987,285.45	
F2. Gardening	3,972,757.86	
Total		7,960,043.31
G. Labor		
G1. Cattle	9,826,875.00	
G2. Gardening	12,105,000.00	
Total		21,931,875.00
H. Net profits		
H1. Cattle	5,787,103.82	
H2. Gardening	26,552,042.14	
Total		32,339,145.96

$$\frac{\text{Profit}}{\text{Investment}} = \frac{32,339,145.96}{132,667,386.73} = 24\% \text{ or } \$452,748 \text{ net profit}$$

* This value is not included in the rest of the account for reasons detailed
in the cattle accounts below.
† Differences between the data gathered in the socioeconomic census and
the figures generated from the accounts lead to the discrepancy of 225,240
pesetas between this total and that found in Chapter 2, p. 37.

The system need not be explained formally because one of its virtues is simplicity. I will thus present, without explanation, the total accounting for agriculture in Fuenterrabia which combines the results of the cattle-raising and gardening accounts. Then I will present separate cattle accounts for each exploitation level and a general accounting and commentary on cattle raising, followed by a similar analysis of gardening. Finally, the results will be analyzed in terms of the relations between profits and the distribution of the factors of production.

The accounting will be done in outline form for ease of reading and reference. Each account will be followed by an explanation keyed by letter and number to the sections of the account, explaining the exact means of calculation of all figures.

The first account will be presented without indication of the method of calculation because these figures will be explained in the subsequent accounts. This account is the total value in pesetas of profits in cattle raising and gardening from September 1, 1968 to August 31, 1969 (Table 3.4). The account will take on more meaning after its components have been explained, but some points can be made: Agriculture operates at a profit. If net profits are added to interest and payments added to labor, the resulting figure approximates the total income generated for farmers by the farm economy. As the accounting is explained, this reasoning will be clearer. Suffice it to say here that total farm income, calculated in this way, is 62,230,998.44 pesetas. Divided by the 168 farms, this gives a per farm income of 370,422.60 pesetas or about $5,186–a substantial income. In reality, this is not divided up equally, so that some farms make much more and others, much less. Also, while there are cattle on nearly all the farms in Fuenterrabia, cattle raising contributes only 20 percent of the net profits while gardening accounts for 80 percent. This indicates the enormous profitability of gardening relative to cattle raising, and will be the focus of much of the analysis that follows.

Table 3.5 presents the general cattle account. In the following pages I will provide a summary of the data inputs and then accounts for all three exploitation levels separately, with all the calculations explained (Tables 3.9, 3.10, and 3.11). This is the reverse of the actual calculation procedure, but is a more logical order in which to read it.

Turning to Table 3.5, the machinery value in the Capital section is given as if all machinery were purchased in 1968. As noted before this is because I could not get detailed information on the age of machinery from which to make up a depreciation scale, and be-

Table 3.5. *General cattle accounts, 9/68–8/69 (in pesetas)*

A. Land	671,904,885.00*
B. Capital	66,454,755.73
C. Production	31,568,225.75
D. Costs	11,966,961.48
E. Gross profit (C − D)	19,601,264.27
F. Interest	3,987,285.45
G. Labor	9,826,875.00
H. Net profit (E − [F + G])	5,787,103.82

$$\frac{\text{Profit}}{\text{Investment}} = \frac{5,787,103.82}{66,454,755.73} = 9\%$$

* This exclusion will be explained following this accounting.

cause much of the machinery was introduced so recently that there is no used machinery market. Building value is set by observations of building conditions and values in 1968.

This summary of cattle raising shows that the dairying and beef-raising contribution to total agricultural activity is not only small in percentage but is also far under the profit-investment ratio of 24 percent showing for agriculture as a whole. This is not an accidental result and it is the beginning point of my analysis of the rise of gardening.

In these accounts the value of land employed in cattle raising is not included even though it is very large. To include this would necessitate either that it have an alternative use or that it could be sold. The problem is that these farms generally range from 2–10 ha. in size. The largest garden size in Fuenterrabia is 7,000 m², this size being held down by the market organization. Thus the only alternative demand for large parcels of cattle land is the summer home market. However, the summer home builder wants only 5,000 to 10,000 m² plots for the building sites. He does not want to buy whole farms. In addition, sites suitable for a home (having a good view and easy access) are usually few on any given farm. Thus the sale of a cattle farm as a unit becomes a problem. Many farmers would sell if they could find a buyer willing to take the whole farm. This contention is supported by what happened in one barrio. The Jaizkibel Country Club, Inc., wanted to accumulate about 60 ha. of land for a construction. By offering to buy whole farms at a low price (20–40 pesetas per m²), they were able immediately to purchase 15 cattle farms. In fact only two of the farms in the area refused to sell and a few others are holding out for a higher price. This illustrates the point that, if a buyer is willing to take the whole farm, cattle farms are readily sold. If only small parcels are wanted, the farmer waits, feeling that it is more secure to keep farming and wait for a large buyer. To sell in parcels might make the farm unexploitable and leave the farmer with a number of poor, unsaleable parcels. Furthermore, the cost of inheriting many farms is only that of settling with siblings, which may make the land acquisition cost lower than the market price, providing inheritance conflicts do not develop. Thus, for cattle farms the effective opportunity cost for land used in farming is zero, and therefore it is not added into the accounts. I include the value in the account only to show how high the land market value would probably be relative to other factor values and to show why, when a sale is possible, it usually is made without hesitation.

The land value itself is arrived at by using the municipal *plus valía* index (p. 127). The farms are categorized according to the *plus valía* and then the square meters of land are multiplied by four times the *plus valía* to get the market value.

In the garden accounts the land used is included in the accounting because these small plots have alternative uses, namely cattle raising. The ultimate effect of this is to favor cattle raising in the accounting, but even so the profitability of cattle raising is far below that of gardening.

Before doing the accounts for each exploitation level I will present a summary of the data inputs derived from the previous section (see Tables 3.6, 3.7, and 3.8). The classification of farms into the exploitation levels corresponding to different feeding practices was done through observation and cross-checking with the local veterinarian who has lived for many years in Fuenterrabia and knows all the farms and farmers well. Though there is bound to be some error, it is likely to be slight because the use of factory feeds is the main source of differentiation. As this has repercussions in the weight and production of the animals and requires weekly visits from the feed dealer, most people know how much each farmer uses.

As mentioned before, in these accounts milk and beef production are combined. This is unfortunate because it disguises the differences between these two types of cattle raising. On a small scale, milk production is more profitable than beef raising, as will be shown in the individual case studies. However, I could devise no means to separate the amounts of capital used for each type of animal, especially since the actual mix of the animals in the stable varies greatly. Only in those cases observed firsthand for a year, could I do this. The total number of animals may be constant over the year but the relative number of cows and calves depends on the time of year and other factors. As my census itself was done over a six-month period, I do not feel confident enough about the

Table 3.6. *One-year costs to be used in cattle accounts*

Specialization	Item	Costs (pesetas)
Dairy	Milch cow	35,000.00
	Bedding	173.38
	Miscellaneous	1,200.00
	Feed	
	level 1	8,456.10
	level 2	3,884.20
	level 3	2,705.20
	Upkeep	5% of building and machinery value
	Labor per cow	11,250.00
Beef	Calf	4,000.00
	Bedding	146.00
	Miscellaneous	250.00
	Feed	
	level 1	6,503.44
	level 2	2,324.77
	level 3	2,209.20
	Labor per calf	5,625.00

Table 3.7. *One-year production values to be used in cattle accounts*

Specialization	Item	Values (pesetas)
Dairy	Milk	
	level 1	40,500.00
	level 2	32,400.00
	level 3	27,000.00
	Calves	4,000.00
	Manure	3,250.00
	Slaughter	
	level 1	17,298.00
	level 2	15,004.00
	level 3	13,206.00
Beef	Slaughter	
	level 1	22,500.00
	level 2	20,250.00
	level 3	18,000.00
	Manure	1,250.00

Table 3.8. *Census data for cattle accounting*

Exploi-tation level	Number of farms	Cows		Calves		Fixed capital value (pesetas)
		Total	Per farm	Total	Per farm	
1	29	172	5.9	83	2.9	9,383,347
2	84	396	4.7	237	2.8	20,103,312
3	35	101	2.9	89	2.5	5,933,618
Total	148*	669		409		35,420,277

* Three cases are unclassified.

numbers to separate out actual specializations within cattle raising. The two specializations are not alternatives, more likely they are a result of holding one or two calves born in the stable for fattening. I was unable to get accurate information on the real lactation cycles of the cows in order to see whether or not there was an attempt to target milk production for the summer. My impression, and that of the farmers I asked, was that milk production was not targeted for the summer months.

With this information, the accounts with the derivation of the figures, where relevant, can be presented. The first account (Table 3.9) is for exploitation level 1; an explanation of the derivation of these figures, keyed to the account by letter and number, follows.

A. This value is from the census.

B1.a. There are 172 cows at this level at a value of 35,000 pesetas each giving 6,020,000 pesetas.

B1.b. There are 83 calves at 4,000 pesetas each for 332,000.

B2. These figures are taken from the census.

B3. Circulating capital in cattle raising is estimated at ½ of the total costs. In this case, costs D are 3,816,991.43 which divided by 2 gives 1,908,495.71. This method of calculation is used because cattle raising cannot really be divided into a one-year operation, and money spent the previous year is paying off this year, etc. This represents the minimum amount of cash a farmer needs to raise cattle.

C1. Milk production at level 1 is computed as follows: There is a 20 percent loss of milk production due to lost calves or failure to have the cows inseminated. Thus only 80 percent of the cows produce or .80 × 172 cows = 137.60 cows in production. At level 1 each cow produces milk valued at 40,500 pesetas per year which multiplied by 137.60 gives 5,572,800.00 pesetas.

C2. The number of calves produced has been determined in C1. With the 20 percent loss of calves a total of 137.60 calves are raised at 4,000 pesetas each giving 550,400.00. It should be noted that fractions of cows and calves are included because the 20 percent loss is an approximation, and is not made more accurate by rounding off.

C3.a. Given an active life of 8 years for a milch cow, this means that yearly ⅛ of the cows must be replaced on the average. Thus, ⅛ of the cows (or 21.5 cows) are slaughtered per year. At level 1 a

Table 3.9. *Level 1 cattle account (in pesetas)*

A. Land		163,620,360.00
B. Capital		
B1. Livestock		
a. cows	6,020,000.00	
b. calves	332,000.00	
B2. Buildings and machinery	9,383,347.00	
B3. Circulating	1,908,495.71	
Total		17,643,842.71
C. Production		
C1. Milk	5,572,800.00	
C2. Calves	550,400.00	
C3. Beef		
a. cows	371,907.00	
b. calves	1,680,750.00	
C4. Manure		
a. cows	559,000.00	
b. calves	103,750.00	
Total		8,838,607.00
D. Costs		
D1. Feed		
a. cows	1,454,449.20	
b. calves	539,785.52	
D2. Bedding		
a. cows	29,821.36	
b. calves	12,118.00	
D3. Replacement of cows	752,500.00	
D4. Purchase of calves	332,000.00	
D5. Miscellaneous		
a. cows	206,400.00	
b. calves	20,750.00	
D6. Upkeep	469,167.35	
Total		3,816,991.43
E. Gross profits		5,021,615.57
F. Interest	1,058,630.56	
G. Labor	2,401,875.00	
Total of F + G		3,460,505.56
H. Net profits		1,561,110.01

$$\frac{\text{Profit}}{\text{Investment}} = \frac{1,561,110.01}{17,643,842.71} = 9\%$$

slaughtered cow produces 17,298 pesetas; multiplied by 21.5 this gives 371,907.00 pesetas.

C3.b. The calves are sold at one year for slaughtering. During the year there is about a 10 percent loss of calves from illness or accidents, meaning that 74.7 survive to be sold. Each is worth, at level 1, 22,500 pesetas which, multiplied by 74.7 gives 1,680,750.00 pesetas. The lower number of calves is taken from the census.

C4.a. As explained earlier cows produce 3,250 pesetas worth of manure × 172 cows = 559,000 pesetas.

C4.b. Calves produce 1,250 pesetas worth which multiplied by 83 gives 103,750 pesetas. In this case I did not feel these estimates accurate enough to lower them by the percentage of calves that die.

D1.a. At level 1 feed cost per cow is 8,456.10 × 172 cows = 1,454,449.20.

D1.b. At level 1 feed cost for calves is 6,503.44 × 83 calves = 539,785.52. I did not reduce this by the calves lost since I could find no meaningful way of estimating the feed used and lost.

D2.a. Bedding costs 173.38 per cow per year × 172 = 29,821.36.

D2.b. Bedding costs 146.00 per animal × 83 = 12,118.00.

D3. As cows have a useful life of 8 years, on the average, ⅛ of the stock must be replaced each year; ⅛ × 172 = 21.5 which multiplied by 35,000 pesetas per milch cow = 752,500.00.

D4. The yearly purchase of calves is 83 × 4,000 pesetas per calf = 332,000 pesetas. I had doubts about including this since most farmers get calves simply by raising a few born in the stable. However, a calf still costs the farmer 4,000 pesetas because he foregoes that amount by not selling the animal. For that reason the calves must appear as produced value in section C and as costs in section D.

D5. Miscellaneous includes medicines, fees for the veterinarian, etc.

D5.a. These are estimated at 1,200 pesetas per head per year × 172 = 206,400.

D5.b. These are estimated at 250 pesetas per head per year × 83 = 20,750.

D6. Upkeep refers to repairs of the stables and of the machinery and other tools. After questioning farmers I set this at a flat 5 percent per year for all types of capital. Thus 5 percent of 9,383,347 = 469,167.35.

E. Gross profit is figured simply as produced value minus costs or 8,838,607.00 − 3,816,991.43 = 5,021,615.57.

F. This category requires some explanation. In Padre Lecuona's accounting this refers to interest on the land value and on the capital based on the idea that 6 percent per year must be paid to this value and profit must be considered over and above this interest. I think this is a useful concept since I am looking at the alternative applications of value to production. For this reason, explained earlier, I exclude interest on land and figure interest as a flat 6 percent of capital section B. If I had the data (which I do not) it would be better to calculate the real interest paid on buildings and machinery. The rest, livestock and circulating capital, are readily convertible into cash and thus have alternative uses and banking the money alone would earn the 6 percent. Thus section F actually deducts the cost of not utilizing this capital in some other pursuit, namely saving it at a fixed rate of interest; therefore it is really interest and opportunity cost combined. Ultimately this lowers the final profit figure more than other methods would, but has the great advantage of including the cost of not doing something else with the value employed.

The calculation is simply 6 percent of 17,643,842.71 = 1,058,630.56. Loan payments are not included in these accounts because I found almost no loans being taken. Thus the interest category serves to cover the subject of opportunity costs for the capital and land employed.

   G. Labor is calculated at 11,250 pesetas per cow and at 5,625 pesetas per calf. Thus 172 cows × 11,250 = 1,935,000 pesetas labor for cows and 83 calves × 5,625 = 466,875 pesetas labor for calves. Then 1,935,000 + 466,875 = 2,401,875 pesetas.

In Padre Lecuona's accounting system labor is placed here rather than in the cost category, and I have followed this practice. In family farming the wage for personal labor is rarely paid in cash and is seldom accounted for. Thus it does not enter the cost picture as something actually to be paid as do the other costs. Instead it is usually included by the farmer within the concept of profits. For my purposes this fits in very well because labor in this context is similar to opportunity cost in that the value of labor is calculated to see if it is being paid for at a comparable level as in some other occupation such as factory labor. In this case the value of farm labor was set as 90,000 pesetas per year which is the average earning foregone by not working in the factories. The fact that the wages are foregone explains why the labor value must be calculated and why it is placed in the section of debits against gross profits.

It must also be noted that a farm family can manipulate its labor. A farmer can decide to keep four cows or eight calves and still manage to hold an urban job at 90,000 pesetas a year, if he wishes, and if his wife and family can do the light stable work. However, such arrangements indicate either a farm too small to support more cattle and unsuited to gardening or a family in the process of moving out of agriculture.

   H. Net profit is simply E. Gross Profits minus F. Interest, and G. Labor or 5,021,615.57 − (1,058,630.56 + 2,401,875.00) = 1,561,110.01 net profit for the September 1, 1968 through August 31, 1969 period, at level 1 exploitation.

In this case total production is about one-half the capital employed while costs are about half the gross profits and interest, and labor, the other half.

The next account (Table 3.10) is for level 2 exploitation in cattle raising. Here the explanation of calculation will be left out as the means of accounting are identical to those previously followed.

Table 3.10. *Level 2 cattle account (in pesetas)*

A. Land		322,347,342.00
B. Capital		
B1. Livestock		
a. cows	13,860,000.00	
b. calves	948,000.00	
B2. Buildings and machinery	20,103,312.00	
B3. Circulating	3,206,244.88	
Total		38,117,556.88
C. Production		
C1. Milk	10,264,320.00	
C2. Calves	1,267,200.00	
C3. Beef		
a. cows	742,698.00	
b. calves	4,319,325.00	
C4. Manure		
a. cows	1,287,000.00	
b. calves	296,250.00	
Total		18,176,793.00
D. Costs		
D1. Feed		
a. cows	1,538,143.20	
b. calves	550,970.49	
D2. Bedding		
a. cows	68,658.48	
b. calves	34,602.00	
D3. Replacement of cows	1,732,500.00	
D4. Purchase of calves	948,000.00	
D5. Miscellaneous		
a. cows	475,200.00	
b. calves	59,250.00	
D6. Upkeep	1,005,165.60	
Total		6,412,489.77
E. Gross profits		11,764,303.23
F. Interest	2,287,053.41	
G. Labor	5,788,125.00	
Total of F + G		8,075,178.41
H. Net profits		3,689,124.82

$$\frac{\text{Profit}}{\text{Investment}} = \frac{3,689,124.82}{38,117,556.88} = 10\%$$

Any question can be cleared up by consulting the explanation for the account of level 1.

In this account the picture is quite different from level 1. Production (C) is half the value of the capital (B) but in this case costs (D) are more than one-third the value of production. The source of the difference in costs is the difference in feed costs only. Thus the restriction of factory feeds from the cattle diet lowers costs greatly while overall production remains high. The interest and labor costs are a little under half the value of production. Thus a technically inferior method of production results in an increase of the profit-investment ratio, and the fact that the majority of the farms use this method indicates that this is not unknown to the farmers.

The reasons for the superiority of a lower level of exploitation are partly a matter of speculation. However, I offer one explanation. Exploitation at level 1 is only efficient if the enterprise is large enough to profit from the economies of scale, as a later individual case of a large cattle farm will show (case 1, Chapter 5). As most farms have between five and ten head, this optimal diet is not compensated for by increased revenues.

Why any farms operate at level 1 is an interesting question. In most cases the farms are big. It is already known that the labor force is not readily expansible and larger farms cannot increase the labor force much. If a large farm decides to exploit near the land carrying capacity, the labor force is not sufficient to produce grass and forage for many head in quantities sufficient to substitute for the factory feeds in the diet. Thus at these levels of production there is probably little choice but to employ the level 1 diet.

At level 3 of exploitation, the picture is quite different (Table 3.11). In the case of the level 3 farms, profits are lowered. It must be remembered that in this method of accounting the 6 percent interest to capital and payments to the farmers' labor have already been deducted.

What makes the difference in this case is that the further decrease in the quality of the diet reduces costs a little more, but not enough to compensate for the loss in milk and meat production, and net profits are thus sharply reduced.

Farms operating at this level tend to be those with very few cattle. The farms either are only marginally involved in agriculture or are keeping cattle to have manure for the gardens and to cover home consumption of milk, selling the small excess.

The use of capital to bring production up to level 1 causes some increase in revenues but the overall profit-investment relationship

Table 3.11. *Level 3 cattle account (in pesetas)*

A. Land		185,937,183.00
B. Capital		
B1. Livestock		
a. cows	3,535,000.00	
b. calves	356,000.00	
B2. Buildings and machinery	5,933,618.00	
B3. Circulating	868,740.14	
Total		10,693,358.14
C. Production		
C1. Milk	2,181,600.00	
C2. Calves	323,200.00	
C3. Beef		
a. cows	166,725.75	
b. calves	1,441,800.00	
C4. Manure		
a. cows	328,250.00	
b. calves	111,250.00	
Total		4,552,825.75
D. Costs		
D1. Feed		
a. cows	273,225.20	
b. calves	196,618.80	
D2. Bedding		
a. cows	17,511.38	
b. calves	12,994.00	
D3. Replacement of cows	441,000.00	
D4. Purchase of calves	356,000.00	
D5. Miscellaneous		
a. cows	121,200.00	
b. calves	22,250.00	
D6. Upkeep	296,680.90	
Total		1,737,480.28
E. Gross profits		2,815,345.47
F. Interest	641,601.48	
G. Labor	1,636,875.00	
Total of F + G		2,278,476.48
H. Net profits		536,868.99

$$\frac{\text{Profit}}{\text{Investment}} = \frac{536,868.99}{10,693,358.14} = 5\%$$

is lowered. Reducing units of capital from level 2 to level 3, however, brings about a decrease in revenues and lowers the profit-investment ratio considerably. Thus level 2 maximizes the profit-investment ratio in this situation, a fact the farmers are clearly aware of. Fifty-six percent of the cattle farms operate at level 2.

Table 3.12. *Levels of exploitation and percentages of profits in cattle raising*

Level of exploitation	Number of farms	Percent of total farms	Percent of net cattle-raising profits
1	29	20	27
2	84	56	64
3	35	24	9
Total	148	100%	100%

My general case for the relationship between the level of exploitation and the number of cattle is given strong support in the case of milch cows by the phi correlation. This correlation is $-.53$ and is significant at the .001 level, meaning that high levels of exploitation are associated with larger numbers of cows on a farm and lower levels with fewer cows.

Table 3.12 shows the distribution of exploitation levels and profits. It demonstrates that over half of all the farms work at level 2 and account for a total of 64 percent of the total net profits. Given the fact that this level has the highest profit-investment ratio, it is clear that the choice of method tends toward the technique giving the highest profits, all without a formal accounting system. This information alone provides ample justification of the complex accounting techniques employed here. In spite of the makeshift nature of the data and the degree to which the accounts depend on estimates, clear relationships, with some quantitative basis, have emerged.

Two very important lessons of wider import have also been learned. First, even within a sample of 160 farms, the amount of technical variation is not only great, it is of critical significance in understanding what is happening in agriculture here. For example, it can be seen that any major deterioration in milk and/or meat prices will very likely force the level 1 farms down to level 2, as profits are erased, or out of cattle raising entirely. If costs remain equal I would predict that the level 3 farms are most likely to leave cattle raising next. Thus in future analyses of economic change, the variations in technique must be taken into account in detail, and the technically homogenized view of the countryside subjected to skeptical scrutiny.

The second lesson is that even in such small-scale farming as that existing in Fuenterrabia, variations in farm size produce significant variations in appropriate and profitable techniques. Level

2 is probably optimal in this case, with level 1 only being useful on very large farms and under extenuating circumstances, primarily the scarcity of labor. On the other hand, too little investment lowers profits greatly.

In short order it will become apparent that the gardening specialization has very different characteristics from those found in cattle raising. As before, I will present a general garden account, first without explanation of the calculations and then with detailed specific accounting by exploitation levels (see Table 3.13).

Many striking differences between this and the general cattle account appear. The first is that the profit-investment ratio is four times as great in gardening as it is in cattle raising. Production, instead of being half the value of the capital, is double the value of the capital. Thus capital employed in gardening is about four times as productive as it is in cattle raising.

The reader will have noticed that the value of land is included in this accounting, while it was excluded from the cattle account. There are reasons for this. Garden plots are small and tend to be flat. They are easily sold for house sites. Also this land does have an alternative use—it can be used to produce forage crops for cattle raising. All garden plots can be used this way. The reverse is not true because most land in grass, suitable for cattle raising, is not suitable for gardening. Furthermore, the area of cattle-raising land may be 1 to 2 ha., which is larger than a local garden can be, and therefore cannot be converted in its entirety into garden, even if physically suitable. For these reasons the value of the land has

Table 3.13. *General garden account, 9/68–8/69 (in pesetas)*

A. Land		41,741,770.00
B. Capital		
B1. Buildings and machinery	16,486,041.00	
B2. Circulating	7,984,820.00	
Total		24,470,861.00
C. Production		50,614,620.00
D. Costs		7,984,820.00
E. Gross profit		42,629,800.00
F. Interest	3,972,757.86	
G. Labor	12,105,000.00	
Total of F + G		16,077,757.86
H. Net profit		26,552,042.14

$$\frac{\text{Profit}}{\text{Investment}} = \frac{26,552,042.14}{66,212,631.00} = 40\%$$

been included here as have the 6 percent interest paid on this value as opportunity cost.

In terms of total municipal agricultural production from these two specializations, gardening accounts for about 80 percent of the total profits while cattle raising accounts for only 20 percent. Table 3.14 summarizes the data inputs for these accounts. First, I determined that the labor of one individual was sufficient to culti-

Table 3.14. *Garden accounting: inputs by level of exploitation*

Exploitation level	Total area of garden (ha.)	Gross value of production per m² (pesetas)*	Paid out costs per m² (pesetas)	Total land value (pesetas)	Total fixed capital value (pesetas)
1	10.6	269	39	24,694,250	7,216,904
2	6.3	215	35	12,811,080	6,468,731
3	5.3	161	31	4,236,440	2,800,406
Total	22.2	–	–	41,741,770	16,486,041

* Thirty percent of the value of produced vegetables is deducted as an estimate of normal losses due to weather, market conditions, or miscalculations. This was done by working through specific production histories of a number of gardens which led to the setting of the 30 percent figure.

Table 3.15. *Level 1 garden account (in pesetas)*

A. Land		24,694,250.00
B. Capital		
B1. Buildings and machinery	7,216,904.00	
B2. Circulating	4,130,100.00	
Total		11,347,004.00
C. Production		28,487,100.00
D. Costs		4,130,100.00
E. Gross profit		24,357,000.00
F. Interest		
F1. Land	1,481,655.00	
F2. Total capital	680,820.24	
G. Labor	5,760,000.00	
Total of F + G		7,922,475.24
H. Net profit		16,434,524.76

$$\frac{\text{Profit}}{\text{Investment}} = \frac{16,434,524.76}{36,041,254.00} = 46\%$$

vate and sell the produce of 1,650 m² or .17 ha of garden. This exact-sounding figure is actually the result of observation of work and the division of a number of garden sizes by the number of people working them. Nevertheless it is fairly appropriate. Again I did not rely on the census for this data because it was impossible to get people to separate the time they spent working in the garden from the time spent tending cattle and performing other chores, and I had to rely on an estimate which fits fairly well with the census data.

The first account (Table 3.15) is that of the level 1 exploitations; in other words, those making the most intense and continuous use of the land.

Key to Table 3.15:

A. This comes from the census data on land.

B1. This comes from the census data on capital.

B2. Circulating capital in the case of gardening is set at the total amounts of costs D, or 4,130,100.00. In the cattle accounts it was set at one-half this amount because cattle raising is not really geared to a yearly production cycle with complete turnover. In gardening, one year sees the investment in costs turned into profit in all cases, and thus the entire amount of costs is used. For those who disagree with this reasoning, the effect is to favor the cattle industry and cut down the profit-investment ratio in gardening.

C. Production is simply calculated using the output in pesetas per square meter at level 1–269 pesetas. Thus 269 pesetas $\times$ 105,900 m² of level 1 gardens = 28,487,100.00. As I mentioned before, this production figure includes a deduction of 30 percent of the total value per m² to take into account losses due to weather, gluts, etc. This 30 percent figure was set on the basis of a sample of the production of five gardens for one year.

D. Costs are calculated by reference to Table 3.14, taking 39 pesetas per m² cost and multiplying by 105,900² of level 1 garden = 4,130,100.00. As discussed earlier, these costs are the results of specific ethnographic analysis and represent all the variable costs of producing each vegetable.

E. Gross profit is simply production minus costs, or 28,487,100.00 – 4,130,100.00 = 24,357,000.00.

F1. Interest is calculated on the land factor because it does have alternative uses and thus must earn at least 6 percent of its own value yearly in order to make this employment of it more profitable than merely banking the value in cash. Thus 6 percent $\times$ 24,694,250.00 = 1,481,655.00 pesetas per year.

F2. Here buildings and machinery are added to circulating capital. All of these are readily convertible into cash or applicable to alternative ends, and thus must earn at least 6 percent per year to be employed

profitably in gardening. Thus 7,216,904.00 + 4,130,100.00 =
11,347,004.00 × 6 percent = 680,820.24 pesetas per year interest.

G. Labor is calculated at the same value as in cattle raising, or 90,000 pesetas per year as the opportunity cost of employing labor in agriculture as opposed to factory or trade work. Since one person can cultivate and sell the produce of 1,650 m² of garden, the total m² of garden,
105,900, is divided by 1,650 m², giving 64 labor units: 64 × 90,000 pesetas per year = 5,760,000 pesetas per year labor value in level 1 gardening.

H. Net profit is E − (F + G), or 24,357,000.00 − 7,922,475.24 =
16,434,524.76.

The reader is likely to find this accounting rather hard to believe. I admit to having not believed it at all when I reached these
results in the field. Consequently, I rechecked all the quantities
and concepts used, to ensure that errors had not been introduced.
A second method of checking was to do this accounting for individual farms and then try to relate their profits to known investments they had made and to casual comments about the daily take
at the market. This painstaking process during the last six months
of fieldwork produced some modifications, but the phenomenal
profit rates and levels continued unchanged.

The key to this profit margin is that even after deducting 30 percent of the entire year's crop as a total loss, costs are less than one-
seventh of the gross value of the produce. Moreover, the interest
and labor amount to less than one-third of the value of the produce. Thus the key to the high profits is in section C, Production.

That costs are very low could be a reason. However, most of the
elements entering into the variable costs are items like chemical
fertilizers, lime, sand, and manure, items that are at least as costly
here as anywhere in Spain. Though proof would be difficult for
lack of comparative data from other areas, I do not think that low
costs are the reason for high profits. High prices and volume seem
to lie at the root.

If we accept informant testimony and personal observation,
most garden farms operate at either a loss or break even from
about September to March. In April to June and September to No-
vember there is a small profit, but from July to August, profits soar
both because of prices and of volume. During July and August the
avalanche of tourists enters the area, increasing the population by
at least four times its size. The familiar complaint of the farmers
about low sales changes to anguish over the day not being long
enough to grow and harvest more vegetables. They sell all the lettuce, beans, peas, and tomatoes they can produce. I could not estimate what the monthly profits during these months are, but as

they average out to 40 percent per year when the rest of the months are slow, they must be huge. Thus the enormous profitability of gardening is in large part due to the demand situation created by tourism.

Tables 3.16 and 3.17 provide the accounts for levels 2 and 3. I will not reproduce the method of accounting here because it is

Table 3.16. *Level 2 garden account (in pesetas)*

A. Land		12,811,080.00
B. Capital		
B1. Buildings and machinery	6,468,731.00	
B2. Circulating	2,220,400.00	
Total		8,689,131.00
C. Production		13,639,600.00
D. Costs		2,220,400.00
E. Gross profit		11,419,200.00
F. Interest		
F1. Land	768,664.80	
F2. Total capital	521,347.86	
G. Labor	3,465,000.00	
Total of F + G		4,755,012.66
H. Net profit		6,664,187.34

$$\frac{\text{Profit}}{\text{Investment}} = \frac{6,664,187.34}{21,500,211.00} = 31\%$$

Table 3.17. *Level 3 garden account (in pesetas)*

A. Land		4,236,440.00
B. Capital		
B1. Buildings and machinery	2,800,406.00	
B2. Circulating	1,634,320.00	
Total		4,434,726.00
C. Production		8,487,920.00
D. Costs		1,634,320.00
E. Gross profit		6,853,600.00
F. Interest		
F1. Land	254,186,40	
F2. Total capital	266,083.56	
G. Labor	2,880,000.00	
Total of F + G		3,400,269.96
H. Net profit		3,453,330.04

$$\frac{\text{Profit}}{\text{Investment}} = \frac{3,454,330.04}{8,671,166.00} = 40\%$$

identical to that for level 1 except that the inputs for level 2 (Table 3.14) are used. It is worth noting that the profit-investment ratio is much less favorable here than in level 1. Most of the lowering of profits, in comparison with level 1, occurs in categories F and G, which together amount to 42 percent of the value of the gross profits. In level 1 they are only about 33 percent of the value of gross profits.

The account for level 3 (Table 3.17) shows surprising results. In the case of the level 3 gardens the profits rise again to nearer the level 1 ratio. Here the production is again worth about double the value of the total capital. Also the value of the land is below that of the capital in this case, thus lowering interest and increasing the profit-investment ratio.

Table 3.18 presents the percentage distribution of farms by level and percent of profits. It shows that although level 1 farms are not the majority, they dominate the profits taking a total of 62 percent, while the level 2 farms, which are 51 percent of the farms, have only 25 percent of the profits. Most farmers feel, and the accounts suggest, that they may be right, and that further applications of labor and capital would bring even higher profits in gardening.[12] What this essentially means is that at this small scale of gardening, production bottlenecks that cause the rate of profit to diminish do not yet appear. The reason that more than 7,000 m² of garden are not exploited on any single farm is that the labor force is insufficient. Such an exploitation would require about four full-time laborers, a situation only six farms approach at this time. As the domestic cycle progresses their labor force, too, will decrease. Thus the main limitation on the extension and intensification of gardening is the limit of the domestic group labor force, since outside labor cannot be obtained. If a farmer pays double the factory wage all year he feels that he is paying money for nothing and is unwilling to do it. If he offers the high wage only in summer and

Table 3.18. *Levels of exploitation and percentages of profits in gardening*

Level of exploitation	Number of farms	Percent of total farms	Percent of net profits
1	28	37	62
2	39	51	25
3	9	12	13
Total	76	100%	100%

fall, the laborer will be better off working at a steady, year-round pace in the factories. If the farmer does not pay more than the factory wage, the laborers prefer the ease and prestige of factory labor to farm labor.

It should be noted that the level 1 of garden exploitation correlated with large garden size in a phi correlation of . −23 which is significant at the .01 level, but of course the small labor force keeps more farms from moving to this level. Another reason for exploitation at lower levels is that the enormous majority of the farms combines gardening with cattle raising and this additional labor requirement inhibits high-level garden exploitation.

In this general discussion, I have given absolute profit figures, though I have focused attention on profit-investment ratios as a convenient shorthand device. I have already indicated the per farm income figures deriving from these accounts. In Chapter 5, I will give six case studies with full accounts to show the levels of profit on a variety of farms, and to provide an idea of the standard of living these profits can underwrite. For the moment, I merely point out that farming is profitable and that, in most cases, it provides a considerably higher income and standard of living than could be earned in urban jobs.

Two important objections to this accounting which require extended discussion have been raised by Julius Rubin (personal communication). First, cattle raising and gardening might be mutually interdependent and thus be joint products. This means that the separation of accounts and specializations would misrepresent the situation.

The argument rests on the question of whether the manure necessary for gardening must be supplied by the farms' own cattle. There is a market for manure and it can be easily purchased by anyone. In point of fact, nine gardening farms with no cattle do very well in this way, and the market value of manure is used in my accounts.

In no other way is there any necessary interdependence between the two specialties. In Chapter 5 it will be shown that the two specializations coexist in many cases because of the limited land appropriate for gardening and the limitations on the marketing of vegetables. However, this is a separate issue.

A second objection voiced is that what I call profits in my accounting are really, by definition, implicit rents. The economists argue as follows:

Even if you were a farmer who owned your own land, it would be a mistake to think that rent does not enter into your costs of production. After you had paid all your other bills, including wages to yourself at least as great as you could earn elsewhere in the market, there would have to be left an amount at least equal to the market rental value of your land. For what if there were not? Then you would soon find that it would be better for you to rent out your farm on the open market and hire your own labor to somebody else. (Samuelson, 1967:533)

This would supposedly apply to cattle raising which does not produce enough profit to pay off 6 percent of the land value per year as rent. Also it applies to gardening by saying that the present high profits in gardening merely show a transitory situation in which the value of the land has not risen to match increases in productivity. When it does, these profits will be reduced.

The error in this argument is that it assumes that the land values are being set by agricultural forces and thus are related to agricultural productivity. I have been at pains to show that they are not. Urban developers control the price of land; the price is set according to nonagricultural criteria such as the view of the bay, nearness to the beach, and beauty of rock outcroppings. Therefore, the argument that gardening profits are merely rent and that an adjustment upward of land value in response to gardening profits is likely, is false because land values and agricultural profits are not directly related in this situation. Thus the profits are indeed profits, and not rent.

In the case of the cattle farms, the nature of the demand for land for summer homes is such that cattle farms are not readily salable as units, although land values are high. Thus the opportunity cost of rent for the use of the land in cattle raising is zero until the nature of the demand for land changes.

Another question is why, with such high profits available, does competition not flood this market and drive profits down. In cattle raising, Gurelesa provides the element of competition, and indeed, profits in cattle raising are much lower than in gardening, and show signs of further decline. Thus in cattle raising it is only a matter of time until the profits are considerably reduced.

In gardening the situation is more complex. The importance of freshness of vegetables and the proximity of the farms to the market centers permit farmers to do their own selling and thus maintain their incomes. However, until recently the local farmers were the only suppliers in this regional market. The Navarro truck farmers had to cross a high mountain pass on poor roads to sell in Irún-Fuenterrabia. Now, the demand for produce surpasses Fuenterrabia's production and an excellent, all-weather road connecting Navarra with Irún has been built. Since this time the Navarros have increasingly made this trip and made great profits in this market.

The movement of the Navarros into this market has partly been slowed up by the nature of the demand. The Irún market gives good prices during the summer tourist rush only. During the rest of the year it is hardly worth the transport costs to come up to Irún. However, with good profits in summer a relative certainty, the Navarros seem to be targeting more production for the good summer months and making alternative arrangements for the rest of the year.

This may be the beginning of the end of the extremely high profits for the Fuenterrabia farmers. I believe that the Navarros will continue to increase their participation in this market and ultimately reduce profits to more average levels. Therefore, I think gardening is at the beginning of a period of adjustment in which the profit margin has become high enough to attract competition from outside into the local area. Until this happens, however, profits will continue to be profits, not rents, and the farmers are watching these developments vigilantly.

From all of this data on gardening, a number of facts become clear. In the first place there is a fundamental difference between gardening and cattle raising in economic terms. Gardening is the more profitable at all production levels. Part of this profitability has been attributed to the demand for vegetables created by tourism, but there is more to it. In gardening, the relation between the levels of exploitation, meaning the application of capital to the productive process, is such that increasing applications of capital bring in quite considerable increases in revenues. This relationship is somewhat obscured by the problem of land values in the accounts. In fact, the land used in level 3 exploitations happens to have a relatively low per m² value while the most costly land is found in the level 2 gardens. This is a function of the unrelatedness of land values to the specific agricultural qualities of plots, but it does tend to obscure the profits produced by capital somewhat. However, compared with cattle raising, gardening shows that more capital can be added to production with profit. Cattle raising is most profitable at level 2 and shows a diminishing profitability of capital use at level 1.

Gardening makes intensive rather than extensive use of land in a municipality in which the land values are going up. Gardening responds with increasing profit-investment ratios to the intensification of production via applications of more capital and labor, while cattle raising at level 1 already begins to show a diminishing profit rate. However, the disadvantage of gardening, shared with cattle raising, is that it requires a considerable labor force to expand production under the present conditions. Thus gardening fulfills the conditions for successful agriculture better than does cattle raising, but it also comes up against the lack of labor–52 percent of the men living on farms prefer factory work to farming. Thus the explanation of the total condition of agriculture will have to account for the migration of labor out of agriculture despite the favorable profit margins.

On the basis of the information presented so far, gardening should logically be expected to take over in Fuenterrabia and cattle raising should disappear. This has happened to a large extent and can be attributed to the farmers' perception of the higher profits in gardening. However, gardening has not done away with cattle raising for a number of reasons.

I have already shown that the land factor limits large-scale gardening to only about half the farms, those which do not have clay soil. In addition, there are a few farms that have dedicated themselves to cattle raising even though gardening is possible. As cattle farms are not easily sold in their entirety, a number may be hanging on in cattle raising, awaiting the right buyer. Furthermore, cattle raising can be combined with factory work, if there are a couple of able-bodied people on the farm, while gardening requires full-time labor. All these circumstances support the continuation of cattle raising.

A few of the farms that continue with cattle when they could garden are actually in the process of emphasizing the garden more and phasing out the cattle. This transition is done slowly and cautiously. Perhaps most important of all are the limits on gardening imposed by the organization of the garden produce market. Since a family cannot both cultivate and sell the produce of a garden larger than 0.70 ha., they choose to employ the remaining factors of production in cattle raising, preferring to make a small profit in cattle raising to making no profit at all by leaving the factors idle. This is a reasonable and economically-comprehensible choice, and I think it accounts for the main part of the co-occurrence of gardening and cattle raising.

There is no point in overdoing this, however, since there are a few farms that raise cattle when they could garden, and thus are making a choice on which they are losing money. Some do this because they are not aware of the profits they are losing. An exception is those farms committed to cattle raising as a way of life, the life styles of the cattleman and the gardener being quite different.

I have also demonstrated that in gardening, the returns to increasing applications of capital are high while in cattle raising they are not. The figures presented show that a large number of farms exploit the garden or the cattle at the level that yields the best profit-investment ratio. There is an ambiguity in my analysis here in that garden market limitations and the restriction of gardenable soil may, as mentioned, force the farmer to raise cattle to keep the factors profitably employed. This lowers the overall profit-investment ratio for a farm, and also brings the exploitation level down by draining off capital and labor. For example, a farm that would be exploited at garden level 1 will only be employing three-fourths of its factors of production and will add a cattle enterprise to the gardening to increase the gross profits. However, the addition of the cattle may split up the available capital and labor in such a way that the garden may move down to a level 2 exploitation. Support for such a point would have required more individual farm studies than I could carry out.

Farmers often explained to me, in their own terms, that cattle raising and gardening were different and that it did not pay to capitalize cattle raising too much, while this limitation did not apply to gardening. My accounts show that these ideas are essentially correct and that the farmers have an explicit awareness of the different profit-investment ratios within the specializations as well as an awareness of the major difference in profitability between the two. They are thus highly sensitive to their economic situation and while none carries on formal accounting, the basic structure of the farm economy is no mystery to them.

In sum, the data in Chapters 2 and 3 provide crucial links in my argument. Historically, cattle raising and gardening have developed as different specializations out of a primarily subsistence economy as a response to demand for farm products. Gardening has extended practically to the absolute limits imposed by soil conditions, the market organization, and the scarcity of labor, while cattle raising continues mainly on those farms where no alternative is possible or where the ungardened land can be kept in production by raising cattle. The accounts show that gardening is far more profitable and I thus attribute the rapid expansion of gardening to the farmers' awareness of its greater profitability. This I take to be proof of an awareness of the possible profits and of an ability to earn them. I have also argued that there is some evidence to show that the farmers are aware of the different profit-investment ratios within each specialty and that they adjust their activities accordingly.

I do not say that agriculture is technically perfect here, nor that all farmers operate their farms equally well, but my data support the contention that the farmers do perceive, with considerable sensitivity, the avenues of profit in agriculture and have adjusted their use of the factors of production in order to maximize their involvement in the highest profit specialization and level of exploitation.

The efforts expended provide a picture of a profitable agricultural system evolved by a group of basically uneducated farmers in response to economic conditions that developed in this century. The land is not ideal and the techniques are not the best, but the profits are large. While I admit that my economic analysis of agriculture is rather crude, it does make it clear that rural depopulation cannot be explained away as an automatic result of low farm profits.

Thus for the purposes of this work, I now take the profitability of farming and the economic acumen of the farmers to be demonstrated and I therefore discount low agricultural profits and/or the inability of the farmers to perceive and to take advantage of those profits as a total explanation of the present rapid, rural depopulation in Fuenterrabia. Were it not for the fact that from 1960 on, these farms are being abandoned at a rapid rate, the economic data I have just presented could almost be used as examples of the activity of "economic man." But the fact remains that these profitable farms are being abandoned and a strictly economic analysis of agriculture can provide no explanation of this apparent paradox.

So it is that the presentation of the formal-aggregate analysis has led straight into an anomaly that such an analysis can in no way explain. The farms are commercialized and reap high profits. The distribution of the factors of production among the alternative specializations and techniques is such that the good profits are earned. Yet by 1969, the number of farms had dropped to 168 from the previous number of 256 operating in 1920, and the farms abandoned were not merely marginal ones. The average age of the farm head has increased to over 50 years of age and the average farm domestic group size has dropped to 5.5 per farm. The people moving out were all going into lower-paying factory work, paying high urban rents and food prices, and having minimal job security.

Whether or not this situation is typical cannot be judged from the study of one municipality, though I suspect this has happened in more cases than might be imagined. What is clear is that the utility of the formal-aggregate mode of analysis is at an end here. It cannot explain how farmers who maximize in agriculture choose to sacrifice economic gains in order to leave it. The culture of the

Basque farmer here holds the key but it requires a different kind of analysis, developed in the following chapters.

It comes as no surprise that formal economic analysis should not be able to explain all facts of the behavior of a particular group of people. Economy, after all, is only part of culture. What I have done is to dramatize both the contributions and limitations of formal economic analysis in this particular case.

That this mode of analysis has led to the posing of questions that it cannot answer is not a criticism of it, but rather a clear indication of its worth. The idea that a scholar must choose between "economic man" and "traditional man" instead of being free to reproduce some of the complexity of human life is to substitute doctrine for observation. Here I have shown that quantitative economic analysis does not necessarily lead to the negation of the complex cultural dimensions of human life. Properly used, it can focus attention precisely on the complexities of behavior that it cannot explain.

The rest of the book develops a cultural interpretation of farming and rural depopulation and explains why the Basques are willing to sacrifice economic rewards in the service of other goals.

4

The agrarian history of Fuenterrabia from 1920 to 1969

THE SUBSTANTIVE-AGGREGATE VIEW

To portray adequately the institutions and ideas which are at once the basis for the success and the decline of agriculture in Fuenterrabia, an exceedingly wide range of data is required. As the farms are both enterprises and family units, profits, markets, and social structure are complexly intertwined. Beyond this, the farmers have their own interpretation of the meaning of life and this has interacted with the other elements in their situation to bring about the collapse of agriculture here.

At this point it is useful to combine the data on profits and markets with a consideration of the ways in which farmers are able to assemble the factors of production on their farms. An understanding of these two points brings out clearly all of the institutional conditions to which farmers must respond. Following this is an analysis of the farmers' view of the cultural significance of farm life and their hopes for a better future in the cities.

It is important to repeat that the ordering of the presentation does not reflect an attempt to weight the importance of the various factors. The high profitability of agriculture, the institutional context of farming, and the farmers' vision of life and hopes for the future all interact in the commercialization of agriculture and its subsequent collapse in Fuenterrabia.

The first section deals with the means by which farmers gain access to the land, capital, and labor they need–that is, how they get control over the factors of production. This analysis shows that it has become increasingly difficult to assemble the factors of production for farming. Current conditions favor agricultural activities that make intensive rather than extensive use of land, that respond with considerable revenue increases to purchases of additional units of capital, and that do not require a large labor force to produce an acceptable level of profits. Under these conditions, gardening is decidedly advantageous. It is land intensive, yields high returns to additional capital, and requires a small labor force to produce high profits. In gardening, labor, which is scarce, is easily substituted with capital. By contrast, under present conditions, cattle raising requires more land, provides lower returns on capital, and requires a great deal of labor. Thus the tendency for gardening to supplant cattle raising, where possible, represents a sensible response, not only to the specific profit levels and ratios given in the last chapter, but to all the institutional conditions affecting access to the factors of production.

The analytical framework

Before proceeding, a brief review of the methods and concepts used will be helpful. The substantive-aggregate view corresponds to what is found in most studies under, e.g., "the institutional context of economic activity."[13] The discussion of Basque ideas about life and the dignity of work corresponds to what is generally called "the cultural context of economic activity."

This is an aggregate mode of analysis because it states the most common relationships and ideas discovered in my research. After all, analyses of institutions and systems of ideas are made up of statements about the frequencies of certain behaviors. When an observer reports that in a particular society the major means for raising a dowry is by selling cattle, he is saying that in most cases, people behave this way. It is an aggregation of observations which is stated in the form of a rule or a relationship. Thus the substantive-aggregate parallels the formal-aggregate analysis because both consist of statements of the frequencies of certain occurrences.

But the similarity between these two kinds of aggregate analyses is only partial. Both modes are based on observation and interviewing, but the results are organized differently. The formal-aggregate analysis is a statistical picture of the results of behavior expressed as magnitudes and intercorrelations. The substantive-aggregate analysis attempts to formulate the rules, institutions, and ideas that affect observed behaviors.

This chapter does not pretend to provide a full ethnographic coverage of Fuenterrabia. Rather I set out a minimal amount of information about the rules, conditions, and ideas affecting the options open to the farmers.

One major assumption is made: The way the factors of production are brought together on a farm will strongly affect the way they are or can be employed. Through this approach, the constraints and opportunities facing the farmers are revealed, and it is possible to make sense of the increasing emphasis on gardening. Ultimately it sets the stage for the analysis of farmers' decisions to abandon agriculture entirely.

Throughout, the ways in which the factors of production are assembled for farming are called the *means of access to the factors of production.* This idea is borrowed from Emrys Peters,[14] though the concept is current in social network and decision-making theory. The aim of this method is to explain peoples' behavior by understanding the rules for behavior and the conditions under which they are applied. In this case, an understanding of the changes in means of access to the factors of production shows the increasing emphasis on gardening to be an adaptive response to a definable set of conditions. Such information is usually found in anthropological studies under the rubrics of marriage, inheritance, kinship, and so on. In shifting the organization of this chapter away from that mold, I am not trying to increase the reader's difficulties. I find that this procedure allows treatment of marriage, inheritance, purchase, rental, and other means of access from a unified point of view and provides a sense of the farmers' situation.

Basic definitions

The terms land, capital, and labor are used in a conventional way and need no special definition. The means of access to the factors of production are marriage, inheritance, purchase, rental, reciprocal arrangements, production, and appropriation. This ordering reflects my vision of their importance in Fuenterrabia, marriage being the most important and appropriation, the least.

Marriage is viewed as the passage of ownership and/or control over the production factors by entry into a conjugal relationship. *Inheritance* is a passage of ownership and/or control of them from one generation to the next via testamentary or nontestamentary means. In *purchase,* ownership of the factors is gained by paying cash or services in return for definitive legal possession. *Rental* is the payment of an amount of cash, produce, and/or services in return for control over selected factors of production and for the rights to the resulting net profits. *Reciprocal arrangements* refer to various temporary passages of control over certain factors of production in return for similar or equivalent privileges at the same or some future time. *Production* means the creation of factors by expenditure of land, capital, and/or labor; *appropriation* refers to use of the factors with no claim other than the exercise of one's own labor.

This list of means of access does not exhaust the logical possibilities. There could be more means of access and a greater precision of definition, just as there can be more than three factors of production and a variety of ways of defining them. I am working within pragmatically set limits in that I elaborate them only as much as my argument requires.

Means of access to the factors of production:
The socioeconomic context of farming
in the twentieth century

I will begin with a general presentation of the rules, conditions, and ideas affecting access to the factors of production. Following this are specific data for 1920 and 1969 reflecting changes in the areas presented and a discussion of the relatively favorable situation of gardening under these conditions.

Marriage

Land. Land is not transmitted by marriage, but anyone marrying into a farm domestic group gains the right to work the land and to receive bed and board from its produce. The single heir chosen by the parents is allowed to marry, but he or she will not own the land until the parents' death. An in-marrying person may never gain legal control over the land, even upon the spouse's death, since marriage only creates a right to work and a right to usufruct. An in-marrying female works the land in some capacity–probably selling its produce–and performs household duties. An in-marrying male is required to labor on the land. Thus marriage does not transfer ownership of the land to the marrying couple, nor does it allow them to direct the production process. It establishes the right to usufruct and the potential for ownership by the selected heir.[15]

Capital. Marriage does not establish ownership of capital, but creates limited rights of usufruct. The only right clearly established by marriage is the right to material sustenance resulting from the use of the farm's capital. There is some movement of capital since a female marrying onto a farm brings a trousseau and provides the new couple's bedroom with linen and furniture. An in-marrying male pays for the wedding clothes of both families, for the wedding ceremony and banquet, and for the honeymoon if they have one.

In-marrying spouses cannot appropriate farm capital or sell it. They generally cannot gain ownership of it even at the death of the parents-in-law[16] or of the spouse. When a spouse dies, the surviving in-marrying partner will ordinarily have rights of usufruct to the third of betterment (defined below) during his or her lifetime.

Dowries are not stipulated in formal marital contracts in Fuenterrabia, though such contracts are common in other parts of the Basque country (Douglass, 1975). The farmers argue that the health and moral character of a potential spouse is the most important consideration because even a large dowry is insignificant when compared to the value of a lifetime's labor.

Labor. At the beginning of a marriage, the heir's parents, if not incapacitated, control the labor of the in-marrying spouse. Upon their death or incapacitation, the authority pattern must be worked out between the spouses. Authority usually rests with the farm owner, though there are cases of the in-marrying spouse exercising effective control. I have seen no cases of fully equal exercise of authority, but I am not very confident about the precision of my information on this point.

Marriage can be said to produce a labor force—the in-marrying spouse and the children of the marriage. This is quite important in Fuenterrabia since only one heir in each generation is given the right to bring a spouse to the farm. If the heir's parents die or become incapacitated before the heir's children reach working age, the burden of farm work falls entirely on the heir, the unmarried siblings, and the spouse. These periods in the development of a family present difficult problems about which little can be done.

Inheritance

Land. Inheritance provides definitive control of land to farmers, whether they are owners or tenants, but the rules of inheritance are extremely complicated. They involve two conflicting legal systems: the Spanish Civil Code and Basque customary law. The conflicts between these two systems is an old one. Although Basque customary law was formally suppressed in the nineteenth century (Echegaray, 1950), and the farmers publically obey the Spanish Civil Code, they still practice important aspects of customary law. As a result it is necessary here to present elements of both legal systems and then to indicate the important sources of conflict between them and the local solutions most often employed.

In the order of inheritance of the Spanish Civil Code, the legal heirs are: (1) children and legitimate descendants of the testator or of the testator's parents; if none of these exists, (2) the parents or other legitimate ascending relatives of the testator; and (3) the widow or widower, children out-of-wedlock who are legally recognized, and the father or mother of these children (*Código Civil,* Art. 807). If no one belonging to any of these categories exists, anyone the testator wishes may inherit. Otherwise only a portion can go to nonkin (Art. 763). It should also be noted that inheritance can only take place at the death of the testator (Art. 657), thereby delaying the passage of ownership to the chief heir until he or she has reached middle age.

The property subject to inheritance must be divided into thirds: a third for the legitimate offspring, a third for the betterment of legitimate offspring, and a third of "free choice."[17] The Basques oppose division of the land, so that the usual process is to place a value on the land and to divide the value among the heirs. The chief heir gets the farm. His or her siblings receive their corresponding fraction of the third of the legitimate offspring.[18] The third for betterment is given to any child the testator wishes to favor–usually the chief heir–but is initially held in usufruct for the testator's surviving spouse. Finally, the third of "free choice" can go to anyone.

If a farm owner wants to give the chief heir as much as possible and to keep the farm intact, he will give him or her the third of "free choice," the third for betterment, and the corresponding fraction of the third for the legitimate offspring. The heir then pays to the siblings the value of their respective shares of the third for the legitimate offspring and keeps the farm intact (*Código Civil*, Art. 808)

There are many possible permutations, given these complex rules. In the case of testamentary inheritance, the testator may make the distribution of the property known before death and formalize it in an open will. Or an executor may be appointed to divide the property (*Código Civil*, Art. 1,057). The heirs themselves can divide the property, and must do so if there is no will (Art. 1,058). When there is no will or when a will is contested, failure to divide the property to the satisfaction of all concerned forces the matter into court (Art. 1,059).

In all cases, the farm must be assigned a cash value. If the heirs get along well, this is easily done, determining an average price per m² of farmland by taking the varying values of different parts of the farm into account. This value is then divided among the heirs in satisfaction of their claims to the inheritance. Any heir who does not accept the average price can bring the matter to court. When this happens, the court undertakes a complete inventory of the farm (*Código Civil*, Art. 1,010). This is an infavorable procedure for the farmers, because the court usually inflates the value of the farm to increase the inheritance tax; moreover, the heirs must pay the court-hired assessor's salary.

Property acquired by the testator after marriage comes under the category of mutual property (*bienes gananciales*), half of which belongs to each spouse. A will can only apply to the testator's half of the property (*Código Civil*, Arts. 1,392–5, 1,413, and 1,426).

In cases of nontestamentary inheritance, the Spanish Civil Code's ranking of relatives establishes the order for entering claims (*Código Civil*, Arts. 915–23, 930–8). This ranking was discussed above. Inheritances of this type almost always end up in court and the farmers claim that they lose in inheritance taxes and court costs as much as 70 percent of the value of the farm. It is not infrequent for the farm to be sold in order to pay the court costs.

Tenants obviously do not inherit land, but the holders of long-term leases can will the rights to continue as the tenant on a particular farm. Heirs of a tenant farmer receive their shares of the mutual property accruing to the testator and spouse after their marriage, but it is the chief heir who usually ends up with most of it.

Basque customary law runs counter to much of the Spanish Civil Code, thereby creating certain predictable conflicts. The Basques assert that only the following persons have rights in a farm: those kin born on the farm or having worked on it for a long time, and those spouses having married in and having worked on the farm for some time. One heir, who may bring a spouse to the farm, has the right to live on the farm and to direct production after the parents' deaths. The other heirs have the right to live on the farm all their lives if they choose not to marry; or they can receive a dowry, an education, or a sum of money to help them get a start in life off the farm. When farms are bought after some of the children have left home, the absent children have no inheritance rights over the farm. The physical farmstead is conceived of as an indivisible unit. The chosen heir, ideally selected for agricultural talent, is given the farm and the rest are taken care of in other ways.

Thus the first major conflict between the Spanish Civil Code and Basque customary law centers around who has the right to inherit and whether any one child should be favored over the others. The Spanish Civil Code favors division of the property and presses for some equality in inheritance. Interestingly, the Basque customary system ordinarily results in a larger inheritance for the siblings of the chief heir than would the strict application of the rules of the Civil Code. Using the Civil Code, a child may receive only that fraction of the third for the legitimate offspring which pertains to him, a sum generally smaller than the worth of the dowry or the education that Basque customary law requires. The Basques, like many people, feel that the state has no right to intervene in family matters and thus do not feel morally bound to satisfy the requirements of the Civil Code.

The farmers' perception of an ideal outcome to a division of property is as follows. A son or daughter, of proven farming ability, stays on the farm after marrying. The other children are given a start in life outside the farm. The parents, invalid children, and unmarried members of the domestic group live and work on the farm until death, in return for room and board. This is all arranged before the parent's death. Thus the inheritance does not break up the moral unity of the family.

Another source of conflict is the Civil Code's requirement of a unitary valuation of the property. Placing an average price on the land is a complex matter requiring a good deal of negotiation. The chief heir generally wants a low average value to lower inheritance taxes and the amount of the shares to be paid to siblings. The siblings generally want the opposite. One sibling's refusal to agree to the average price can break down the previous arrangements. When this happens, the wishes of the parents are often not observed and much of the value of the property is lost.

Basque customary law itself contains sources of conflict. One is the problem of a child who wants to inherit the farm but is not selected chief heir. He or she will often turn resentment into quarrelsomeness, endangering the plans of the rest of the heirs. Another problem is the quality of life of the siblings who remain on the farm without marrying. They must submit entirely to the authority of the chief heir which means, from the Basque point of view, that they remain forever in the status of children. This often works well, especially while the siblings are young, but when they reach middle age, family relations may become extremely troubled.

Beyond the conflicts intrinsic to the Civil Code and to Basque customary law, other problems arise when farmers attempt to subvert the Civil Code. The prime source of difficulty is that application of the Civil Code can easily lead to a division of the land or to sale of some of it. This runs directly counter to the fundamental tenet of the Basque system, the indivisibility of the farm.

In addition, the Civil Code is cumbersome, making the complex matter of inheritance even more problematic, especially because settlements must await the death of the parents who then cannot mediate the disputes. Inheritance taxes are actively evaded because they are considered immoral. The farmers suspect that the Civil Code is complicated intentionally, to enable the government to deprive them of their property.

A farm bought after some children have grown up and have left home creates a serious problem because the Civil Code gives them full rights to the parents' property. Basque customary law gives rights over a farm and its produce only to those living and working on it for some time. Under these conditions, there is a strong temptation to subvert the application of the Civil Code in order to effect an acceptable customary solution.

However, parents can also use the Civil Code in order to give certain of their children a smaller inheritance than Basque customary law would require. Thus, strict adherence to Spanish law may cause an impropriety when parents and children do not get along.

Inheritance must formally await the death of the parent. If the parent lives to old age, he or she will make known the plans contained in the will by selecting the chief heir who will then marry and work on the farm. At the parent's death, the chief heir may be middle-aged, and have had dedicated his or her adult working life to the farm. If an inheritance battle erupts and ends up in court, the chief heir may lose a great deal of money and occasionally may lose the farm.

Because there are so many sources of conflict and because the conflicts are so serious, a number of conventional mechanisms have been developed to deal with them. The ideal legal inheritance has already been described above. Other mechanisms used are illegal.

The first is a "simulated sale" of the farm. Instead of passing the farm on in a will, the surviving parent feigns sale of the farm to the chief heir. This is done by making a notarized statement to the effect that the farm has been sold and the payment received. No cash actually changes hands, though the sale requires payment of a 5 percent tax on one half of the assessed liquid assets of the farm. This frequently used measure is quite risky because the Civil Code states that all property received in dowry, gifts, or other transactions must be included in the estate for the computation of the property value (*Código Civil*, Art. 1,035). This subterfuge divides the family and if the siblings know the law, they can require that the bill of sale be included in the estate.

Another risk is created by a land reform law stating that sales of properties smaller than 1 ha. must be made known to the owners of adjoining properties. These neighbors then have the right to purchase the property within a period of eight days simply by paying the price on the bill of sale. Since a low price is given on the bill of sale to reduce taxes and there are a number of farms smaller than 1 ha., carelessness can result in the loss of the farm. Still "simulated sale" is used because it is the last resort of a parent who is sure that division by legal means will not work.

Voluntary repudiations of the inheritance constitute another illegal means of avoiding the physical division of the farm. The legal division of the property is made on paper, and then the siblings with small shares, satisfied that they have been well cared for, refuse their legal inheritance. This is risky because it depends on a covert agreement among the siblings before a parent's death. Since the inheritance cannot be refused until the actual division, 15 or 20 years may intervene between making the agreement and the actual refusal of the inheritance. Any falling out among the siblings or the deterioration of the economic situation of any one over the years, may endanger the agreement.[19] If the siblings get along well and feel that they are treated fairly by their parents and by the chief heir, the arrangement is quite successful.

Bringing together the threads of this discussion, it is clear that the inheritance of farms is very complicated. Between the Civil Code with its cumbersome system of thirds and Basque customary law with its requirement that farms be inherited intact, endless problems are created. In a way, the surprising thing is that the system works; the Basques generally succeed in passing farms from generation to generation with only minor alterations in the land base.

As a result of the inheritance system, people adjust their social relations to fit a fixed land base. The number of farms sets the number of chief heirs in the community and thus forms the foundation on which all of the other aspects of social life are erected. The success of the system can be measured in the local archives where most of today's farms are easily identified in census data over 250 years old. (For documentation of similar practices in other Basque towns, see Douglass, 1975.)

Capital. Capital inheritance is the same as the inheritance of land because the rules apply to property in general rather than to separate factors of production. Thus the above discussion applies to capital as well, with only the following qualifications.

Dowry, educational expenses, and inheritance are all seen as part of the inheritance, but in Fuenterrabia they are given at different times. That is, the dowry or educational expenses are received when needed, while formal inheritance cannot be said to have occurred until the death of the parents. In other parts of the Basque country, these matters are dealt with simultaneously at the marriage of the chief heir by means of formal marriage contracts (Douglass, 1975).

In practice this may mean that in Fuenterrabia, an in-marrying spouse can bring in a sum of capital as a result of an inheritance settlement on the spouse's natal farm. This is particularly likely in the case of contested inheritances in which the heirs who have married out ultimately embroil a large number of families in court action. It can also occur that the chief heir pays cash to his or her siblings in return for the land that came to them as a result of the application of the rules of the Civil Code.

The one rule never transgressed seems to be the prohibition on dividing up the farm capital. My questions about this brought a look of horror to the peoples' faces.

Labor. Inheritance does not create labor nor does it place a specific person in charge of it; rather all but one of the potential heirs are excluded from the possible exercise of that authority and are subordinated to the chief heir. Thus inheritance gives authority over the disposition of labor to a particular married couple in each generation.[20] As noted before, authority tends to reside with the chief heir, but there are exceptions in which the in-marrying spouse exercises most of the authority.

Purchase

Land. Purchase is the most direct way to gain permanent title to a farm or a piece of farmland. The most important influences here are the long-run market for land and the availability of capital for farm purchase.

Until recently, the goal of all farmers was to own a farm, and purchase was often the only way to achieve this. Early in this century, 77 percent of the farms were tenant-operated, but between 1930 and 1955, many tenants purchased their farms from the owners. Most of these people attest that getting the money together required years of work, sometimes being the result of two generations of effort. But with work, frugality, and the good fortune to avoid illness and natural disasters, farm purchase was possible. A powerful aid in this was the passage of laws governing farm rents which so favored tenants that the owners were willing to sell (see below, p. 131–2).

Capital. Due to the Basque approach to pecuniary matters, capital for farm purchase was not accumulated through bank loans. The Basques feel that both personal independence and privacy are seriously compromised when loans are contracted with nonkin. In addition, they believe that the payment of interest involves an unacceptable moral commitment to outsiders.

Even so, purchase has been an important source of acquiring housing materials, tools, clothes, chemicals, livestock, and recently, machinery. A market for these items has long existed and they have been widely purchased. The only restriction is that purchase must be made directly out of savings. Most purchase of capital items has been restricted in the recent past by the lack of machinery, chemicals, and seeds suited to the particular agricultural conditions in Fuenterrabia. However, purchase has now become the prime means of access to capital because of the expanded range of useful items for sale.

Labor. The purchase of labor has been possible with full-time, live-in farm laborers or part-time wage laborers only. Neither category has been abundant in this century and most farms have only employed the labor of their own domestic groups. The few available laborers have long had the options of fishing, factory work, and urban odd jobs, and have shown a decided preference for such employment. The greater personal independence offered by fishing and by urban jobs, coupled with the fact that the slow seasons in farming and fishing coincide, has meant that wage labor is rarely available when needed. In the end, the farm domestic group has been able to count only on its own labor force, and has been unable to counter the fluctuations created by changes in the composition of the family over time (see p. 129–30).

Rental

Land. Three types of rental arrangements are used in Fuenterrabia: long-term, protected leases; short-term, unprotected leases; and various sharecropping arrangements.[21] The long-term, protected lease was widely used in the Basque country. With this lease, the advantages rest with the lessee because he or she has the right to operate the farm, can pass on this right to a chosen heir, and cannot be evicted unless paid an indemnity agreed upon by both the tenant and the owner. The rent cannot be raised at the owner's whim because rents were calculated in accordance with a national rent formula (see p. 131–2). Thus a long-term lease results in a relationship to the land that is similar to ownership. The short-term, unprotected lease was also used. It stipulates the exact period of the lease and can be terminated at the end of the period without the payment of an indemnity.

When the absentee landowners lived on rental income, it was in their best interest to give long-term leases to guarantee themselves a consistent flow of earnings and to regularize their relations with tenants. The leases given were highly idiosyncratic in the specification of money payments, payments in kind, and the requirements of services to be provided the owner. For the farmers, such leases provided security and predictability in life, making their own planning easier.

The short-term lease was used, apparently, when the landowner was interested in trying to raise the rent or when the farmer was not certain that he or she wanted to make a firm commitment to a particular farm or set of leasing conditions. Informants felt that this lease was prevalent between about 1900 to 1936, when farms changed hands often. This cannot be directly confirmed because of the absence of regular census data for the period and because the municipal records specify only that farms were owner-operated or tenant-operated and do not describe the lease involved.

Capital. In the case of tenants the farm building is rented as part of the lease and is included under the same conditions and restrictions I already described for the rental of farmland. Farm machinery and hand tools are not part of the lease. Rental of the latter items, without obligations beyond payment in cash or in kind is rare. Rental of a team of oxen for plowing always includes the work of the team owner, and takes on the form of a social reciprocity involving mutual labor obligations. Recent rentals of farm machinery follow this pattern, as will be noted below; but rental has not been an important source of tools and machinery.

Labor. As for labor, there is a definitional problem here in that wages can be viewed as either purchase or rental of labor. I have chosen to consider them as purchase, a preference consistent with my emphasis on labor as a produced commodity. Thus there is no category of access corresponding to the rental of labor.

Reciprocal arrangements

Land. Reciprocity with regard to land has always been limited. Its major form has been the *aparcería* (sharecropping) in which the landowner supplies the land to an *aparcero* who supplies the labor, and they divide the product on a year-to-year basis. Exact arrangements vary. The owner may supply the land and seed or some other item necessary for production, but the *aparcero* always supplies the labor. The profits may be divided in equal or unequal shares. *Aparcería* has not been widely used in this century because the *aparceros* felt that their labor was worth much more than the share they received.

Capital. Given the restricted number of capital items available until recently, there has been little to exchange. Brabant plows were usually lent as part of the general labor reciprocity but reciprocity played a minor role in access to capital.

Labor. Reciprocal labor arrangements were once very widespread in the Basque country (Echegaray, 1933), evidently because the most scarce factor of production was labor. These arrangements are the only reliable hedge against illness and other problems created by the variable size of the farm domestic groups. Residential proximity and/or kinship have been the prime conditions for participation in these labor arrangements.

The most popular form of labor reciprocity has been work teams. The work is socially pleasant and hard work by all parties is assured by mutual cajolery. In addition, a farmer cannot accumulate many reciprocal labor obligations before paying them off or calling them in. So the reciprocities cannot be manipulated to create permanent relations of superiority over others. Team tasks frequently undertaken are plowing, haying, and road maintenance. Mutual aid given in times of crisis more often comes from kin and relatives by marriage without the requirement of immediate payment.

Much of the sociability of farm life was built around these reciprocities. When most farmers were poor, the labor reciprocities were a vital component in the success of any farm. Their contemporary disappearance shows how profound recent social changes have been.

Production

Land. By production of the land factor I mean the creation of land where none existed previously, or the transformation of clay into sandy soil suitable for intensive cropping. From an economic point of view, this produced land could be discussed as capital because of the extent of its transformation. The production of land has played a key role in farming because it both improved soils and increased the amount of land available.

Reclamation of river bottom land was extensively practiced, giving rise to 88 ha. of new land. This process began around 1825,[22] was intensively practiced until about 1930, and ended by about 1945. Transformation of clay soil began much earlier and has been vitally important. The total amount of transformed soil is about 50 ha. When one realizes that all the profitable gardening is now carried out on a total of 22 ha. of sandy soil, it is clear that soil transformation has played a major role in the agricultural history of Fuenterrabia.

The actual process of transformation required the carting in of river sand which was spread over the clay soil and subsequently covered with a heavy application of manure. The soil was then plowed. By repeating the process twice a year, the farmer could hope for improvements in the soil within 5 years, and a complete transformation of it after 30 years or so. The resulting land is ideal for gardening in this climate.

Capital. While there are a number of capital items produced on the farms, capital-producing activity is not very extensive. House building has generally been done under the supervision of a specialist, though remodeling and light work are carried out by the farm family. All steel tools are purchased, but the wooden handles are bought in rough form and are shaped and fitted by the farmers. Work clothing is often sewn at home but the cloth is purchased. The most significant capital items produced on the farm are seeds and plants to be used in farming, and milk cows raised on the farm (see p. 137–40).

Labor. The concept of production of labor requires some theoretical clarification. Labor can be produced in two senses. First, viewing labor as produced by humans is derived from Marxian analysis. A person produces labor for application to various purposes and may or may not, depending on circumstances, be able to control the uses to which it is put. In this sense the primary source of labor in Fuenterrabia is production. All farms, except one, are worked by the domestic group living on them, thus producing their own labor through their own efforts.

Human reproduction is the second sense in which labor is produced. Reproduction produces labor force which in turn produces labor. Such a perspective indicates the pivotal nature of marriage in assembling the factors of production. Where the labor force is almost totally dependent on the fluctuations of the domestic cycle, marriage is the key means for producing the labor factor in the long run.

Appropriation

Land. Appropriation of land, in the sense of willful disregard of another's legal claim to land is illegal and is severely punished. All farms and properties have boundary stones and the owners watch these with great care. Incursion into another farm is taken very seriously and usually leads to legal action. The relationship to communal lands can be viewed as appropriation. These lands are held by the municipality in communal tenure. For centuries they have been available to all residents for the collection of firewood, cutting of fern, and the grazing of semiwild cows. At certain times of the year, pigs were set free to root and to eat nuts on these lands. All farms had these rights by virtue of community membership and exercised them in accordance with their needs and the relative availability of the resources from year to year. Because the communal lands were so large, covering one fourth of the municipality, these rights were quite important.

After the Spanish Civil War, the municipal government planted the land with pine as a source of income for the town. The trees severely restrict the use of the land because they inhibit the growth of hardwood trees, and they impede the development of grass and fern.

Other forms of appropriation are strictly illegal, though I know of at least two cases. One is a garden plot on communal lands. The other case is that of a farmer who works as a gardener for the owners of various summer homes. In the winter he gardens there without the owner's knowledge.

The appropriation of capital in the Basque country is considered to be stealing and as such is not a source of capital. The same is true for labor.

Means of access to the factors of production:
A comparison of farming conditions in 1920 and 1969

The above general description of the means of access in Fuenterrabia refers to this century as a whole. I will now develop specific data about access to the factors of production in 1920 and 1969, documenting the changes that took place between these dates. In this way, the changing availability of the factors is fitted together with the changes accompanying agricultural commercialization.

This part of the analysis is particularly vulnerable to "presentism," in which the past is rewritten to fit the present. Yet the past was not a mere prologue to the present. I have tried to correct for this bias by combining the testimony of aged informants with data gathered in the municipal archives. Still the reconstruction is highly schematic.

Major changes in the availability of the factors of production have taken place between 1920 and 1969, with the pace of change accelerating after about 1955. Together these have affected the kind of production choices possible, and have led to the increasing emphasis on gardening. This is crucial information for the understanding of the rural depopulation now occurring.

Table 4.1 presents a summary of the most important changes. The following discussion is devoted to explaining each of these major alterations in means of access to the factors of production and their significance for farming in Fuenterrabia. Special emphasis is placed on the implications of the decreasing number of ways

Table 4.1. *Comparison of the means of access to factors of production in 1920 and 1969*

	1920			1969		
Means of access	Land	Capital	Labor	Land	Capital	Labor
Marriage	Yes	Yes	Yes	Limited	Limited	Limited
Inheritance	Yes	Yes	Yes	Limited	Limited	Limited
Purchase	Yes	Yes	Yes	No	Yes	Limited
Rental	Yes	Limited	–	No	Limited	–
Reciprocal arrangements	No	Limited	Yes	Limited	Limited	Limited
Production	Yes	Yes	Yes	No	Yes	Yes
Appropriation	Limited	No	No	Limited	No	No

available to farmers to assemble land, capital, and labor in order to continue farming.

Marriage

1920. As discussed above, marriage was a means of access to land. Because of the prevalence of tenant farms in 1920, marriage usually meant that a person worked the land and received income from that work, but had no further right to it. Marriage established usufruct rights to capital as described above and provided rights over a spouse's labor, as well as the possibility of producing children–an additional labor force. The notion of marrying a strong, hardworking man or woman so that the future of the farm would be secure was primary in all marital choices. A constant theme in informants' accounts was the bad luck of marrying a sickly person or one who suffered an incapacitating injury.

I do not argue that marriage was a purely exploitive relationship, for it had many other dimensions. It was conceptualized as a partnership in work. Given the importance of work in the Basque self-image, it is no exaggeration to say that work was fulfilling in itself as well as being a means to an end. One cannot speak of marriage with an old couple in Fuenterrabia without discussing work, for work and marriage are parts of a single idea (see p. 153–5).

Marriages were apparently easily contracted with either males or females marrying onto the farms. At this time, even those having very poor farms could expect to find a hardworking spouse to share life's burden. Many children who desired to farm, but were not chosen chief heirs on their natal farm, used marriage to become farmers elsewhere.

1969. Continuity of a farm requires that each generation bring an outside spouse onto the farm, giving them usufruct of the land in return for their labor and the formation of a new nuclear family unit. But in 1969, marriage, as a means of access to land, labor, and capital, was in a state of crisis. Only 1 of 168 farms was able to choose a willing chief heir. The males were unwilling to become farmers in spite of the economic advantages offered by farming. They drifted off into factory work or fishing, while the parents attempted to attract them back. The failure to select a willing heir for the farm has made marriage onto the farm impossible.

For the women, the crisis has been even more acute. On the farm the woman must care for the children, keep house, work in the fields, and sell the produce at the market. Labor saving appliances simply free their hands for more intensive field labor and sales work. In the city, they have only the children, the home, and the shopping to take care of. While it is no easy life, most young women believe that the city alternative is far better.

The greater amount of money earned on the farm cannot be used to satisfy the desire for nice clothes, beauty care, and the development of the lifestyle to which these women aspire. A farm woman is a farmer, no matter how much money she has. A young girl feels that farming is a lifelong commitment to a low-class mode of living. The result is that if the parents succeed in finding a male chief heir, his prospects of finding a wife are very dim.

Because neither males nor females are willing to farm, marriage is no longer used as a means of access. Marriage itself has not been closed off, but the decline of the commitment to agriculture is visible in the unwillingness of young people to tie their futures to farming through on-farm marriages. Without the foundation of a new nuclear family in each generation, farming is destined to die out at the retirement of the parents, at which time the farm is sold.

Inheritance

1920. Impartible inheritance through free parental selection of the chief heir worked in the way described above. The large number of tenants made the selection of a chief heir easier since the land and the right to be a tenant could not be divided. There was little personal property to divide. The ease of leasing farms permitted a sibling wanting a farm a good chance to become a tenant on other farms in the municipality or nearby, for there was considerable turnover of tenants. The potential for conflict between heirs was slight.

The small volume of capital simplified the selection of the chief heir and the division of the capital. The indivisibility of productive capital was a clear rule then as now, though small dowries or sums of money were provided for the other children.

The inheritance of rights over the disposition of labor, that is, succession to a position of authority, was vested in the chief heir. Conceptually the authority over labor was part of the single notion of inheritance of the "farm" with land, capital, labor, and their associated symbols. The location of this authority in the chief heir at the death of the parents was unambiguous, there being no remembered cases of the other siblings remaining on the farm ever usurping the chief heir's authority, regardless of their relative capabilities as farmers.

One point worth further investigation is the question of authority within the marriage of the chief heir. Though I could not presently prove it, it appears that the sex of the in-marrying spouse did not affect the distribution of authority. If the chief heir were female, she generally retained authority over the farm operations. I think more could and should be done in the analysis of these authority patterns, for as will be seen later, they can exercise a decisive influence over the fate of farming under changing external conditions.

1969. Inheritance, too, has been in a state of crisis. While it continues to be a means of access to farmland, inheritance has little significance when a marriage cannot be contracted to carry on the farming. In addition, inheritance gives rise to further problems. Thus, in the past parents faced the problem of selecting among their children, a number of whom wanted the farm. Sibling conflict and manipulation of parents are often-mentioned features of Basque life; but lately the problem has been reversed. The parents are faced with children who are competing to leave the farm and family politics center around parental attempts to entice a child back into agriculture. Young people now say the sibling chosen for the farm is generally the most shiftless child, the only one who could not make it in the "modern" world.

To the parents, who often spent their working lives either buying or improving a farm, this is bitterly disappointing. It deprives their lives of the conclusion they had worked for and raises the specter of a lonely old age, perhaps spent in a nursing home.

Added to this is the huge increase in the market value of the farmland over the last generation. Though no child wants to farm, most are tempted by the vision of the money they could receive if the farm were sold and the proceeds either given to them singly or divided among them. I have already described the complexity of the Basque inheritance system and the points at which it conflicts with the Spanish Civil Code. These complications and the great worth of farmland on the market often put siblings at one another's throats over the inheritance. If the parents choose a chief heir, the rest of the children often demand a settlement favorable to them, threatening to invoke the Spanish Civil Code. In the event that the chief heir cannot or will not meet these demands, the others may take him to court and force a division of the value of the farm. Generally this results in the sale of the farm.

The changing value of the farms and the unwillingness of the heirs to farm have placed so much pressure on the Basque customary inheritance system that it is in a state of virtual collapse. Undivided inheritance of the farm was the answer, for a few centuries, to a certain kind of agricultural problem: the viability and continuity of agricultural units. Now that solution is collapsing because the continuity and viability of the farms are less important to the heirs than the cash value of the land.

In some cases families get along and inheritances are settled to the satisfaction of all. But these are the exceptions. It is not that the inheritance system has failed; the goals of the people have changed in response to changing social conditions, and the inheritance rules no longer satisfy the requirements of the new goals.

The next section shows that the crisis in heir recruitment is also related to the difficulties surrounding the succession to authority. Because authority is only passed at the death of both parents, the chief heir may live for many years as a grown person and parent but directly under the thumb of his parents. His siblings, in the meantime, are in the city living what most young people consider to be more independent lives.

Purchase

1920. Purchase was a means of access to land. Land prices for 1920 are not available, but even if they were, the purchasing power of money at the time would be hard to establish. Informants indicate that becoming a landowner was a general goal. While land prices were low, cash income was not great, making the purchase of a farm difficult. Evidently a farmer who purchased a farm could pay off the debt gradually, but accumulating the initial sum was difficult. It appears that land values were not influenced by nonagricultural demand, and that a skillful farmer could indeed hope to become a landowner. More than 35 farmers succeeded in becoming owners between 1920 and 1969, indicating that purchase was a valid means of access.

Cow carts, Brabant plows, hand plows, and iron parts of other tools had to be bought, making purchase an important means of access to capital. Purchase was limited by the farmers' small cash resources, but the interest in labor-saving capital, so apparent today, was already visible in the purchases of plows in the 1920s. The farmers point out that the purchase of a Brabant plow in the twenties was a big investment, comparable to the present purchase of a garden tractor or a car; yet many were purchased. But as noted before, even if the farmers had had abundant funds, the access to capital would have been limited by the lack of tools and chemicals appropriate for local agricultural conditions.

In 1920 wage labor was available to a greater extent than in 1969. Factory employment was very limited then and fishing was not very profitable. Paid labor in agriculture was wage or live-in labor. Large families occasionally sent adolescents to work and live on other farms in return for room and board. However, the 1920 data show that farmers made very limited use of this; there were only eight clearly identifiable live-in laborers. I could not get detailed information on the use of wage laborers, but my impression is that it was slight.

1969. Since 1955 a veritable revolution in the land market has occurred due to the appearance of large-scale developers eager to buy sites for apartments and summer homes. Because this change is so important, I will discuss it in detail, with special reference to the effects that development land-pricing, unrelated to farming value, has on the farm economy.

In addition to the inheritance taxes discussed earlier, the government receives important revenues from property taxes and taxes on land transactions. To determine the annual tax paid by each family head, the Ministry of Finance assesses land value by classifying land in terms of types of agricultural production. These assessment values are unrelated to the actual market value of the land, since the developers dominate the market and use different criteria of valuation. For them a good site must have a view, relative independence from other dwellings, and a good access road. Often land which is poor for farming commands a high price, using these criteria, and good farmland receives a low price. Thus land prices vary a great deal and often bear little relationship to the agricultural value of the land.

The municipal government is well attuned to the interests of the developers. Its involvement ranges from attracting tourists and awarding construction contracts to the approval of construction plans. In all of this, it watches land values closely because some prime development sites command prices 25 times greater than those for nearby lands. When land is bought and sold in the municipality, the local government is entitled to the *plus valía*, part of the tax on the transaction. To aid in the levying of this tax, the local government triennially tabulates these values for all the municipal land. The government's interest is in assigning as high a value as possible to land, in order to get the maximum tax from each sale. I found that the *plus valía* paid averaged about one-fourth of the land's market value. The *plus valía* figures show that it is largely the developers who set the price for land.

It happens that much of the optimal gardening land also is optimal for construction. The wealthy developers can usually buy it because their investment in land is not part of a profit structure built on agricultural markets. One tiny farm (0.49 ha.) was sold for over $105,000. High net profits in gardening enable a farmer to afford even such high land prices, but cattle-raising profits cannot offset these high land costs. In 1969, a large cattle farm of 7.17 ha. was sold at the low price of $41,000. The cattle accounts show that this price is too high to permit purchase for profitable cattle raising.

The general situation, then, is not favorable to the expansion of agriculture; it encourages agricultural contraction. No farms have been bought for agricultural purposes since 1961, and nine or ten farms stand vacant while their owners speculate in the land market.

Another major influence on the land values has been the Country Club of Jaizkibel. This organization began buying land in a lowland barrio five years ago when the land was worth 6 to 26 pesetas per m^2. In acquiring 60 ha., the company never paid more than 40 pesetas per m^2. With the 60 ha. the company holds more than half the barrio lands, giving it legal rights to control all building codes within the barrio. Thus it prohibited farm building improvements and the building of summer homes around the Club, refusing even to permit farmers to renovate their own farm buildings. Their prohibitions on livestock around the Club are forcing some of Fuenterrabia's biggest cattle farmers out of business.

The Country Club is constructing homes on its own grounds. Its apparent aim is to get people to become members of the Club and pay the high prices that it reportedly charges for land and homes.

Fuenterrabia's airport, located on the river bottom land, has also influenced land values. This land was worth about 10 pesetas per m² in 1960. With the coming of the airport and associated highways, land was expropriated and the owner indemnity was paid at about 165 pesetas per m². Two more highways are soon to be built on this land.

Finally, the municipal government has a detailed urbanization plan which is in the final approval stage. This massive plan will have the effect of reclassifying much of the rural land as urban. The urban classification will probably include the entire strip of high *plus valía* land referred to earlier. Once the classification is changed, the municipal government can prohibit livestock, as soon as it supplies street lighting, curbs, and sewers. However, under present legislation, gardening cannot be prohibited. The government also will have greater control over all construction on farms. The local government's interest is in getting the farmers out and getting the wealthy Spaniards in, and the pressure on the farmers never abates.

A second influence on the land market, this time from the farmers' point of view, is the availability of money for farm purchase. The only source for cash, outside of personal loans, is the savings and loan associations. Loans are granted for three purposes: the purchase of a farm by its tenants, paying off debts incurred by tenants in buying their farm, and purchase of a farm or an additional parcel of farmland.[23] The savings and loan association hires an agricultural engineer to assess the value of the farm and then lends up to 70 percent of that amount. Interest is at 5.75 percent per year plus 0.15 percent trimesterally, making a yearly total of 6.20 percent, and the interest is figured on the balance remaining to be paid. When the number of years of payment is agreed upon,[24] the interest for the entire period is calculated. This total interest is divided equally among the payments so that the initial interest burden is spread over the entire period of repayments. Payments may be speeded up if the farmer wishes, and the interest is reduced accordingly. The association has the right to cancel the loan if the farm is sold, or if the occupants abandon farming as an occupation even though they continue to live on the farm. These loan conditions clearly do not extend special help to the farmer in the face of inflated land prices nor are there any government programs to aid in farm purchases. However, the farmers have never considered loans to be a correct way of accumulating money. The few loans that were discussed with me were taken from kinsmen, but most people felt that lending to kinsmen was a poor idea. It is difficult to obligate a kinsman to pay, and often the loans result in family problems. At present, professional and personal loans are little used.

Thus, a farmer wishing to acquire a farm for himself faces a nearly hopeless situation if he must purchase one. Purchase is simply not a means of access to farms in Fuenterrabia. The high land values make it impossible for a farmer to work off the price of purchase in cattle raising. The desirability of the optimal garden land for building sites makes for high prices, though the prices still permit profits in gardening. However farmers fear that the political power of the developers may later result in expropriation of their land with the payment of a low indemnity, and they find such an investment too risky.

It is easier to buy isolated small pieces of land, but these are not very useful. Parcels for sale are small and spread out so that the farmer has to move long distances to farm them. In the case of gardening it would be hard to police the crop and small parcels are of little use to cattle farmers.

Almost all farm machinery is purchased, and falls into the category of mutual ownership between spouses. It can be sold only by mutual consent and only half can be left in a will by either spouse. Because farm machinery is important and has been used here only since 1957, a problem is likely to arise in the future. This machinery greatly increases the value of capital in the category of mutual ownership. Not only are two wills required to pass it on to heirs, but this increased value automatically increases the size of the indemnities to be paid by the chief heir to the siblings. Between the two wills and the increased value, it is fair to assume that the already difficult division of property will become even more troublesome.

Purchase is the prime means of access to capital. There is a wide variety of suitable capital available and its use can partially offset the production limits imposed by the small size of farms and the scarcity of labor. Nearly all farmers are committed to the search for and testing of new capital items. The introduction of farm machinery, chemicals, and recently greenhouses, has been rapid and decisive. This costly capital is usually purchased with personal savings; loans are not used for the same reasons discussed above with reference to the purchase of land.

The purchase of labor, while always limited, has now become virtually impossible. The pool of wage labor has simply dried up for reasons related to the general crisis in farming. I will describe the lack of wage labor as a fact here, and in the next section provide detailed reasons for the young Basques' refusal to farm at any wage (p. 144–56).

In 1969, five farms, all specialized in cattle raising, had full time, live-in laborers. They received room, board, a salary, and social security payments from their employers. If we include the value of room and board, and the salary of about 90,000 pesetas per year, the wages for such labor are higher than those of unskilled factory workers. A few of the farms used part-time wage laborers in heavy periods, paying about 35 pesetas per hour without food or 25 pesetas per hour with the noon meal. Both types of labor would be extensively utilized if the supply were greater and more reliable. A few farmers stated that they would expand production considerably if they could get laborers.

Farm work is extremely unpopular among wage laborers and cannot compete with fishing and factory work, even though the wages in these latter occupations are lower. While I could not get figures for fishermen, the salaries for unskilled factory labor range between 62,400 pesetas and 88,400 pesetas per year, including social security and sickness insurance payments.[25]

Thus the wages in nonfarm work do not explain the shortage of farm laborers. The situation has a complex cultural component. Farm labor is despised as a sign of backwardness and involves a loss of pride. Though they are aware of the better income and security in farming, most people prefer urban jobs.

Farm labor needs are seasonal. Cattle farms need large amounts of labor in the fall for haying, but in the winter they need very little. The gardener needs help during the summer, but during the nine months of slack demand and bad weather his main interest is in cutting losses by lowering production and production costs. Thus a farmer must pay more than the factory wage to get labor in the summer and fall and be willing to continue paying this wage during the slack months. Even so, some farmers are willing to do this, but they still are unable to get wage laborers to work for them consistently.

Rental

1920. The rental of farms was the prevalent means of access to land. As I noted, I was unable to differentiate between short-term, unprotected leases and long-term leases in the archival documents. The farmers said that many people changed farms each year. I assume that this implies short-term leases, but I am informed by Douglass (personal communication) that such shifting was common in the Basque country, even with long-term leases.

In any case, the tenants moved, looking for better land, buildings, or leases. As they had little movable property, they could shift around fairly easily, three or four residence changes being common during a farmer's lifetime.

Though leases varied considerably, a common one included a rent of half the apple crop, 20 kilos of corn, plus an amount of cash. To make ends meet and pay the rent required planning, although landowners evidently did not evict tenants often. The situation was clearly the reverse of what it is now. The landowners wanted to get long-term tenants while many tenants wanted to shift around until they found a favorable situation. The landowners had few alternative uses for the land.

The rental of capital was a very limited matter. The only example I found was rental of a Brabant plow with a team and operator, in sort of the arrangement I have already described above. Other than this, no capital could be rented.

I treat rental of labor definitionally as purchase and have dealt with it above.

1969. Significant changes have taken place in the rental of farms. Rental has effectively disappeared. Legislation enacted years ago to favor tenants has, under present conditions, made landlords unwilling to enter long-term leases with farmers. Many now leave their farms empty while they speculate in the land market.

To understand this it is necessary to show how the rural rents are calculated. These calculations are complex, and are based on a national rent formula designed to control the exploitation of tenants by landlords. The Ministry of Finance, as part of the general tax assessment process, calculates the taxable assets of each farm every five years. The basis of the calculation is the soil type and product classification. This initial tax calculation results in the liquid assets (*base liquidable*) of the farm, which are halved to arrive at the taxable liquid assets (*líquido imponible*).

If there is a rent figure that had been agreed upon before July 1, 1939, it is stated. This figure is divided by 50 pesetas, the price of 100 kilos of wheat in 1939, which results in a transformation of the initial rent figure into a number of 100 kilo units of wheat. With these figures the rent can be calculated. The number of 100 kilo units is multiplied by a price fixed yearly by the Spanish government expressly for rent calculation. The total figure is then augmented by 50 percent, a supplement the government permits. To this basic rent figure is added a social security payment calculated at 15.9 percent of the liquid assets. The municipal tax is 5 percent of this, and another 5 percent is paid to the provincial farm syndicate, rural pest control agency, and the local brotherhood of farmers. Fire insurance premiums, if any, are divided equally between owner and tenant. Finally, any improvements on the farm made by the owner are paid off at a rate of 8 percent of the total value of the improvement per year. These figures are added to determine the yearly rent, which is usually paid in two installments. In addition, most tenants supply the owner with two chickens at Christmas.

In spite of the complexity of this calculation, the rent accruing to the landlord is very small. To make this clear let us look at the rent for a specific 1.5 ha. farm. The annual rent is 800 pesetas. The farmland is worth 350 pesetas per m^2, or a total land value of 5,250,000 pesetas. Were the landlord to sell the farm, bank the money, and merely collect the 6 percent interest, it would yield him an income of 315,000 pesetas per year.

However, these leases can only be terminated by the consent of both parties or by failure of the tenant to pay the rent. Eviction is practically impossible because the law supports the tenant. When a farm is sold, the buyer has the right to evict the tenant after he has taken in the year's crop and after the former owner pays an indemnity that the tenant agrees upon (*Código Civil*, Art. 1,571).

In this way there has been a gradual decrease in the number of tenant farms. However, the situation is complicated by another law giving a tenant the right to pay the same price paid by the buyer for the farm and take the farm for himself, within eight days of the sale. The common practice in sales between landowners is to place a low figure on the bill of sale in order to reduce taxes, but this exposes them to the danger that the tenant will buy the farm. Thus the seller approaches the tenant in advance of the sale, tells him that the farm is to be sold, and quotes a higher price. If the tenant is not interested in purchasing at that price, he is asked to sign a statement that he does not wish to buy the farm. Then the sale is made at the lower price. If the tenant is literate and knows the law, he may assert his rights, but most tenants cannot. Sales without prior notification to the tenants have resulted in court action in which large indemnities are usually won by the tenants.

A case in point is that of a very small tenant farm. It has a total of 0.3 ha. of land around it and uses rented river bottom land nearby for gardening. In 1968 the landlord sold the farm without notifying the tenant. She took the matter to court and won. As an indemnity she received ownership of the farmhouse and 0.1 ha. of land around it.

A further complication is that the seller has to pay the indemnity to a tenant on the property he sells. This fact gives the tenant a strong bargaining position and often delays sale of a farm (*Código Civil*, Art. 1,571). In most cases, knowledge of their legal recourses would give the tenants the chance to gain a large indemnity, but not to continue as farmers. Many tenants lost their rights through lack of knowledge. Now most know at least the essence of their rights and farms are not sold without indemnities.

In 1969, no farms were available on long-term, protected leases, nor are they likely to become available. Since speculation in land and profits from sale of summer home sites are their prime goals, landowners do not wish to tie up land in long-term leases, especially because of the indemnity required to free the land again. They prefer the very small loss of rent incurred in leaving a farm unexploited to renting on a long-term lease. There are now nine or ten abandoned farms for this very reason. Thus there is little chance to gain access to land via these leases.

Sixty-six farms with long-term leases remain, and they are likely to decrease in number due to urban migration and the process of sale and indemnity. This high percentage of tenant farms is atypical for Guipúzcoa where the general tendency, in this century, was to sell the farms to the tenants. According to the *Primer censo agrario de España: Año 1962*, tenant farms make up only slightly under 10 percent of the total in Guipúzcoa (1964:6). In Fuenterrabia, the sale of farms to tenants began in about 1930 and progressed rapidly until about 1955 when the landowners realized that the land prices were rising as demand for summer home sites increased. Since then few farms have been sold to the tenants, and it is unlikely that many will be sold. Thus, development brought about a halt in the acquisition of farms by tenants.

The second type of lease is the short-term, unprotected lease, often called *precaria* and listed under *censos* in the Civil Code. These leases are made on a year-to-year basis, though other arrangements are possible if it is the landlord's wish (*Código Civil*, Art. 1, 604–1, 654), and both parties are free to contract the exact rent to be paid. Landowners are quite willing to rent idle farms on this basis since neither long-term contract nor indemnity is required. For the same reason few tenants are interested in such an arrangement.

On the farms available under these terms, houses are usually in very poor condition and the owner is unwilling to fix them. If the land has been abandoned for more than two or three years, it requires a major effort to make it fit for production again, because

underbrush grows very rapidly. Finally, the amount of capital required, in the form of equipment and animals, makes short-term
rental impractical for the tenants. Thus the empty farms remain
empty.

The only people making use of such leases are five shepherds
who winter their flocks in Fuenterrabia while the inland moun-
tains are snowed in. In two cases they rent an entire farm and in
the rest they rent meadows on short-term leases.

Short-term leases are used frequently in the small parcels of reclaimed river bottom land. This land is readily available since
there are no alternative uses for it, but contiguous parcels are
nearly impossible to find. The leases do aid some farms that are
hard pressed for grass or for good soil for forage crops. Three farms
out of 160 depend entirely on this kind of land for their living but
these specialize in gardening. The principal danger, over and
above theft of the crop, is that the new highways into the municipality will do away with this land entirely.

The general conclusions to be derived from this discussion of
rental are that long-term, protected leases form a strong relationship to the land, but that the pressure exerted by rising land values has stopped this form of rental. Short-term leases, though
available, are undesirable to farmers.

One final point should be made. Most agricultural development
schemes take land ownership for farmers as a necessary condition
for proper husbandry and often as an end in itself. Yet, in this
case, such a notion is at least slightly contradictory. With the legislation designed to protect tenants and the subsequent increase in
land values unaccompanied by rent increases, the tenant is in the
best short-run position because the land costs him very little. In
effect the law forced the landlords to subsidize agricultural development. Of course, now there is great pressure to get the tenants
off the land through payment of indemnities. It is also worth re-
membering that landownership does not prevent expropriation of
land by the government. Under present conditions it is hard to tell
whether the tenant or the farm owner is in the more secure position.

If installment purchase is considered to be rental of capital, then
capital is rarely rented by the farmers. Savings and loan company
loans are avoided whenever possible. The loan conditions have
been discussed above.[26] Tenant farmers can only get loans for construction and/or machinery by having two persons of proven financial strength (called *avales*) sign an agreement to pay off the loan
if the tenant farmer defaults. Farm owners can do this or put up

their farms as collateral. In either case 60 percent of the value of the construction or machinery can be borrowed with five to eight years to pay. The interest is calculated at 6.20 percent per year and is paid off in the way described for farm purchase loans.

The use of *avales* (backers) is extremely unpopular among farmers. They are fiercely private in all their dealings and especially so in regard to money matters. Many refuse to take loans because of this. If the need for the loan is overpowering and collateral is lacking, farmers usually go outside the farm community to find backers, and thus try to maintain their privacy.

Neither the government nor any other institution gives the farmers special credit to aid in the purchase of machinery, livestock, or in the construction of farm buildings. The only help given is fuel-oil coupons to lower the cost of running machinery.

The rental of machinery is very limited and short-term. It always includes both the machinery and its owner-operator, thus retaining some of the characteristics of the older mutual labor arrangements. The following items can be rented: a team of cows or oxen with a Brabant plow and operator, a power reaper and operator, and a garden tractor and operator. The team and plow rent for 300 pesetas for a half day's work. Due to an oversight I did not obtain the rentals on the reaper and tractor but even these arrangements are temporary because the owners are renting the machinery only in order to pay off the loans they took to buy them. Of the two farms that regularly rent a team and plow and the three others that rent other machinery, all use verbal agreements. The farmer requiring these services usually has to wait a number of days before the service is performed. Power tillers and hand tools cannot be rented this way, nor can house-stables be rented separately from the farms. Thus rental constitutes a limited means of gaining access to capital and is suitable only for short-run or emergency needs. One form of rental widely used, is the rental of a bull to inseminate cows. Farms generally do not keep bulls because the expense is too great. However, I failed to get the rental costs in my data gathering.

As stated above, rental of labor is definitionally excluded, payments to labor being considered as purchase.

Reciprocal arrangements

1920. I was unable to find any cases of reciprocal land use. Reciprocal loans of capital were not generally made, but capital or the use of it was often lent in return for labor. A man having a Brabant plow lent it along with his labor, in return for the other farmer's help later in plowing his land. The farms with cider presses would press apples and prepare cider with help from the owner of the apples. In return they received some of the mash and the right to call up the labor of the owner of the apples at some future time.

Reciprocal labor arrangements were widespread. Four-person hand plow (*laya*) teams would turn over the soil on each other's farms. Many people cooperated to bring fern and firewood from the communal land, to care for children, and to perform other chores. Given the lack of capital substitutable for labor, use of such reciprocal arrangements is not surprising. They formed part of a wider network of reciprocity included within the concept of the *vecino* (neighbor) typical of the Basque country, a subject extensively dealt with by Echegaray (1933) and Douglass (1975).

Because of the great ideological significance of work in the Basque self-image, the exchange of labor or team work was an important and intimate expression of mutual solidarity and trust. To render this as a social dimension of labor would be to draw lines where the Basques did not. Rather work, marriage, inheritance, and reciprocity were all part of a single mode of living in which the hard physical labor was in its very essence participation in the main current of social life.

1969. Access to land through reciprocity was very limited. One means of access is through an arrangement in which a farmer or chalet owner allows a man to cut the grass on his property and to haul it away. The grass is given in return for the labor. These are verbal arrangements and are unstable.

Another arrangement is for farmers with large farms but small amounts of livestock to sell grass to other farmers. The owner is responsible for maintaining the meadows; the buyer cuts and hauls the grass. Sometimes formal written agreements with yearly payments, they generally are handshake contracts with payments made whenever feasible. There is a moral obligation for the owner of the grass to continue this arrangement indefinitely because the cattle production of a number of smaller farms may depend on his grass.

Sharecropping or *aparcería* is an infrequent practice, involving only the cultivation of potatoes and garden crops. The landowner provides the land and the farmer provides the labor and capital, the product being divided between the owner and the *aparcero*. The farmers in Fuenterrabia see this as involving excessive returns to the land factor. They prefer to buy vegetables in the market and to use their labor at a higher return elsewhere.

There is infrequent lending of land, occurring in the few families where divisions of land were carried out and small parcels, often in the river bottom, had been distributed among brothers and sisters as their fraction of the third for legitimate offspring. Siblings who do not need this land may lend it to the chief heir, as long as the inheritance division was carried out without creating family strife.

Clearly no major access to land can be gained through reciprocity. These arrangements are stopgap measures for farmers having short-term needs. Long-term dependence upon this is risky, and even then only a small contribution to the total farm's economy usually can be derived from this source.

Reciprocities involving capital apply only to machinery and hand tools. Some kinds of machinery can be lent, but lending usually is restricted to relatives and near neighbors, and is one aspect of kinship and neighborly relations. The most frequently lent items are power tillers and power reapers. This is a relatively important source of capital and at least ten farms depend on it for access to such equipment. Beyond this, reciprocity cannot mobilize capital.

As indicated above, labor reciprocity was an important dimension of social relations in farming and often helped farms over crisis periods. Now this means of access is severely limited. I did not see any cases of direct labor reciprocity, though I have mentioned a few in which one farm supplied the machinery and another supplied the labor.

The complete attenuation of what was once a prime form of productive interaction between farms is striking. The importance of reciprocity in labor at an earlier time is hard to imagine when observing the contemporary scene. Each farm operates as an isolate, being more closed in on itself than perhaps ever before. Agricultural development has produced an unparalleled degree of social isolation in farming, with machinery replacing social ties.

Production

1920. In 1920 there was limited production of land via reclamation of the river bottom and soil transformation on upland plots. Many farms did not have land suitable for the production of the crucial corn, beans, and squash crop. Without these crops the cattle diet would have gone unenriched and the people would have had to do without their staples–cornbread and milk. The farms with poor soil needed good land for these crops; hence the effort at reclamation of land and soil transformation. These small modifications in the environment were the key to survival for small farms because by making them, the farms could support the crucial cow and calf.

Besides the production of seeds, plants, cows, and tool handles, farmers did most of the household repairs. However, self-sufficiency in the production of capital was not the case in 1920 nor does it seem to have been the case for the last 100 years, as far as I can tell from the municipal records. There have always been commercial involvements with nonfarm artisans.

As these were and are "family farms," the production of one's own labor and the regeneration of the labor force in successive generations were and are the prime means of access to labor. In 1920, it was supplemented by wage labor and reciprocal relations.

1969. The transformation of clay soil had been an important means of extending the cultivation of crops on many farms. These processes have all ceased, and farms are bought or sold with the transformed land already developed. Largely this is due to rural depopulation, though machinery and chemical fertilizers make it possible to use some clay soils for crops when market timing is not critical.

Reclamation of the river bottom areas has also ceased. Again this is partly due to rural depopulation itself, but there is another cause. The river involved is an international boundary controlled by a joint Spanish-French commission. Because of fears about flooding, and probably also in response to demands from industrialists who profit by selling sand and gravel, this commission has prohibited all further reclamation. The river bottom areas turned into weed infested land, testifying to an era of land hunger in which farmers, with small holdings, were forced into reclamation in order to grow the basic crops that allowed them and their cattle to survive. The stoppage of this, and more important, the state of abandonment of the already reclaimed land suggest that the era of land hunger has passed and that the shape of agriculture has altered.

The farm-based production of capital has continued to diminish. At present it is limited to the production of seeds and plants to be used in gardening, the preparation of compost, the making of tool handles, and the breeding of some milk and beef cattle. As commercial seeds and plants often fail to give good results due to poor quality control, there is a concerted attempt by farmers to provide themselves with as many seeds and plants as they intend to use. This is not a simple matter. Most plant varieties tend to degenerate after a few generations unless crossed with fresh plants of the same variety. Some of this can be avoided by careful crossing of plants on the farm, but the farmers' lack of knowledge of plant genetics inhibits full use of this recourse. I am familiar with only three cases of successful production of seeds over long periods, and these are clearly exceptional.

In the case of plants, as distinct from seeds, nearly all farms produce their own plants from the seed. Here cost enters as a determinant because commercially grown plants are expensive. The timing of planting must also be precise, and the farmer prefers to grow his own plants to be sure that he has them available when needed. The commercial cost for plants is over 25 céntimos per plant. The on-farm average cost is 7 céntimos. The difference in cost and certainty about the quality of the plants makes home production a very general practice. Recently a number of farms have begun to specialize in production of plants for sale, taking advantage of this excellent cost structure.

Potatoes are generally planted from the previous year's crop, but every four or five years new varieties must be brought in because the yield of a given variety declines greatly by about the fifth year. According to my cost calculations, the cost of producing seed potato on the farm is 23 céntimos per kilo. Seed potato bought on the market varies from between 8 to 12 pesetas per kilo, 35 to 52 times more expensive.

Nearly every farm keeps enough cattle to have the manure needed for cultivation. In this rainy climate, the constant leaching of nutritive elements out of the soil makes large applications of manure necessary. There is a lively debate among farmers as to the profitability of keeping cows for this purpose (and for the milk) as opposed to the cost of taking care of the animals. It is evident that the farmers' own system of accounting, which serves well generally, does not provide a clear answer to this question.

The calculation of costs is difficult because manure is not produced as a primary product but is a useful by-product forming part of the general profit structure of cattle raising. Manure bought outside costs 25 céntimos per kilo.[27] As was shown, the profit investment ratio in cattle raising ranges between 5 and 10 percent per year while in gardening it ranges from 31 to 46 percent per year. Keeping cattle solely for the purpose of providing manure for farming and milk for home consumption is not a profitable employment of the factors of production, although some farmers do it.

Production of handles for hand tools is common on many farms. The 10 to 20 peseta price of the handle is lowered since rough-cut handles bought in stores are used; they are cut on rainy days when other work cannot be done. There is also a personal balance in hand tools that each farmer seeks in order to work most comfortably.

Capital in the form of cattle can also be considered as having been produced. Since milk is sought, the farmer sees to it that his cows are inseminated at the appropriate times. Some of the resulting calves are raised as beef animals, some are sold, and a few are raised as milk cows.

Until recently little attention was paid to the breed of bulls since no one raised his own milk cows. The preference was to buy guaranteed Holsteins. However, since 1958 the price per head of producing Holsteins has increased from 16,000 pesetas to 35,000 pesetas; this has sent many farmers back to raising their own milk stock. When good milk stock is desired, great attention must be paid to the characteristics of the bull, and farmer interest in the quality of the bulls is becoming intense.

Calves raised for meat are generally worth 4,000 pesetas at eight days of age. The farmers feel that this is a low compensation for the milk lost before the birth and the increased food ration given the cow in the last months of pregnancy. In this way most farmers justify raising at least one or two of the calves each year. Specialization in the raising of meat animals is impeded by a low return on investment when it is carried out on a small scale and by the underdeveloped nature of the market for calves. It is often hard to find calves to raise and occasionally a farmer will have to pay as much as 8,000 pesetas at eight days. This is the result of the informality of market arrangements. By contrast, the market for milk cows is excellent, with cows being shipped in and out of Guipúzcoa.

Production continues to be the prime source of labor and certainly is the only reliable one. The domestic group relies on its own efforts to meet its demands for labor. The specter of ill health and the bad years at the beginning of the domestic cycle are major concerns voiced in everyday conversation. With young unmarried siblings moving into urban work roles early in life, the problem is more acute than ever.

The reliance on self-produced labor has given great impetus to the search for more and better labor-saving capital items. Present-day farmers must constantly be on the alert to balance their consumption and production goals against their fixed source of labor.

Appropriation

1920. Appropriation of land was restricted to the limited use of communal lands described earlier in this chapter. The firewood, fern, and grazing areas were important in the farm economy. Appropriation of capital and labor were illegal and were not practiced.

1969. Use of communal land is restricted to inhabitants of Fuenterrabia and includes only the cutting of naturally occurring grass, collection of mountain fern, and gathering of firewood in the form of fallen branches. No trees can be cut. In the last few decades, the municipal government has put large parts of these lands to pine to earn money. When this was done, the pine market was very strong. Now the market has fallen off badly. But the trees remain and restrict the utility of the lands for the farmers.

The importance of these lands to the farmers has also decreased greatly. As wood shavings and sawdust replace laboriously gathered fern for cattle bedding, and the butane gas replaces firewood as a source of heat for cooking and warmth, the need for access to these lands has diminished.

The appropriation of capital is illegal, with one curious exception – Brabant plows. Most farms purchased them because of their superiority over other plows and the many years of use they provide. The present farm abandonment has left a surplus of these plows, which can be taken away merely by asking.

Labor appropriation is illegal and not practiced.

1920–1969: Summary and implications

Referring back to Table 4.1 (p. 122), the numerous changes in means of access to the factors of production from 1920 to 1969 are obvious. In 1920 there was a wide variety of means of access to all the factors. Only reciprocal uses of land and appropriation of capital and labor were definitely not possible. All the factors of production were readily available through marriage, inheritance, purchase, rental, and production, with some appropriation of land and reciprocal uses of capital and labor being possible. In any particular case, the impossibility of using a specific means of access to a factor could be overcome by using an alternative one.

In 1969 the picture was quite different. Land was practically inaccessible, with marriage and inheritance being the only ways to gain access to an entire farm. While appropriation and reciprocal use of land were a very limited matter, marriage and inheritance have been in a crisis of recruitment; and purchase, rental, and production of land were simply not possible.

Capital has been the most easily accessible factor of production and this accords well with the increase in the use of machinery since 1957. Because of the availability of capital and because farm profits have provided ample savings, the purchase of capital is extremely important.

By comparison, wage labor is very difficult to obtain at any price, and with both marriage and inheritance practices in a state of crisis, even the continuity of on-farm labor is in doubt. Reciprocal labor arrangements are only a minor means of access and are clearly insufficient to meet the labor needs of full-time farming.

Thus land is not easily available in any way, capital is only available reliably through purchase, and labor can only be found on a regular basis from farm family members. Land and labor are only fully available through marriage and inheritance. Yet both of these institutions are in a state of severe crisis due to conflicts over the inheritance, the inability of parents to recruit a chief heir, and the inability of a chief heir to find a spouse.

These are no small matters for they indicate the profound social transformation that is underway. A whole mode of life is collapsing in favor of an urban alternative to which the young Basques are firmly committed.

The assertions made at the beginning of this chapter can now be restated. The specialization most adaptive here is the one making intensive rather than extensive use of the land. It also must respond to the purchase of added units of capital with considerable increases in revenues. Finally it must not require the services of a large labor force to produce sufficient profits to ensure an acceptable standard of living. From the analysis of techniques and the accounts presented earlier, it is clear that gardening is at a decided advantage under these conditions. Gardening is land intensive and yields high returns to added capital; gardening capital is easily substitutable for scarce labor. Cattle raising requires more land, provides a lower return to capital, and under present conditions requires a great deal of manual labor.

Thus the analysis of the restriction of the means of access to the factors of production over time provides an understanding of the context in which the ever greater commitment to gardening has developed. It gives some idea of the conditions facing Fuenterrabia's farmers, who have adjusted to the changing conditions by emphasizing that aspect of farming that is best suited to the situation. In this light the development of the specializations of gardening and cattle raising, and the increasing commitment to gardening make sense.

Perhaps the most striking changes in the means of access between 1920 and 1969 are the increasing restrictions under which the farmers operate. In 1920, subsistence agriculture contained a good deal of flexibility. This was a key feature in the viability of this type of farming. Should any means of access to a given factor have failed, a series of alternatives always existed to keep the farm going until the problem could be solved. This flexibility lay at the root of the success of this kind of small family farming.

The concept of "traditional" agriculture, often applied to such cases, usually washes this dimension of flexibility out entirely, leaving us with the image of a uniform, simple, and brittle system of activity. Given the historical changes to which this kind of farming has been subjected over the last 500 years, it seems clear that sources of flexibility, like those outlined here, are crucial to so-called "traditional" agriculture. In fact, I think flexibility should be considered its defining characteristic, as contrasted with the specialized, market-oriented and market-dependent form which has emerged with the spread of agricultural capitalism. It is the restriction of the sources of flexibility that makes sense of the recent changes in farming here. To bracket them under the rubric of the shift from "traditional" to "modern" farming is to cloud the issue.

By 1969, the specialized, capital intensive farms had come to depend on very few means of access. Though highly profitable, this capitalistic form of commercial farming is much more brittle than its predecessor. The concomitants of commercialization have been both increased profits and increased vulnerability to alteration in product markets which are tied to national and international business cycles and the international tourist trade. I suspect that this is typical of the process of agricultural commercialization. The generally optimistic tendency of planners to view commercialization as a major improvement in agriculture, while making sense in GNP terms, is risky if it overlooks the very real costs in increased vulnerability that are paid as commercialization becomes complete.

The combined use of census data, accounts, and analysis of changes in the means of access to the factors of production would seem to be a good way of pursuing these issues in the study of other cases. (For a related line of argument, see Douglass, 1971.)

One question now remains, and it is perhaps the most crucial of all. Why is there a recruitment crisis in farming? The marriage and inheritance systems crucial to the continuation of farming are collapsing because a chief heir and his or her spouse cannot be convinced to stay on the farm. Wage labor is unavailable. Farmers who have extremely valuable land could probably sell it and use the proceeds to buy cheap land in other parts of the Basque country but they do not even seriously consider this option. The lack of heirs, spouses, wage laborers, and the lack of interest in moving on to find cheaper land all stem from the same underlying problem–no young people born on the farms or in the nearby towns are willing to become farmers.

Why are these people abandoning a profitable form of agriculture for a less economically rewarding and less secure working life in the city? Thus far the census, accounts, and analysis of means of access have only shown that these people are astute farmers who know how to perceive profits and how to arrange their activities in order to obtain these profits.

The final lesson to be drawn from the recent history of agriculture in Fuenterrabia is contained in apparent contradiction between the farmers' economic acumen and their willingness to sacrifice known economic rewards. It involves the relationship between their motives of economic gain and other cultural goals. To me it is the most exciting finding of all for it takes all of the economic magnitudes and institutional arrangements I have discussed, and places them in the context of the cultural world within which the Basques live.

Why farming is now an unacceptable way to earn a living

That the farmers' behavior should appear paradoxical is the result of our failure to appreciate the cultural complexity of rural life and to attempt to fit it to the Procrustean bed of "traditionalism" or "modernity." If a rural society must be either one or the other, there is no room left for its human complexity and the history of the ideas that affect peoples' lives.

The concepts of traditionalism and modernism ultimately rely on the ancient commonplace that in human life some things are economic and some things are cultural. This commonplace is the source of the formalist-substantivist debate in economic anthropology and, in an earlier period, it is seen in arguments about the relationship between economics and morality.

The separation of economy from other aspects of culture is an artifact of the application of a specific analytical framework to the study of human behavior. Such a separation is a useful analytical tool and I have employed it throughout this book. But to argue that the simplifications of behavior which help us carry out analysis adequately represent the behavior for all purposes is wrong. It confuses the model with the behavior it is designed to make intelligible.

Much of the difficulty in viewing the economy-society relationship revolves around a single question: what is an acceptable degree of simplification for the analysis of economic behavior? The argument of this book is that, with respect to the behavior of these farmers, neither a simple maximization model for economic gain nor a simple model of the social context of economic activity will do. The two must be combined and interwoven if the results of this case are to make any sense at all. The cultural complexity and historical uniqueness of the process, usually bracketed under the heading of economic development, defy unidimensional analyses.

While depopulation appears to be an economic paradox, it makes good sense in terms of significant dimensions of the Basque cultural system. In Fuenterrabia, rural exodus makes cultural sense. To show this, I present two types of material: first, problems of managerial complexity, domestic group conflict, farm social identity, and collapse of the rural social milieu that are exacerbated by the process of agricultural commercialization; and second, some relevant Basque ideas about work and dignity which have a long history in the area.

From the material already presented, it may seem that an explanation of depopulation is not needed–agriculture seems to have nothing but serious problems. However in looking at other periods in Basque history, one would find that war, plagues, overpopulation, land shortage, famines, and poverty are recurring themes. Yet they have not done away with this form of agriculture. Only now has the whole system begun to collapse and thus the present situation requires special efforts of analysis.

Basque farming has always been a complex matter. The farms are small, the climate not ideal, the soils of poor quality, and the topography very difficult. In 1920 the farmers had to cope with this and balance the production of the farm with the consumption requirements of the family, the rent, and dowry needs as they came due. This was done with a small number of tools and much ingenuity.

When reading accounts of "traditional" Basque rural culture, especially those by urban Basques who yearn for a bucolic ideal in which to root their cultural pride, farm life appears to be an uncomplicated interaction with nature by a fundamentally simple, and usually noble, people. The complexity of farming and its attendant risks are not perceived in an image that is more diagnostic of the dissatisfactions of urban people than of the real situation of the subsistence farmers.

Contemporary Basque farming is also complex in a new way, for the farmer is a capitalist. During a year he makes large investments of capital and he must realize a profit sufficient for present consumption and future investment. Most items consumed are purchased with money. In 1969 it was possible for one to starve in the Basque country for lack of money rather than for lack of land. The balancing of hard work, subsistence, and rent has been replaced by a balancing of cash income and expenditure.

In cattle raising, the milk and beef markets, the costs of machinery and feeds, upkeep of the stalls and machinery, and construction of silos must all be taken into account. The marketing must be handled by the farmers themselves and the costs of this activity must be balanced against the lower return on milk sold to the large commercial dairies on a wholesale basis. In all this, the local demand for the products must be considered. The farmers are thus involved in local product markets and national or even international markets for capital goods. Added to this is the pressure on land and labor created by the speculation in land values by developers and the availability of factory work. The complexity in farming is perhaps not greater, but surely different from that found in 1920.

Gardening presents an even more differentiated picture. More than 20 varieties of vegetables are cultivated, and each has different seasons and requires different cultivating practices. Even the decision about proper successions of crops on different garden plots is an extremely complex matter, requiring experience and much thought. Each vegetable has a different market in which proper timing and the selection of desired varieties mean the difference between high profits and large losses.

Year-by-year decisions must also be made as to the amount of each vegetable to be planted. This requires the marshaling of marketing experience from previous years and speculation about the amount of each vegetable likely to be available in the local market. Each crop also requires the application of different herbicides, pesticides, and fungicides, and decisions must be made about the utility of different types of machinery in cultivation and about use of the different types of seedbeds and transplanting techniques available.

Finally, the vegetables must be marketed with consummate skill or all the labor and expense is for naught. This marketing depends on the affluence of the summer tourists and the development of a fixed clientele of stores and private consumers. As happened during my stay, the imposition of currency exchange restrictions by the French government on French tourists leaving France brought on an immediate crisis in the vegetable market. All of this occurs in the context of a wet climate, poor soils, prevalence of plant diseases and pests, and late killing frosts and hailstorms.

Thus at every turn, the managerial complexity of farming now extends to making decisions and balancing factors over which the farmers have little control. Problems in the capital markets, the national and international monetary system, and the general state of health of the Spanish economy have become the conditions which determine the amount a farmer will actually make in a year. Capitalist farming subjects the farmers to a host of new conditions beyond their control, over and above the permanent and familiar problems of climate and mobilization of a labor force.

Planning and hard work are the farmers' hedges against this situation, but no amount of hard work will make the tourists appear during a bad international monetary crisis, nor will it relieve the inflationary trend in the Spanish economy.

This is a specific description of what is called the "commercialization" of agriculture, but the term is often associated with a positive feeling that commercialization is coterminous with progress and modernization. I emphasize the negative components here, not because of a romantic involvement with the past, but because the process of commercialization is seen in this negative light by the farmers themselves. While they are clearly aware of the high profits they have earned, they are also aware of the costs they have incurred, costs they pay in additional managerial effort, speculation in future markets, and in their subjection to the movements of prices over which they have no control. They accept happily the high profits but this does not lead them to ignore the additional costs.

The farmers speak of the new profits as costing them worry and the loss of the freedom they had as subsistence farmers. This is not simply a retrospective utopianism; it is the recognition that commercialization has altered their relations with the outside world and has made farming into an entirely new occupational role. For reasons I will develop below, they feel that this subjection to outside forces is a liability of commercial agriculture.

Again I emphasize that the changes are not changes away from a "simple" subsistence era into a "complex" commercial one. Not only was there commercial agriculture in the eighteenth and nineteenth centuries, but subsistence agriculture, with the multiplicity of forces farmers had to balance, was a difficult endeavor. Present commercial agriculture is thus not more complex but merely complex in different ways. Since the Basque farmers have withstood three wars and a terrorist movement in this century, all contributing to the instability of their markets, this statement is not unrealistic. That they should lack absolute faith in the world beyond the farms seems patently reasonable.

There are problems at the heart of Basque domestic group organization which have always been sources of conflict, namely those related to inheritance and succession to authority. I have analyzed the recent expression of these problems already, but there is more to be said.

By means of introduction, it is worth noting that the Basque impartible inheritance system did not make its appearance until sometime in the sixteenth century, a fact often overlooked by Basque specialists (Caro Baroja, 1971). The development of such a system involves a cultural choice to adjust social relationships among people to a set of relatively fixed units of land. By contrast, partible inheritance usually parcels out the land in accordance with the number of heirs.

As long as there is more than one heir, impartibility requires that the patrimony be divided in an unequal fashion in that only one heir will receive land. When farming was a sought-after occupation, this always forced parents to introduce distinctions between their children and to reward one child more than others by giving him or her the most desired inheritance of all. While the other children were taken care of, the indivisibility of land was always associated with tension. It was always a potential source of conflict.

The contemporary economic conditions have exacerbated this conflict and are breaking the system. We are seeing the start of a return to equal inheritance in the Basque country. The enormous increase in land values, the collapse of the Basques' commitment to agriculture as a way of life, and the presence of a civil code demanding equal inheritance have set the stage for bitter inheritance conflicts which have crippled the operations of many farms and broken up domestic groups. The parents can no longer guarantee the chief heir his or her patrimony, a fact that lessens the desirability of being named chief heir. Everyone demands a share of the value of the farm and the possibility of achieving a successful transmission of a farm is remote.

The combination of uncertainty and bitterness that surrounds this problem places the entire system in jeopardy, making farming unattractive to nearly everyone. For the parents this is a bitter disappointment–in accordance with their own goals, their lives are incomplete until the transmission of the farm, intact, is guaranteed. Thus an old conflict, in new trappings, breaks the pattern of recruitment.

Actual succession to authority in the domestic group is another old conflict which has become very difficult to resolve under present conditions. Unlike many parts of the upland Basque country in which the passage of authority over farm operations is effected at the marriage of the chief heir and formalized in a written marriage contract, in Fuenterrabia it only takes place upon the death of both parents. This gives rise to situations in which a man or woman of 50, with married children, may be in a subordinate position to a 75 year-old parent.

Further, parental authority is absolute. It is undivided and extends into all areas from farm operation to the smallest home improvement and to the purchase of food. The siblings of the child in authority are totally subordinate as well.

This raises an insoluble problem. As will be shown below, the Basque definition of a true human being is one who exercises full authority over his or her destiny. This very idea makes aging parents unwilling to relinquish their authority, for to do so would relegate them to a nonadult status. But the chief heir also rankles under this parental authority for the same reasons. The years of subordination to parents are years of great personal stress for the heir because he or she holds the same definition of adulthood that makes the parents unwilling to retire. As a result, while the parents live, the chief heir is kept in the sociological status of a child. The marriage contracts in other areas do not solve this problem, but they decide the transmission of authority in favor of the heir, forcing the retirement of the parents as dominant figures in the domestic group.

Always a source of conflict in these domestic groups, the problem of parental authority has grown worse for many reasons. Young people can now move into factory work in their teens and soon take on most of the trappings of adult status. They escape the authority problem by going to the city and establishing a new social identity there. The chief heir is at a decided disadvantage because his or her adulthood may be delayed 15–30 years beyond that of the siblings.

When inheriting the farm was the ideal, and when the chief heir enjoyed prestige in the eyes of the whole community, such a disadvantage was tolerated. Now, with the decline in the prestige of agriculture, the shift toward a more independent youth, and the attribution of rusticity and stupidity to those named chief heirs, the disadvantages of the delayed official adulthood are not offset by social prestige. Even so, parents still find themselves unable to relinquish the authority they have. Thus, the old problem of succession becomes serious enough to discourage nearly all potential heirs from accepting designation as chief heir.

Taken together, the problems of inheritance and succession force most parents to spend years trying to get at least one child to accept the heirship. They generally fail, with only 1 of 168 farms in 1969 having a chief heir designate willing to stay on the farm. As I have shown, even if an heir were found, the chances of finding a spouse willing to marry onto a farm are virtually nil. The inmarrying spouse must not only accept delayed adulthood, but must also spend a lifetime under the authority of the chief heir, working in an occupation with which no prestige is associated.

Another feature of Basque farming that has a respectable ancestry is the means by which the social identity of the farmer is established in the community. As I indicated at the outset, the most stable unit of rural Fuenterrabia is the physical farmstead. The social organization of domestic groups is adapted to maintain a balance between the size of domestic groups and the carrying capacity of these farmsteads. The farmstead itself is the identifiable, persisting unit. As Douglass puts it, "In rural Basque society social continuity is provided not by descent groups but rather by the immutability of households [i.e., homesteads]" (1969:88). This observation is supported by the fact that at least 150 of the presently known farms of Fuenterrabia are found in the same locations and bear the same names as appear in census data going back hundreds of years.

The farmstead itself leaves a strong social imprint upon its occupants. Domestic group composition changes but the farms are conceived as going on forever. Farmers are identified by the names of their farms. In many cases, informants did not know the legal last names of their neighbors. People are known by their first name and the name of the farm they live on. An in-marrying spouse comes rapidly to be known by the name of his or her new farm, though everyone will know the name of the natal farm as well.

If the farm is large and well exploited, the association of one's name with it adds prestige to one's person. A poor farm or a poorly exploited one reduces the prestige of the domestic group members. Therefore much of the social identity of the members of a domestic group is formed by their identification with a particular farmstead. This is a significant part of their identification, categorization, and evaluation by the rest of the people. To be designated heir is to be selected as the custodian of this identity.

The strength with which the farm impresses itself on the social identity of the farmers means that to accept the chief heirship is to be given a lifelong rural identity. With the decline of the prestige of agriculture, this designation is not an honor, but a source of ridicule to be avoided because it excludes the person so identified from participation in the urban, and hence "modern" social milieu. Only recently has "farmer" come to mean "rustic" in Fuenterrabia and young people react by refusing to accept the heirship and the "rustic" identity.

There are other factors that drive people away from agriculture. The increasing privacy of domestic life and the process of depopulation itself have increased the social isolation of the farmers greatly over the last decades. The lapse of reciprocal ties between farms has ramifying effects. The actual decline of reciprocal ties removes a source of flexibility from the farming system, meaning that a single crisis, be it an illness or a fire, can be enough to force people off a farm.

Less obvious but equally important is the fact that the fixed farm units arranged into *vecindades* (neighborhoods) used to constitute a meaningful social and moral universe. The most dramatic symbolization of this is the mapping of the farm landscape on the church floor in Murélaga, as described by Douglass (1969:19–82). Each farm had a place in this universe and was tied inextricably to the other farms. Of course, farmers got into conflicts with each other, but these conflicts occurred within the confines of a universe of accepted meanings. Basing themselves in these meanings, the farmers interacted and cooperated, attended church, died, and were mourned.

The inroads made by chalets, apartment houses, and abandoned farms have destroyed this delicate unity. Those farmers who remain, feel like survivors in a landscape suddenly devoid of meaning. The fixed landscape of farms had a moral significance barely perceived by nonfarmers and once broken, it collapsed definitively. Farm life has lost its geographical-moral dimension. All the older farmers speak as if they were the survivors of a previous age, and, in a sense, they are. A young man or woman hardly wishes to start life as a survivor in a world already dying.

Throughout the discussion of the conditions that make farming difficult and contribute to the social costs of farming, one point has emerged repeatedly–the decline in the prestige of agriculture as an occupation in the sense of an increasingly negative evaluation of farming as a work role. All the other conditions eroding away at farming really follow on the heels of this. Lack of wage laborers, the succession crisis, and the inheritance crisis, all stem from the fundamental unwillingness of young people to farm, a reluctance arising from their perception of farming as a demeaning occupation.

Common explanations accounting for the desire of rural people

to migrate to urban areas often depend more on a variety of teleo-
logical evolutionism or on a "what I would do if I were a peasant"
kind of reasoning than on the analysis of cases. A particularly prevalent explanation, and one I often encountered in Spain, is simply that it is "natural" to want to become part of the "modern"
urban world and that, therefore, migration requires no explanation
at all. Aside from the long-standing Western notions that the city is
the locus of dynamism in history and the country is static and
rustic (Caro Baroja, 1963), this explanation has a certain plausibil-
ity because the migrants often represent their motives in this way.

But such an explanation is based on a theory of history in which
the industrial stage of social evolution is held to be inevitable and
superior to all that preceded. The city is modernity and urban migration is movement toward a better future. The lack of attention
to the explanation of the causes of migration, compared with the
heavy concentration on the migrants' adaptation to the city suggests that this view is widespread.

One version of this has been given a terminological backdrop
that makes it appear more scientific. The migration is accounted
for by the "demonstration effect," the "aspiration effect," or
the "revolution of rising expectations." The external aspects of
industrialism, of necessity, produce these effects. If we accept
this, there is no need for research.

But these "effects" and "revolutions" are not explanations of
migration; they are schematic and imprecise descriptions of migration based on the modernity model alluded to above. The invocation of an "effect" could explain away the Basque rural exodus.
Aside from the uncritical evolutionism and determinism involved
in the view, it is based on a strong prejudice in favor of explaining
social changes solely in terms of changes in ideas, a crude form of
historical idealism.

None of these general explanations need be rejected out of hand
for they all point to significant elements in the process; however,
there is no reason to embrace them wholeheartedly. Their extreme generality, schematic quality, and the historical and behavioral assumptions on which they rest make them blunt instruments
for the analysis of cases for which sufficient data exist or can be
developed.

In order to explain the decline in the prestige of agriculture in
Fuenterrabia and the farmers' decisions to leave high profits behind, we must attend to the Basques' view of man. I admit that I
have only begun to delve into this and expect to devote more effort to it in the future, but my general findings will suffice to close
the argument of this book.

During the Middle Ages, Basque culture in Guipúzcoa and in some valleys of Vizcaya and Navarra gave rise to an unusual phenomenon, the "collective nobility" of the inhabitants of the Basque country. Though much emphasized by Basque intellectuals over the centuries (e.g. Padre Larramendi, 1969), and linked to the researches into the "democratic" form of self-government the Basques used before the abolition of their customary laws (*fueros*), contemporary social scientists have made little of it.

Collective nobility results from the Spanish monarchs' written recognition that all people born in Guipúzcoa and some other areas were *hijosdalgo* (of noble birth). Given the time and the conditions, this is a most surprising idea. It affirms the inherent nobility and equality of all Basques, regardless of occupation, in a Europe of divine kings, blood nobility, warriors, merchants, artisans, peasants, and serfs. In the context of the extreme social stratification of European society, collective nobility is remarkable. That a cobbler should be, in some sense, the equal of a wealthy aristocrat was an idea with very limited appeal to most Europeans. Yet when the Spanish monarchs successively swore to uphold the *fueros* of many Basque regions, they included specific recognition of Basque collective nobility.

In this period, many men applied for entrance into Spain's powerful military orders. For the men the habit of an order meant permission to move into the ranks of the gentry. An important part of the screening process was devoted to proofs that the applicants were of clean blood. This involved an elaborate investigation of the ancestry of the individual in question through the grandparental generation on both sides. But if a man could prove that he was a born Guipuzcoan, the military orders automatically accepted his claim to blood uncontaminated by Jewish, Moorish, or heretic ancestry. This is not to say that all Guipuzcoans who applied were admitted, since the military orders also required that the individual have substantial wealth and be of reasonably aristocratic occupation. Yet the fact remains that the collective nobility of the Guipuzcoans was an accepted fact.

Social stratification existed in the Basque country and was a powerful force in social life, but the concept of collective nobility suggests that Basque peasants and the noblemen recognized a kind of equality that transcended their differences in social station.

I am not prepared to seek the causes of this idea nor to explain its permanent imprint on the Basque country. I present it here to introduce an element of Basque culture which helps explain the present migration. The upshot of collective nobility is that the

Basques draw a clear distinction between the concept of human being and the concept of social role. A person is not simply the embodiment of the social role performed. A Basque farmer is not a *farming* person, but rather a *person* who happens to farm. This contrasts strongly with other versions of the relationship between the concept of human and the concept of social role in which the role itself defines the human qualities of the human occupying it.

Further, in the Basque hierarchy of ideas, the attribute of being a person is more fundamental than the performance of a particular social role. This is simply another way of stating the definition of collective nobility, that is, people all are equal, even though they differ in social role. The key point is that the Basque distinction between human being and social role opens up the possibility that, under certain circumstances, the performance of certain social roles can conflict with the more basic requisites for being human. I believe that this is what is happening in agriculture now.

In speaking about authority and the problem of succession, I indicated that the most important aspect of the definition of a human is that one be free from direct subjection to other human beings in the immediate social milieu. One struggles to dominate the impersonal forces of nature and society that have power over his or her fate. A proper sense of personal dignity is only possible when one is the master of one's own destiny, this dignity being a fundamental human quality. Thus freedom and dignity, so defined, are constituents of the Basque definition of a human being.

Lest I be accused of romanticism, I note that in earlier generations of farmers, this freedom and dignity were not widely distributed within the domestic group. In each generation, the chief heir with his or her spouse monopolized them, holding all of the siblings and children in strictest subordination. For this very reason the succession to authority has always been difficult, for to live without authority over one's own fate is to lead a less than human life. Hence, selection as chief heir was an honor to be sought.

The introduction of the Basque distinction between human being and social role is related to the decline in the prestige of agricultural roles. My argument is that in 1920, farming as a social role, did not conflict with the people's definition of human freedom and dignity; it offered a satisfactory degree of freedom and dignity in spite of the poverty and difficulty of daily life. However, now that agricultural roles conflict with this definition of humanness, the Basques, consistent with their culture, choose to abandon the farming role rather than to abandon their concept of the freedom and dignity of human life. What follows is an attempt to support this argument.

While farming was still ascendant, the farmer's role satisfied the conditions for human dignity in a variety of ways. Each farm was a single, permanent, and relatively independent social unit. Life on the farm was private and the chief heir was the sole authority in the domestic group. Hard labor provided subsistence, but each domestic group was the director of its own efforts and worked mainly for itself.

In a certain sense, not idealized, the subsistence farm had a sort of independence. The main forces to which it was subject were nature and the domestic growth cycle. Weather, growth of the domestic group, marriage of the children, and changing consumption requirements all are forces over which humans have little control. The Basques consider these events to be God's will. All that a human could do was to labor, praise God, and hope for the best. Failure, unless through laxity, was not an affront to dignity so much as a lack of God's grace.

The market, the incipient tourist trade, and the host of slowly encroaching forces only affected the subsistence farm indirectly. Thus in the midst of its general poverty, subsistence farming could be and was an acceptable social role.

However, as seen now by the young Basques, the farming role violates all the conditions of a dignified and free way of life, in spite of the income it yields. The transformation into commercial farming has altered the farmer's role in ways already discussed. The farmer is tied to every fluctuation in the agricultural markets and to every monetary crisis. The prices are impersonal, but they are man-made forces. The farmers view this very much as subjection to the will of other people.

The tourists flock into the area in July and August and the farmers must work 18 hours a day to feed them. The clients cajole, the tourists imperiously demand, and the farmer labors to serve. When the tourists leave, the farmer can rest a bit and then begin to prepare the gardens for the following season. Each transaction, each production decision is made in the light of the anticipated wishes of other people. This provokes a great amount of personal conflict within the farmers, for how can they be free if they are subject to desire of other people? It is the nature of market involvement that the commercial farmer become subject to even minor changes in consumer demand. For the young Basques, this is an unacceptable way of earning a living, a social role that conflicts with their version of a proper human life. Siblings of the chief heir, always in a recognizably inferior position before now, had few off-farm alternatives in the past. They could perhaps become apprentice artisans, members of fishing crews, or migrants to the New World. Now they can stay close to home, move into urban jobs, and by the age of 20 achieve a degree of personal independence they never could have achieved in the past. By contrast, the chief heir, who must wait in the wings until the parents' deaths, is at a clear disadvantage. To be chosen heir now is to enjoy fewer years of adulthood than do one's siblings. This reversal of positions is widely noted and contributes strongly to the desire not to become the chief heir.

The collapse of the rural social milieu has left the farms as islands among large properties owned by outsiders. In the eyes of these outsiders, the farmers are rustics to be spoken to as one would speak to servants. During part of the year, these rich residents and their children virtually dominate the social life of the town with their fancy clothes, cars, and strong sense of social superiority. The farmers resent the treatment they receive from these people, whom they must provide with food in return for money. It embarrasses them to serve and makes them angry.

For the young Basques the situation is intolerable. They mimic the life-styles of the rich, insofar as possible, and attempt in every way to minimize the obviousness of their farm background in order to lessen the very real potential for affronts to their personal dignity. Ultimately the move to the city creates, or at least so they hope, a sufficient degree of anonymity so that they can hold their heads high as members of the "modern," urban society.

Further, the destruction of the physical unity of the farm landscape has already done away with the moral unity of farm life that I discussed earlier. In that moral unity, all farmers were equal before God, so long as they worked hard and kept reasonably free of vice. The meaning of the land and the possibility of affirming one's dignity through work on the farms have disappeared for all but the old farmers. Even farming is now an affront to dignity because it requires meeting the requirements of storekeepers and clients who are happy to remind farmers of their obligations and their social inferiority.

That the Basques should abandon agriculture under these conditions does not seem so paradoxical. They are leaving because the farming role no longer permits them to maintain their sense of personal dignity. It subjects them rigidly to human forces beyond their control. Nor is it surprising that they are choosing to ignore the financial gains of commercial farming—they are pursuing more fundamental goals. The Basques believe that in the city they can achieve a greater degree of independence through work in occupations which, if not inherently prestigious, at least are not negatively charged. They hope to segregate their work identity from their social identity, forming groups of friends who carry on most of their significant interactions in impersonal bars and in the daily *paseo*. The uncertainties of urban work are more acceptable than the demeaning certainties of farming.

It might be argued that this makes little practical sense. The young Basques' move to the city can only result in greater affronts to their dignity, working in factory jobs, at a pace set by the foreman and the machinery, or laundering clothes and cleaning houses at the behest of a fishing captain's wife, jobs hardly more dignified than farming.

Two points are relevant here. First, Basque adaptation to urban life merits study on its own. My impression is that they strive, with some success, to segregate their work role in a specific work setting from their "after hours" behavior. After work, well dressed and combed, they promenade down the *paseo*, sipping wine, chatting and window-shopping. During these evening hours, they are nearly indistinguishable from people with money. They know this and enjoy the feeling of being urban and modern.

Second, I do not argue that the decision to migrate will yield the desired results. There is no guarantee that they will succeed in retaining their dignity in the city, but the farm offers only the certainty of permanent membership in an occupational group with no prestige.

The young Basques are striking a rather desperate bargain in trading economic security for an uncertain urban future. Their action to conserve the old sense of dignity in work forces them to evolve an entirely new life-style under difficult conditions. What is striking is that the very attempt to conserve old values leads them to revolutionary changes in their way of life and sets them on a path toward a most unclear future. Only future studies of urban Basques will determine how much of the Basque concept of human dignity and freedom can survive in the city.

My argument could be phrased differently. Rather than restrict my definition of maximization to pecuniary maximization, I could have said that the Basques place a higher value on social status than on purely economic rewards, and thus are maximizing in their decision to abandon agriculture. However, I refuse to put my argument in these terms. To argue that humans maximize in all their activities is to say no more than that human behavior is goal oriented. Because I do not believe that an analysis of human behavior can be made without this assumption, it does not strike me as the useful conclusion to the analysis of a particular case. Such a strategy leads away from concentration on the unique combination of circumstances that hold in this particular case.

Thus I recognize that my analysis could be phrased in terms of maximization, first of economic gain and then of social status. But I refuse to do so, as it adds nothing to the analysis that is not already present, and distracts attention from the features of Basque culture I wish to emphasize. Modes of analysis that *can* be employed are not always the ones that *should* be.

Lest it be felt that I am portraying a noble drama in which young Basques philosophize about the fate of their souls and then press on, I should make one clarification. The rejection of economic rewards in favor of dignity and freedom is not a conscious act or decision. This phrasing of the decision to migrate is my own, an artifact of the investigation. The young Basques only talk about how miserable farm work is and how much better off they would be in the city. They respond to their discomfort by seeking a way out. It is from a variety of such statements and my own portrait of the profitability of farming that the conclusions I reach here have emerged. Thus I have concocted an explanation that takes account of a variety of features of the local situation and tries to fit them together convincingly.

These last pages make the process of rural depopulation sound stark and dramatic. Before closing, I want to provide a brief corrective to that impression.

Rural depopulation in Fuenterrabia does not take the form of everyone packing up and leaving. Since the parents have a free choice in the selection of a chief heir, they make their choice and if the selected child refuses, they then try another. Because the factories and port are close by, young people can begin early to involve themselves in these occupations without actually moving off the farm. Often they will work in the city for a number of years before really moving out. During this time, the parents court one child after another, trying to attract one into farming.

Years may go by with the succession entirely in doubt. The parents hope that one child will ultimately return to farming and the children often do not clarify their own intentions, partly in order not to restrict their own options and partly out of consideration for their parents' feelings. After all, the parents accepted their role as custodians of the farm domestic group's identity and they strongly desire to fulfill their obligations by ensuring its perpetuation. But as the years pass, the parents find themselves more and more alone on the farm and ultimately give up. While they do not blame their children for choosing urban life, they experience a sharp sense of personal failure made worse by the very real social isolation of their old age. In an earlier time they would·be the aging patriarchs in a house full of grandchildren, leading a full and busy life. Now they are alone.

Thus farm abandonment is a long process with an uncertain outcome for the people involved. Of course this further complicates the inheritance when the parents die, many siblings then claiming to have been the preferred heir. What cannot be given away during the parents' lifetime often becomes the focal point of a bitter struggle when they die.

Terms such as depopulation, rural exodus, succession crisis, and so on, effectively hide the human dimension of social changes which, though undramatic, rob an entire generation of the anticipated completion of their lives. No one is to blame but it is not surprising that the optimistic prophets of the dawning age of urbanism do not find a sympathetic audience among many of these aging farmers.

In conclusion, I would like to return briefly to the problem of traditionalism and modernity. A common feature of the explanations that use "demonstration effects" and "revolutions of rising expectations" is the assumption that there is something so remarkable about "modernity" that it causes a revolution in the mind. People migrate because their traditional values have been superseded by modern ones. For me the most striking feature of the recent history of Fuenterrabia is the long-term historical stability of certain Basque ideas. In my view, the farmers are abandoning agriculture, not because their values have changed, but because their values *have not* changed. The processes of history, some beyond their control and some resulting from their own actions, have changed the role of the farmer so fundamentally that this role now conflicts with their long-held requirements for personal dignity in work. It is the continuity in the values, in conjunction with the economic changes that have come about, that makes it reasonable for them to leave. The young Basques are moving to the cities not because they are rejecting the fundamental ideas of Basque culture in search of some vague substitutes, but precisely because they are so deeply committed to these Basque ideas that they must try to find new work roles. This is, of course, a desperate, and perhaps hopeless, bet. In making such a drastic change in their life-style, they are bound to find their values altering as well. But

I am convinced that they are moving toward an uncertain future guided largely by an attempt to live in accordance with important values derived from their past.

Clearly then, a simple explanation will not do. The events that led to the successful commercialization of agriculture in Fuenterrabia and, at the present, to rapid rural depopulation are a complex mixture of current economic forces and of ideas with a long ancestry in the Basque country. It is only by taking account of this complexity that we can understand how the large amounts of money earned in commercial farming could become such unrewarding wealth.

5

Six case histories of farming

Specific case histories have a double utility. This study has moved from the aggregate results of a socioeconomic census through the techniques, costs and profits in each specialty and into the realm of jural rules and markets affecting the factors of production. Finally I have given a cultural analysis of the ideas and conflicts that could explain farm abandonment. Having moved from the abstract use of statistics into the behavioral world of the Basque farmers, I finish by fleshing out six case histories which serve to contextualize and add dimension to the phenomena I discussed in general terms.

Another reason to include cases is that the foregoing analysis is based on aggregate data. The correlational analysis specifically attempts to wash out variation in order to show trends; the formal accounts do the same. The study of means of access and the cultural context of farm abandonment also are attempts to generalize, to seek the normal state. The problem with such techniques is that social scientists have no reason to assume that the norms and the behaviors of human groups will fall into neat parametric distributions that can be adequately described through a presentation of the mean, median, and modal behavior. Often those behaviors that fall at either end of the range of variation are just as illuminating as any statements about normal behavior, perhaps even more so. The mean or mode may even be grossly misleading.

The six specific cases chosen represent as wide a variation of farm types, domestic group conditions, and farmer personalities as I found. The cases show that my aggregate analysis is an adequate description of what is happening in Fuenterrabia and in this sense they serve to substantiate my analysis. In addition the cases provide one piece of information lost in the aggregate data–here I can calculate the different profit rates in milk and beef exploitations for each farm, showing the relatively lower profits in beef raising.

Each case includes a description of the farm, a production-possibility chart, formal accounts, a farm history, and comments about the present and immediate future of the farm. The material is based on a yearlong study (September 1968–August 1969) of each farm's activities and on structured and unstructured interviews.

The concept of a production-possibility frontier requires clarification here. The production-possibility chart is a formal technique I appropriated because it clearly and succinctly portrays the production choices open to farmers. Graphic representation of production possibilities is limited to two possibilities, though nongraphically more can be accounted for. Since two basic production choices are involved here, the graphic representation is adequate (see Figure 5.1). The chart consists of two axes, one representing increasing production of one good and the other increasing production of the other. The amounts of land, labor, and capital available are then plotted on the chart and the amount of each commodity that can be produced is graphically represented, along with all the various combinations of the two commodities that could possibly be produced.

The thickened line made by combining the lowest parts of each of the factor lines is the production-possibility frontier. Any point along that line, such as point A, represents a combination of the commodities that can be produced with full employment of the factors. Any point under the line, such as point B, leaves some factors unemployed, and any point over the line, such as point C, is impossible. For a full discussion, see Dorfman (1964:127–34).

The concept of a production-possibility frontier provides a ready means of seeing and formulating questions about the range of choices open to a farmer, and allows comparison of cases in terms

Figure 5.1   A sample production-possibility frontier

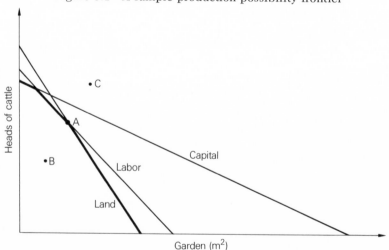

of production possibilities. This probably sets up a falsely restricted choice situation, because cattle raising and gardening are not the only choices, since farmers can also sell out and leave. But for farms that are still committed to agriculture, these charts indicate how much of each commodity they can produce with the resources at hand.

The format of the case studies is to describe the factors of production and then to draw and discuss the production-possibility frontier. The exact product mix chosen is then evaluated against the concrete possibilities. This is followed by a formal accounting of each specialization on the farm from September 1968 to August 1969 and a commentary on the relative profits of each component, these accounts being drawn from direct observation. These case studies did actually provide some of the basis for the general accounts presented earlier. The production activities on each farm will then be discussed in terms of the economic conditions, the production history, the family situation on the farm, and finally the farmers' view of life. The latter includes their concepts of reasonable returns to the factors of production, their view of the economy, and their evaluation of the quality of rural life.

Case 1

The second largest farm in Fuenterrabia and the largest dairy farm in the area is owner-operated and specializes entirely in cattle raising. It has 21 ha. of land[28] including 16 ha. of clay soil and 5 ha. of mountain lands good only for production of fern and pine trees. The only loams on the farm are 0.55 ha. of transformed soil used as a kitchen garden. The land is worth an average of 84 pesetas per m^2, giving a total value of roughly 17,640,000 pesetas.

With a large house-stable in fine condition, a power tiller, a power reaper, a milking machine, and a station wagon, the total value of the fixed capital is 784,767 pesetas.

The domestic group includes the farm owner (age 58), his wife (age 52), and seven boys and a girl from 10 to 24 years of age. There is also one 50-year-old live-in laborer. The farmer and his wife moved to Fuenterrabia as young people. The others were born in Fuenterrabia. Only the farmer, his wife, and the laborer work on the farm, the children have urban jobs or attend school.

As Figure 5.2 indicates, the production-possibility frontier is very restrictive. Having only clay soil restricts choice between 0.55 ha. of garden or the equivalent of 24 head of cattle.[29] This type of frontier is found in 60, or 38 percent of Fuenterrabia's farms which have only clay soil.

The labor line restricts production to 24 head (3 full-time laborers taking care of 8 cows each). This same amount of labor could produce 0.50 ha. of garden if the right soil were available. Capital is no restriction–the machinery makes large-scale forage production possible and the stable can house 32 head of cattle. The same capital could produce at least 1.5 ha. of garden.

The only way the farmer can maximize income is to produce as much milk and beef as possible. He does this, producing at the highest point on the frontier at which the labor line permits, the equivalent of 24 head of milch cows, which in this case means 16 milch cows and 12 beef cattle. The only options open are in regard to the relative number of milch cows and beeves to be kept, and whether to continue in agriculture or not. Any crisis in the markets for milk and meat would threaten this farm immediately.

The farm is considered locally to be a model of perfect production techniques, operating at exploitation level 1. On this large scale it turns a small profit, but in any case there is no choice. Producing at level 2 would require more forage production by a labor force that is already overtaxed with forage production, milking, feeding, and the sale of the products. They save labor by using a stall design requiring little bedding. Bedding can be supplied from the grass and hay that the animals refuse to eat, cutting costs and labor needs.

Figure 5.2   Case 1: Production-possibility frontier

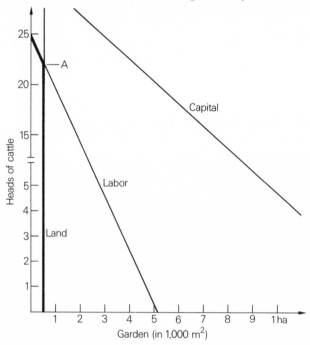

Heads of cattle

Garden (in 1,000 m²)

Milk and beef production are separated in these accounts. I have the data to do this in the individual cases, though I could not in the aggregate. The lower profits in the raising of beef animals will be made clear in this and other cases, providing an indication as to why milch cows predominate in Fuenterrabia.

A production-possibility frontier could be drawn here using milk and beef as alternative products. Given the higher profit ratio in milk production, the optimum point on the frontier would be the maximum production of milk, or 25 cows. The farmer knows this, but argues that he cannot market any more milk than he does presently. Since beef raising requires little market activity, he thus devotes the rest of his land to beef production. In economic terms, cows and eight-day-old calves are "joint products," because milk depends on pregnancy and the production of a calf. But the calf can be raised or sold. Thus beef and milk production are separate enterprises.[30]

I will put only the actual figures into this account (Table 5.1).

Table 5.1. *Case 1: milk production account (in pesetas)*

A. Land		7,660,800.33
B. Capital		
B1. Livestock	560,000.00	
B2. Buildings and machinery	447,317.19	
B3. Circulating	123,431.73	
Total		1,130,748.92
C. Production		
C1. Milk	518,400.00	
C2. Calves	51,200.00	
C3. Beef	34,596.00	
C4. Manure	52,000.00	
Total		656,196.00
D. Costs		
D1. Feed	135,297.60	
D2. Bedding	–	
D3. Replacement of cows	70,000.00	
D4. Miscellaneous	19,200.00	
D5. Upkeep	22,365.86	
Total		246,863.46
E. Gross profits		409,332.54
F. Interest	67,844.94	
G. Labor	180,000.00	
(F + G)		247,844.94
H. Net profits		161,487.60

$$\frac{\text{Profit}}{\text{Investment}} = \frac{161,487.60}{1,130,748.92} = 14\%$$

To review the categories and inputs, the reader may consult pages 59–71.[31]

Key to Table 5.1:

A. 160,000 m² × 84 pesetas per m² = 13,440,000 pesetas total farm value. Cows require about 57 percent of this land or 7,660,800.33 pesetas in land value.

B1. 35,000 pesetas × 16 head = 560,000 pesetas.

B2. 57 percent × 784,767 pesetas = 447,317.19 pesetas.

B3. D costs are 246,863.46 pesetas ÷ 2 = 123,431.73 pesetas.

C1. 80 percent of cows produce; so 80 percent × 16 = 12.8. 40,500 pesetas of milk per cow × 12.8 = 518,400 pesetas.

C2. 80 percent of cows have calves, or 12.8 calves × 4,000 pesetas = 51,200 pesetas.

C3. 1/8 of cattle must be sacrificed each year or 2 cows × 17,298 pesetas = 34,596 pesetas.

C4. 16 cows × 3,250 pesetas per cow = 52,000 pesetas.

D1. 8,456.10 pesetas per cow × 16 cows = 135,297.60.

D2. None.

D3. 1/8 of cows, or 2 head, must be replaced. 2 × 35,000 pesetas = 70,000 pesetas.

D4. 1,200 pesetas × 16 cows = 19,200 pesetas.

D5. 447,317.19 pesetas of buildings and machinery × 5 percent = 22,365.86.

E. C − D = 409,332.54

F. 6 percent × 1,130,748.92 pesetas = 67,844.94 pesetas.

G. Labor is 16 cows × 11,250 pesetas = 180,000 pesetas.

H. E − (F + G) = 161,487.60 pesetas.

The beef accounts (Table 5.2) show a very different picture:

Table 5.2. *Case 1: beef production account (in pesetas)*

A. Land		5,779,200.00
B. Capital		
B1. Livestock	48,000.00	
B2. Buildings and machinery	337,449.81	
B3. Circulating	72,956.89	
Total		458,406.70
C. Production		
C1. Beef	243,000.00	
C2. Manure	15,000.00	
Total		258,000.00
D. Costs		
D1. Feed	78,041.28	
D2. Bedding	–	
D3. Purchase of calves	48,000.00	

Table 5.2. (*Cont.*)

D4. Miscellaneous	3,000.00	
D5. Upkeep	16,872.49	
Total		145,913.77
E. Gross profits		112,086.23
F. Interest	27,504.40	
G. Labor	67,500.00	
(F + G)		95,004.40
H. Net profits		17,081.83

$$\frac{\text{Profit}}{\text{Investment}} = \frac{17{,}081.83}{458{,}406.70} = 4\%$$

Key to Table 5.2:

A. 13,440,000 pesetas total land value × 43 percent of the land used for beef production = 5,779,200 pesetas.

B1. 12 head × 4,000 pesetas = 48,000 pesetas.

B2. 784,767 total value × 43 percent = 337,449.81 pesetas.

B3. D costs are 145,913.77 ÷ 2 = 72,956.89 pesetas.

C1. 10 percent loss of animals; so 90 percent × 12 head = 10.8.
10.8 × 22,500 pesetas = 243,000 pesetas.

C2. 1,250 pesetas per head × 12 head = 15,000 pesetas.

D1. 6,503.44 pesetas × 12 = 78,041.28.

D2. None.

D3. 12 head × 4,000 pesetas = 48,000 pesetas.

D4. 250 pesetas × 12 head = 3,000 pesetas.

D5. 337,449.81 pesetas in buildings and machinery × 5 percent = 16,872.49 pesetas.

E. C − D = 112,086.23

F. 6 percent × 458,406.70 = 27,504.40 pesetas.

G. 12 × 5,625 pesetas per calf = 67,500 pesetas.

H. 112,086.23 − 95,004.40 = 17,081.83.

The total combined profit-investment picture looks like this:

$$\frac{\text{Profit}}{\text{Investment}} = \frac{178{,}569.43}{1{,}589{,}155.62} = 11 \text{ percent}$$

These accounts raise some questions and resolve others. They demonstrate that at a roughly similar scale, beef production earns 4 percent profits while milk production earns 14 percent profits. This fact was lost in the general accounts because of the problem of distributing the capital among the two kinds of cattle raising. Nevertheless it is clear that raising calves is less profitable. The relative limitation of beef production indicates a general awareness of its low profitability.

The low profits in beef production do not necessarily lead to an increase of milch cows, though it might decrease the number of calves kept. The farmer and his wife spend four hours a day distributing milk to clients in Irún. As mentioned, he cannot sell to the cooperatives because his profits on milk would be lowered to 7 percent by selling at 6 pesetas per liter. The farmer is aware of this and limits milk production to what he can sell. By his reasoning he continues to make money, though at a lower profit rate, by using the remaining land, capital, and labor to produce beef. The lower profits in beef production cause the overall profit-rate to drop to 11 percent. The accounts reveal that the farm is totally dependent on the market for milk. Any problem in milk marketing will drive this farm out of business.

Attending to actual profits, rather than to rates, this farm produces a profit of 426,069.43 pesetas when net profits and payments to labor are summed (roughly $6,000). This is an adequate income, especially when the values of milk and garden vegetables are added to it. Still the comparison with garden farms will show these profits to be low.

There is another aspect to this case. The sum of total profits, payments to labor, and interest is 521,418.77 pesetas. If the farmer could sell the farm as a unit and collect 6 percent interest on the money annually, he would receive 1,058,400 pesetas, far above the profits from farming, and without working. Though he might be expected to move out of agriculture when a buyer for the whole farm appears, the decision to sell is a hard one, as his entire life and social identity are built around the farm and the work.

In the domestic cycle this farm is fortunate, since both parents are still active and there are three boys and a girl over 18. However, two of the boys have other jobs; one is a mechanical engineer and the other an industrial engineer. Another is still in school, and the girl gives piano lessons. None works on the farm nor intends to. The couple's other children are also receiving an education up to the university level, and all have expressed the conviction that they will not farm. This explains why a live-in laborer is employed.

The ultimate fate of the farm is clear. By the time the last child is through school it will be sold, unless the milk market collapses before then. The inevitability of this outcome is not easily accepted by the farmer and his wife, considering the history of the farm.

In 1915 the farmer's grandfather and father came from another town where they were tenant farmers, and leased this farm for 20 years. It was in poor shape, and it took years to clean up. By 1919 they began to produce milk for sale and for the next 40 years they carried milk to San Sebastián by horse cart every day. They had 14 cows and raised no calves.

The major production problem was haying and obtaining the bedding for the stalls. For their needs, it required the labor of three men a month for the hay and for three months to cut fern and haul it to the farm.

After the Civil War, there was a great demand for milk and the family made a good deal of money. By 1940 the Holsteins replaced the Swiss cows, raising milk production. At that time they had 16 cows and began to raise animals for beef as well. In 1949 the owner bought, sight unseen, the first power reaper in the region, because the family could not hand cut sufficient grass for over 20 head of cattle. In 1955 they remodeled the stable area. The cows had been in two lines, facing each other. They were shifted to a one-line arrangement, making cleanup much easier. Finally in 1965 they installed the short-bed type of stall with a trough for manure and urine right behind the back legs of the cows. In this way the stall stays clean and dry and does not require the use of fern, thus removing the need for the labor of three men for three months.

However, in 1965, the national campaign against tuberculosis in cattle came to Fuenterrabia and tests showed that all of this farmer's cows had contracted the disease. All were slaughtered, with only small compensation paid. It took him until 1969 to recover.

In 1950 they purchased the farm for 75,000 pesetas or about .36 céntimos per m². Their neighbors felt they would be ruined by this investment, but the rise in land value began soon after. It was a good investment, the land now being worth 84 pesetas per m².

What may happen to this farm in the near future is probably reflected in what already happened in 1959. The big cooperative Gurelesa came into San Sebastián. All those who had previously established milk routes could only continue if they became members and sold milk to Gurelesa for processing. The farmer now feels he could have made a good living by continuing the route, but at the time he got disgusted and shifted to Irún. Though he has built up a good clientele, the cooperative pushed him out of San Sebastián and will probably do the same in Irún.

The production history of the farm is a long and profitable one, but the intervention of Gurelesa and the tuberculosis campaign seem to indicate that the tide is turning. In this context it is easy to understand why the farmer and his wife were anxious to educate all the children. At the same time, it is obvious that they are accepting the fact that all of their struggles with the farm will not attract any of the children to hold on to it.

Though the number of cows on the farm has always ranged between 12 and 16, there have been changes in techniques, including the introduction of factory feeds, the power reaper, and the modification of the stable. In every case, these choices have been made to replace scarce labor with capital.

The farmer's own perception of the economy emphasizes marketing organization more and the factor markets less. He feels that Gurelesa's presence keeps him from raising prices as costs increase, yet at the same time he realizes Gurelesa's sales out of the province keep the local price from dropping. As costs go up and prices do not, he realizes that profits are diminishing and that additional capital cannot hold this off much longer. Thus in his mind, the question is not whether he will be forced out, but when it will happen. His rather unrealistic hope is that finding an heir can somehow avert this.

The farmer and his wife are very proud, hardworking people; their main source of pride is that they are the best cattlemen here and that they have educated their children through their own hard work with cattle. They like the independence of farming, because they stress their freedom to set production levels and working hours. Besides it is a morally good way of life. Neither has any love for urban living, though they are glad their children will not have to work as hard as they have.

This farm is actually the product of two generations of labor in the sense that both father and son worked until it could be purchased. And it is a farm to be proud of with a large, well-kept house, clean barn, and beautiful location. These people's love for their children is evidenced in the considerable sacrifices made to educate them. Yet the fruit of this effort does not include continuation of the farm into the next generation. Though it is one of the best farms in the area, not one of the children even considers taking it over and even now they refuse to work on it during school vacations. The parents understand this attitude but experience a sense of sadness over the future of the farm. Their lives and dreams were built around it and now they cannot give it away. The fact that the children have not begun to squabble over the inheritance is itself a tribute to the strong family relationships and the degree to which the parents have treated the children equally and fairly.

Here then is a case of a fine farm, well administered, producing some profits, and lived on by a unified family. Yet in ten years it will be abandoned.

Case 2

This small farm is run by tenants who combine a small cattle business with small-scale gardening. The farm is 1.74 ha. in size, of which 0.40 ha. is sandy river bottom land located far from the farm, over 1.10 ha. is flat clay located on the farm, and another 0.20 ha. is steep sandy soil also located on the farm. The latter is a result of transformation of clay soil. Within walking distance of the Fuenterrabia urban nucleus and close to the main bus and truck line to Irún, the land is worth 3,202,022 pesetas. Sale is a very attractive idea for the landowner.

The farm is capital poor, having only hand tools and a Brabant plow. The house is a very small one, in fair condition, having electricity, but lacking running water. The family carries water from a creek a quarter of a mile away. The total value of the fixed capital on the farm is about 168,000 pesetas.

The domestic group consists of an elder couple, a man (age 82) and his 80-year-old wife. The younger couple, made up of one of the elder couple's sons and an in-marrying wife, are both 42 years old; they have seven children ranging from 1 to 15 years of age. All were born in Fuenterrabia. The tenant is the 80-year-old woman, her husband having married in. Their son is the chief heir.

Everyone works. The old man feeds and milks the cows and the grandmother babysits and does odd jobs. The son works an eight-hour day as a bargeman, bringing in about 90,000 pesetas a year, a job the old man held until age 75. The son does the heavy physical work on the farm before leaving in the morning and upon his return. His wife cultivates the garden and sells the vegetables by herself, and the 15-year old daughter delivers the milk. Given the limited work capacities of the elder couple, the labor on the farm can be set at about the equivalent of three persons.

The farm exploits cattle at level 2, and conducts its small gardening enterprise at level 2 of exploitation.

The farm's production-possibility frontier does much to explain the product mix chosen (see Figure 5.3). This production-possibility chart shows a frontier made up by the limits of land and labor, there being capital and labor for more cows than the land permits. I set the labor line at the equivalent of two gardeners (0.17 ha. each) or 16 head of cattle (8 each). Because the elder couple can perform chores only close to the house, their

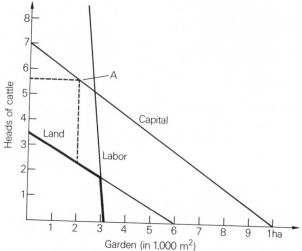

Figure 5.3   Case 2: Production-possibility frontier

labor, though productive, cannot be substituted between these two specializations.

The chosen product mix is the equivalent of 5.5 milch cows (actually four cows and two calves) and 0.20 ha. of garden. This is puzzling on the surface because it far exceeds the farm's land possibilities. The chief heir works outside, bringing in capital used for the purchase of grass. He also cuts grass on a number of farms converted into summer homes, getting the grass in return for the labor. Part of the reason he works outside is his realization that the family's tenure on the farm is in danger. He thus keeps an outside job to fall back on when they must leave the farm. By employing the labor in this fashion more feed is brought in and more cattle are kept than the size of their farm permits.

They produce cattle at level 2 because they do not feel that the level 1 costs are compensated. The woman does the gardening at level 2 because alone she simply cannot work it more intensively. In the accounts that follow (Tables 5.3, 5.4, and 5.5) I will again separate milk and beef production.

Key to Table 5.3:

A. The land value is not included as these farmers are tenants. I was unable to find out the amount of rent they pay.
B1. 35,000 pesetas × 4 heads = 140,000 pesetas.
B2. I estimate that one-half the fixed capital can be applied to cattle raising (an estimate), so 168,000 pesetas fixed capital divided by 2 = 84,000 pesetas. Of the cattle, the cows are 2/3, so 2/3 × 84,000 pesetas = 55,944 pesetas capital employed for milk production.

Table 5.3. *Case 2: milk production account (in pesetas)*

A. Land		–
B. Capital		
B1. Livestock	140,000.00	
B2. Buildings and machinery	55,944.00	
B3. Circulating	20,663.76	
Total		216,607.76
C. Production		
C1. Milk	103,680.00	
C2. Calves	12,800.00	
C3. Beef	7,502.00	
C4. Manure	13,000.00	
Total		136,982.00
D. Costs		
D1. Feed	15,536.80	
D2. Bedding	693.52	
D3. Replacement of cows	17,500.00	
D4. Miscellaneous	4,800.00	
D5. Upkeep	2,797.20	
Total		41,327.52
E. Gross profits		95,654.48
F. Interest	12,996.47	
G. Labor	45,000.00	
(F + G)		57,996.47
H. Net profits		37,658.01

$$\frac{\text{Profit}}{\text{Investment}} = \frac{37,658.01}{216,607.76} = 17\%$$

B3. D costs are 41,327.52 ÷ 2 = 20,663.76 pesetas.

C1. 80 percent of cows produce, or 3.2 × 32,400 pesetas = 103,680 pesetas.

C2. Calves are also produced at 80 percent or 3.2 × 4,000 pesetas = 12,800 pesetas.

C3. 0.5 of a cow each year × 15,004 pesetas for level 2 = 7,502 pesetas.

C4. 3,250 pesetas × 4 = 13,000 pesetas.

D1. 3,884.20 pesetas × 4 cows = 15,536.80 pesetas.

D2. 173.38 pesetas × 4 = 693.52 pesetas.

D3. 0.5 cows per year × 35,000 pesetas = 17,500 pesetas.

D4. 1,200 × 4 = 4,800 pesetas.

D5. 5 percent × 55,944 = 2,797.20 pesetas.

E. C − D = 95,654.48 pesetas.

F. 6 percent × 216,607.76 pesetas = 12,996.47 pesetas.

G. 4 cows = 1/2 the labor of one adult or 45,000 pesetas.

H. E − (F + G) = 37,658.01 pesetas.

Key to Table 5.4:

A. There is no land figure as they are tenants, and I do not have the rent.
B1. 2 × 4,000 pesetas = 8,000 pesetas.
B2. 1/2 of fixed capital = 84,000 pesetas. As calves are 1/3 of the cattle
    produced, 1/3 × 84,000 = 27,972 pesetas.
B3. D costs are 14,840.13 ÷ 2 = 7,420.06 pesetas.
C1. 10 percent loss, so 1.8 calves a year × 20,250 = 36,450 pesetas.
C2. 1,250 pesetas × 2 head = 2,500 pesetas.
D1. 2,324.77 pesetas × 2 = 4,649.54 pesetas.
D2. 146 pesetas × 2 head = 292 pesetas.
D3. 2 × 4,000 pesetas = 8,000 pesetas.
D4. 250 pesetas × 2 head = 500 pesetas.
D5. 5 percent × 27,972 pesetas = 1,398.60 pesetas.
 E. C − D = 24,109.86 pesetas.
 F. 6 percent × 43,392.06 pesetas = 2,603.52 pesetas.
 G. 5,625 pesetas per head × 2 head = 11,250 pesetas.
 H. E − (F + G) = 10,256.34 pesetas.

Table 5.4. *Case 2: beef production account (in pesetas)*

A. Land		–
B. Capital		
B1. Livestock	8,000.00	
B2. Buildings and machinery	27,972.00	
B3. Circulating	7,420.06	
Total		43,392.06
C. Production		
C1. Beef	36,450.00	
C2. Manure	2,500.00	
Total		38,950.00
D. Costs		
D1. Feed	4,649.54	
D2. Bedding	292.00	
D3. Purchase of calves	8,000.00	
D4. Miscellaneous	500.00	
D5. Upkeep	1,398.60	
Total		14,840.14
E. Gross profits		24,109.86
F. Interest	2,603.52	
G. Labor	11,250.00	
(F + G)		13,853.52
H. Net profits		10,256.34

$$\frac{\text{Profit}}{\text{Investment}} = \frac{10,256.34}{43,392.06} = 24\%$$

Table 5.5. *Case 2: garden production account (in pesetas)*

A. Land		
B. Capital		
B1. Buildings and machinery	84,000.00	
B2. Circulating	70,000.00	
Total		154,000.00
C. Production		430,000.00
D. Costs		70,000.00
E. Gross profits		360,000.00
F. Interest	9,240.00	
G. Labor	109,200.00	
(F + G)		118.440.00
H. Net profits		241,560.00

$$\frac{\text{Profit}}{\text{Investment}} = \frac{241,560.00}{154,000.00} = 157\%$$

Key to Table 5.5:

A. As this is a tenant farm, the land value is not included, and thereby inflates the profit-investment ratio.
B1. 168,000 pesetas fixed capital $\div$ 2 = 84,000 pesetas.
B2. Enter total costs D = 70,000 pesetas.
C. 2,000 m^2 $\times$ 215 pesetas per m^2 = 430,000 pesetas.
D. 2,000 m^2 $\times$ 35 pesetas per m^2 = 70,000 pesetas.
E. C $-$ D = 360,000 pesetas.
F. 6 percent $\times$ 154,000 pesetas = 9,240 pesetas.
G. At 1,650 m^2 for 90,000 pesetas, 2,000 m^2 = 109,200 pesetas.
H. E $-$ (F + G) = 241,560 pesetas.

The composite profit-investment ratio is:

$$\frac{\text{Profit}}{\text{Investment}} = \frac{289,474.35}{413,999.82} = 70 \text{ percent}$$

The first question is why such a phenomenal profit-investment ratio appears in gardening. This is because on this tenant farm the 377,000 pesetas worth of land used in gardening are not included in the ratio. Though I could not get the rent figure it is certainly not more than a total of 7,000 pesetas a year.

This case again shows gardening to be far more profitable than cattle raising, although both milk production and beef production show a profit. The question remains as to why this particular product mix was chosen, or more specifically, why gardening is not expanded. There is a double reason. First, around the farmhouse there are only 0.20 ha. of sandy soil, the rest being clay. The other 0.40 ha. of sandy soil, located far away in the river bottom, are difficult to police, and require long absence from the house when worked. As the chief heir's wife does most of the work and the vegetable selling while taking care of the children and the house, work in the river bottom is impractical. Moreover, alone and without a vehicle, she cannot market more vegetables. She must go to the market, sell quickly, and return home early. This problem could be corrected in a few years when her daughter can take care of the sales.

Gardening brought in 241,560 pesetas during the period under consideration and this is a small income for a family of eleven. Thus cattle are raised to further supplement income. Also, cattle raising can employ the labor of the elder male, labor that cannot otherwise be employed, as he cannot garden on the steep garden plots. Adding the net profits and payments to labor from the accounts gives a total income of 454,924.35 pesetas or about $6,400. In addition the chief heir earns 90,000 pesetas per year in barge work. This is not a large income, although it is adequate. Rent is extremely low and much food is produced on the farm. It is a much better income than could be earned in the city and it should be noted that this small farm produces more income than the large, highly capitalized farm in case 1. This good income allows for savings, though the appearance of the farm belies this. The reasons for the difference between appearances and reality will be explained later.

The family's point in the domestic cycle is important. In one sense, they are lucky because the elder couple is still able to work. Though they cannot do heavy jobs, their contribution is very important, allowing both members of the younger couple to dedicate themselves heavily to cash-producing activities. On the other hand, this small farm with poor soil strains the young couple greatly. There is a race against time as the first children near working age and the grandparents become older. Thus far, the farm has done well because of the elder couple's longevity.

The combination of farming and outside labor has always been true of this farm. The elder male married onto this farm in 1919 when the woman's parents were tenants. The heiress was born on the farm across the road, lived on another small farm down the road as a youth, and married here.

When she married, they rebuilt the house because it was falling apart. There was no transformed soil, and no gardening was possible. The husband began transforming soil so they could grow vegetables near the house, rather than in rented river bottom lands. They had two cows at that time and between the cows, apples, barge work, and the woman's employment as a maid, they managed. Her parents died soon after the marriage and from 1919 to 1939, they worked the farm alone. Renting more river bottom land, the couple increased their cows to four and had begun some gardening by 1929.

There is no doubt that this small farm is more self-supporting now than ever before, largely because of the increased profitability of gardening.

I was unable to get a good picture of their views on agriculture and on rural life. Though people were often reluctant to talk to me, these were by far the most secretive. These people are tenant farmers and the landowner apparently is being pressured by his children to get the tenants off and build summer homes for them. There have been various negotiations over the last few years, with the owner becoming more insistent. The tenants have carried on a conscious program of appearing to be absolutely poverty-stricken, in spite of the fact that they are making enough money to save something every year. They have not brought in running water nor invested in machinery though they can afford to, because they want to appear poor. The tenants must receive an indemnity for leaving and the poorer they look, the better their negotiating position.

This is not a game. There is an element of real desperation here, because this large family will have a hard time making ends meet in the city, particularly after having made an adjustment to farm life. They are carrying on a small-scale deception in order to improve their bargaining position with the landlord and to buy more time, for each year the children are closer to the age at which they can help their parents in the city.

This situation seems to be broadly typical of the small tenant farms and is one human aspect of the figures on low capitalization and abandonment of tenant farms. The cleverness with which this is carried out here, and the balancing of a host of contingencies, demonstrate clear knowledge on the part of the farmers of the exact nature of their situation and the means by which they can maximize their resources.

This case supports the notion I put forward in earlier chapters about the advantages of tenancy over proprietorship of land. The landlord has to stand the low rent because of the lease laws. The result is that tenant farming in gardening is profitable because the tenants pay little for the land. Of course, this very imbalance in rent makes the owner willing to pay a high indemnity to get the tenants out.

The present condition of this domestic group is actually the result of the labor of two generations of adults. During a lifetime and a half, the men have worked almost full time at two jobs and the women have born the brunt of the gardening in order to keep the family solvent. Neither generation has had good prospects for educating their children beyond the age required by law, and the inevitable move into the city will be a move into unskilled laboring jobs for all. Their goal is not to pass the farm on, but to gather sufficient funds to make a good start in the city, hence the importance of the indemnity.

The family itself is very close-knit and no hands are ever idle. The grandparents are sad at the thought that the farm will be abandoned, but their sadness is tempered by the difficulties they have experienced in relative rural poverty. They do not want their grandchildren to lead the hard life they did.

Given the conditions and goals of the people, this farm is run astutely and yields good profits. The fact that it will soon be empty, profits or no, is the common theme in Fuenterrabia.

Case 3

The third case is that of a farm of 1.20 ha. of land, owned by farmers engaged almost entirely in gardening. It is one of the major garden-specialized farms in the municipality. The land is in two plots with 0.90 ha. around the farmhouse and another 0.30 ha. in the river bottom far away. The 0.90 ha. is all hand-transformed sandy loam, and the river bottom land is also sandy. The total value of the land is 2,271,000 pesetas.

The family has much fixed capital and a new house. This is the only case in the municipality of a farm with a separate house and stable. When the old house was torn down, the new one was built in the form of three one-floor apartments, two of these to provide rental income to the farmers. The stable was separated in order to allow all three floors to be used for habitation and still stay within height limits set by zoning laws. They have a power tiller, a station wagon, two motorcycles, and a motorbike. The house is fully equipped with modern appliances. The total value of fixed capital used in agriculture is 646,830 pesetas.

This family is exceptional in every sense. It is composed of an elder couple, the man aged 57 and the woman 51, along with two unmarried sons, two married sons and their spouses, and one granddaughter. This situation will be explained below.

Both members of the elder couple were born in Fuenterrabia, but the first two sons were born in Lezo, a bordering municipality west of Fuenterrabia. The eldest is 26, and the second is 24 and is married to a non-Basque girl from western Spain. The third son is 21, was born in Fuenterrabia, and is married to a foreigner. They had a daughter in 1969. The youngest is 20 and was born in Fuenterrabia.

Only the elder couple works full time in agriculture. The eldest son works in a factory and helps on the farm during the afternoon. The others are, in order of age, a carpenter, a house painter, and an electrician. Counting the three women, the part-time help of one son, and the full-time work of the parents, I place the labor employed in agriculture at the equivalent of three full-time laborers.

The point on the frontier in Figure 5.4 is 0.55 ha. of garden and one milk cow. The labor line on this farm was hard to draw because the labor is not perfectly substitutable. In fact, all the sons help a little at very critical times and this allows a larger exploitation in gardening than would otherwise be possible. It does not help in cattle raising where the work has to be consistent. Thus I increased the garden labor to the equivalent of 3.5 persons, while leaving the cattle labor at 2 persons.

Figure 5.4   Case 3: Production-possibility frontier

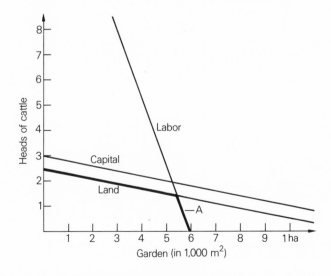

Table 5.6. *Case 3: milk production account (in pesetas)*

A. Land		598,000.00
B. Capital		
B1. Livestock	35,000.00	
B2. Buildings and machinery	20,000.00	
B3. Circulating	5,316.29	
Total		60,316.29
C. Production		
C1. Milk	25,920.00	
C2. Calves	3,200.00	
C3. Beef	1,875.50	
C4. Manure	3,250.00	
Total		34,245.50
D. Costs		
D1. Feed	3,884.20	
D2. Bedding	173.38	
D3. Replacement of cows	4,375.00	
D4. Miscellaneous	1,200.00	
D5. Upkeep	1,000.00	
Total		10,632.58
E. Gross profits		23,612.92
F. Interest	3,618.98	
G. Labor	11,250.00	
(F + G)		14,868.98
H. Net profits		8,743.94

$$\frac{\text{Profit}}{\text{Investment}} = \frac{8,743.94}{60,316.29} = 15\%$$

On this frontier there is very little choice between cattle raising and gardening because only 2.5 head could be raised, a number which would not support these people. The most profitable point would be at 6,000 m², and the farm is exploited nearly at this point. However, they keep a cow, a fact I will explain below.

The cow is kept at a level 2 diet (Table 5.6); garden is exploited at level 1 and is very productive (Table 5.7).

Key to Table 5.6:

A. 3,000 m² of river bottom land at 40 pesetas per m² + 2,000 m² of land around the farm at 239 pesetas per m² = 598,000 pesetas.

B1. 1 × 35,000 pesetas = 35,000 pesetas.

B2. Estimate.

B3. Costs D ÷ 2 = 5,316.29 pesetas.

C1. In any given year there is an 80 percent chance that the cow will produce milk, so 80 percent × 32,400 pesetas per year = 25,920 pesetas.

C2. There is also an 80 percent chance, so 80 percent × 4,000 = 3,200 pesetas.
C3. With 8 years of life, a cow's slaughter value can be distributed over 8 years by dividing final value by 8; 15,004 ÷ 8 = 1,875.50 pestas.
C4. 1 × 3,250 pesetas = 3,250 pestas.
D1. 1 × 3,884.20 = 3,884.20 pesetas.
D2. 1 × 173.38 = 173.38 pesetas.
D3. 35,000 distributed over 8 years = 4,375 pesetas per year.
D4. 1 × 1,200 = 1,200 pesetas.
D5. 20,000 pesetas buildings and machinery × 5 percent = 1,000 pesetas.
 E. C − D = 23,612.92 pesetas.
 F. 6 percent × 60,316.29 total capital = 3,618.98 pesetas.
 G. 1 × 11,250 pesetas per cow = 11,250 pesetas.
 H. E − (F + G) = 8,743.94 pesetas.

Key to Table 5.7:

 A. 5,500 m² × 239 pesetas per m² = 1,314,500 pesetas.
B1. 646,830 pesetas − estimated 20,000 pesetas for the cow = 626,830 pesetas.
B2. Enter Costs D, 214,500 pesetas.
 C. 269 pesetas per m² × 5,500 m² = 1,479,500 pesetas.
 D. 39 pesetas per m² × 5,500 m² = 214,500 pesetas.
 E. C − D = 1,265,000 pesetas.
 F. 6 percent × 2,155,830 total investment = 129,349.80 pesetas.
 G. Estimate based on observation.
 H. E − (F + G) = 820,650.20 pesetas.

Table 5.7. *Case 3: garden production account (in pesetas)*

A. Land		1,314,500.00
B. Capital		
B1. Buildings and machinery	626,830.00	
B2. Circulating	214,500.00	
Total		841,330.00
C. Production		1,479,500.00
D. Costs		214,500.00
E. Gross profits		1,265,000.00
F. Interest	129,349.80	
G. Labor	315,000.00	
(F + G)		444,349.80
H. Net profits		820,650.20

$$\frac{\text{Profit}}{\text{Investment}} = \frac{820,650.20}{2,155,830.00} = 38\%$$

The combined farm profit-investment ratio is the following:

$$\frac{\text{Profit}}{\text{Investment}} = \frac{829,394.14}{2,216,146.29} = 37 \text{ percent}$$

These accounts show the cow producing a 15 percent profit and the gardening producing a tidy 38 percent profit. Net profits plus payments to labor amounted to 1,155,644.14 pesetas or $16,179. The unmarried sons also brought in wages from their urban jobs, while the married ones began to have separate budgets in midyear. In addition the farmers sold 0.31 ha. of garden land in 1967 to a builder for 500 pesetas per m^2 and banked the money. It is now earning an interest of 90,000–95,000 pesetas a year. To say the least, this farm is a very profitable operation and is in a strong financial position.

The keeping of the cow has only a partly economic explanation. The farmers want the manure for gardening, so that they can prepare it according to their standards, also, they like to have the milk produced at home. Keeping one cow forces them to keep the meadows in shape and keep the underbrush from taking over some plots. The presence of one cow keeps open the option of shifting back into the cattle raising specialization if market conditions were to require it. Once all cattle are removed, the meadows lapse into disuse and rapidly become overgrown; it is a major job to bring them back into production again. However, the profit-investment ratio is very much lower for the cow, and the capital, land, and labor would be more profitably employed in gardening. They like having the cow and say they would feel insecure without it. Given their profits, this is a luxury they can afford.

The elder female is the farm owner, her husband having married in. Her mother's father (1849–1933) bought this farm. At that time, as now, there was one farm building, divided between two separate families having separate land. Her father's father, who was a fisherman, moved into this farm originally because, before the extensive land reclamation, it was close to the fishing port. He married a woman from a local farm and had four children, three girls and a boy. The eldest girl, born in 1882, was this woman's mother. She began to emphasize farming, and through the use of extensive holdings in the river bottom area, kept six cows and four calves. All plowing was done by hand. In addition to daily trips to the river bottom for forage, there were two trips a day to the commons to collect fern and firewood. The land around the farmhouse was then clay.

The mother married one of the sons of the farmer living in the other half of the farm building and he moved over to live on this side. The mother ran the farm and made all the decisions. They had five children, four girls and a boy. During this period there was intense activity in transforming soil to sandy loam around the farm, and a lessening of emphasis on cattle, reducing the number to four cows and a couple of calves. Simultaneously they began to plant more garden vegetables. The reason given for this change was that the division of some of the river bottom land occasioned by inheritance left them with less land to support cattle.

The present farm woman married a farmer from Fuenterrabia and they moved to the town of Lezo, where the man made a living as a fisherman. Two other sisters did the same, leaving a single sister and brother on the farm with the parents.

Soon the sister decided she did not want to marry, nor did she want to take care of her old parents. Thus she became an urban maid. This left the brother who was deeply involved in contraband and was often in trouble. He did not take care of the aged parents and often fought with them. Ultimately the parents pleaded with the present owner to return to the farm. Her husband was reluctant but finally she convinced him. They came back to the farm in 1943. Soon the brother was caught by the police and spent some time in jail. He now lives in France, having lost his share of the inheritance.

Her parents, both bedridden, did not die until 1950. During that time the younger couple had a very difficult life, being forced to farm as the parents saw fit. There were many apple trees occupying good land but they were not allowed to cut them. They wanted to get rid of some of the cows and do more gardening, but the parents interpreted this as laziness. In addition they had huge medical bills. In all of this, the other sisters were not obliged to help.

When the parents died, the heiress reduced the number of cattle to four cows, increased the garden, and began to recover their losses. By 1964 they had enough to rebuild the farm building, and they then reduced the cattle to two cows and in 1968 to one, each time increasing the garden size and their profits. In all this the woman directs production.

Because of the farm's high location and excellent view, the value of the land has been climbing. Recently the woman, as I indicated, sold 3,080 m² for over 500 pesetas per m².

The situation in 1969 was unusual because three married couples lived in one farm building. The eldest son, who was unmarried, had been selected by the mother to be the chief heir, but he was not very bright nor did he like to work. After a year of trying, he took a factory job and helped out in the afternoon to keep his claim to the major part of the inheritance alive. In taking this step, the next two brothers saw their chance at the inheritance suddenly reopen.

I mentioned earlier that the house was built as a triplex to bring in rental income for the elder couple. The second and third brothers married quickly and moved into these apartments. The eldest brother was quite unhappy about this but could not stop it; the future of the youngest brother is unclear.

As the land price went up, three of the sons who had originally struck out on their own became very interested in the inheritance again. The resulting situation is not unlike a gathering of predators. None of the sons intends to farm and so this very profitable farm will soon be dismembered. This infighting is mainly due to the enormous value of the land on the farm.

Though I am most familiar with this case, this situation is not unusual–on most owner farms, the cash value of the inheritance has become very great. The children are not content to see this prize go mainly to one sibling, at least not without a fight. Such a situation is likely to speed up the abandonment of farms even more.

In terms of ideology and life style the elder couple is thoroughly committed to farming and considers it to be a good way of life, now that they have made the farm profitable. Their gradual reduction of the cattle on the farm and increase of the gardening shows a clear perception of the relative profits and a desire to maximize returns. The continued presence of one cow is probably a legacy of their past involvement in cattle raising.

Their view of the economic situation of farming is quite realistic. They realize that the farms are profitable, when involved in gardening especially, but that the presence of competition, urbanization, and developers are threats to them. In line with this they have saved money and intend to be self-supporting, even when they can no longer work.

By contrast, their sons think farming is backward, an abomination. Though they earn very modest incomes in urban jobs, they would never return to farming. They dislike farm work, as a matter of concerted policy, and are very much taken by the life-style of the tourists. They all have relatively long hair and never wear Basque berets. Two of the sons affect a love for rock music and motorcycles, both very much in vogue with the tourists.

Here again is a farm, which through two generations of hard labor was brought to its present, favorable economic position. It is one of the best garden farms in the area. The parents did not achieve this success until rather late in their married life and still fervently hope that one of the boys will take the farm. The family conflict and the clear work preferences of the boys make this an idle dream. Moreover, the parents know how complicated farming is and that none of the sons has the experience to carry it on.

Perhaps more than any other case, this shows how strongly the young people feel about leaving the farms. Their minds seem to have been made up for a long time, suggesting that this decision is made in early adolescence, and no force could change it. Although the parents have the company of their children and grandchild, they feel cheated because their goal was to leave this fine farm to the children.

Case 4

The fourth case is the domestic group occupying the other side of the divided farm just discussed in case 3. In relation to the woman of case 3, the farmer is her father's brother's youngest son. This farmer is famous throughout the region for his entrepreneurial talents.

The land is similar to that of case 3 except that around the farm there are 2.20 ha. of land and there are 0.60 ha. of river bottom land. Of the plot around the farm building, only 1.20 ha. have been transformed to sandy loam, the remainder being clay. Altogether the farm has 1.80 ha. of sandy soil and 1 ha. of clay. The land is worth a total of 5,366,000 pesetas.

Capital value is very high on this farm; in fact, it is second highest in the municipality. The house-stable is large and new, having been built at the same time as the house in case 3. It is worth 600,000 pesetas. The farmer has a power tiller and a large truck capable of carrying loads up to 4,000 kilos. The total value of the fixed capital is 922,830 pesetas.

The farm is occupied by the blind sister of the farmer (49), the farmer (39) and his wife (36). The farmer and his sister were born on the farm and the wife is from a nearby town. She is the farmer's father's sister's daughter. They have five children: four boys—seven, five, four, and one year of age, and a girl just a few months old.

The family has a small labor force due to its point in the domestic cycle, and must wait ten years before the situation will improve. To make up for it, the farmer has two occasional wage laborers and he would have two full-time laborers if he could find them. He is presently trying to attract one of the wage laborers

into a permanent arrangement by offering a profit-sharing agreement in addition to salary and subsistence.

The farm has 0.69 ha. of garden at level 1, making it the second
largest producer in Fuenterrabia. There are two cows and four
calves raised at level 2. The farmer also sells factory feeds, raises
chicks to laying age, keeps 20 pigs, and even tears up old cars for
scrap. He is a restless entrepreneur. I could only keep track of the
gardening and cattle raising, which provide the greatest amount of
the annual income.

The production-possibility frontier shows that the land can support six milch cows and could produce 15,000 m² of garden (Fig.
5.5). There are only 12,000 m² of sandy loam, but the farmer informed me that about 3,000 m² of clay were marginally transformed and were adequate for some crops in which the market
timing was not critical. There is sufficient labor for 7,500 m² of
garden or about 36 milk cows. Capital limits cows to eight head
because of limited stable space, but would be sufficient to cultivate 15,000 m² of garden.

The difference between cattle raising and gardening is clear
(Tables 5.8, 5.9, and 5.10). Six cows would not produce sufficient
income to keep the family going, but 0.75 ha. of garden would result in a very high income. The question is why the cattle are retained at all, at the expense of the more profitable gardening. After
the accounts I will explain this.

Figure 5.5   Case 4: Production-possibility frontier

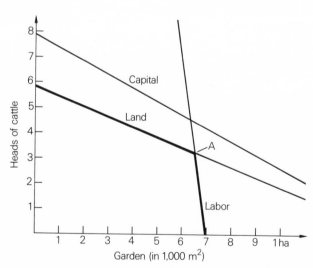

Table 5.8. *Case 4: milk production account (in pesetas)*

A. Land		1,172,000.00
B. Capital		
B1. Livestock	70,000.00	
B2. Buildings and machinery	76,950.00	
B3. Circulating	11,556.33	
Total		158,506.33
C. Production		
C1. Milk	51,840.00	
C2. Calves	6,400.00	
C3. Beef	3,751.00	
C4. Manure	6,500.00	
Total		68,491.00
D. Costs		
D1. Feed	7,768.40	
D2. Bedding	346.76	
D3. Replacement of cows	8,750.00	
D4. Miscellaneous	2,400.00	
D5. Upkeep	3,847.50	
Total		23,112.66
E. Gross profits		45,378.34
F. Interest	9,510.37	
G. Labor	22,500.00	
(F + G)		32,010.37
H. Net profits		13,367.97

$$\frac{\text{Profit}}{\text{Investment}} = \frac{13,367.97}{158,506.33} = 8\%$$

Key to Table 5.8:

A. 6,000 m² of river bottom at 40 pesetas + 4,000 m² of land around the farm at 233 pesetas per m² = 1,172,000 pesetas.

B1. 2 × 35,000 pesetas = 70,000 pesetas.

B2. I estimate 230,000 pesetas for the whole stable. Cows are 1/3 of livestock, so .33 × 230,000 pesetas = 76,950.

B3. Costs D ÷ 2 = 11,556.33 pesetas.

C1. 20 percent failure to produce on the average = 1.6 producing cows × 32,400 pesetas = 51,840 pesetas.

C2. 20 percent failure to produce = 1.6 calves × 4,000 pesetas = 6,400 pesetas.

C3. 2 cows with 8-year life distributed yearly means that 0.25 cows' slaughter value can be assigned yearly, or 0.25 × 15,004 = 3,751 pesetas.

C4. 3,250 pesetas × 2 cows = 6,500 pesetas.

D1. 3,884.20 × 2 = 7,768.40 pesetas.

D2. 173.38 pesetas × 2 = 346.76 pesetas.

D3. To compensate for C3; 0.25 of the value of a new cow must be distributed yearly, or 25 percent × 35,000 = 8,750 pesetas.

D4. 1,200 pesetas × 2 = 2,400 pesetas.

D5. 5 percent × 76,950 pesetas buildings and machinery = 3,847.50 pesetas.

E. C − D = 45,378.34 pesetas.

F. 6 percent × 158,506.33 total capital = 9,510.37 pesetas.

G. 11,250 pesetas per cow × 2 = 22,500 pesetas.

H. E − (F + G) = 13,367.97 pesetas.

Table 5.9. *Case 4: beef production account (in pesetas)*

A. Land		3,106,356.00
B. Capital		
B1. Livestock	16,000.00	
B2. Buildings and machinery	153,180.00	
B3. Circulating	17,271.04	
Total		186,451.04
C. Production		
C1. Beef	72,900.00	
C2. Manure	5,000.00	
Total		77,900.00
D. Costs		
D1. Feed	9,299.08	
D2. Bedding	584.00	
D3. Purchase of calves	16,000.00	
D4. Miscellaneous	1,000.00	
D5. Upkeep	7,659.00	
Total		34,542.08
E. Gross profits		43,357.92
F. Interest	11,187.06	
G. Labor	22,500.00	
(F + G)		33,687.06
H. Net profits		9,670.86

$$\frac{\text{Profit}}{\text{Investment}} = \frac{9,670.86}{186,451.04} = 5\%$$

Key to Table 5.9:

A. Each calf requires 3,333 m² of land. So 4 calves × 3,333 m² = 13,332 m². This × 233 pesetas per m² = 3,106,356 pesetas.

B1. 4 × 4,000 pesetas = 16,000 pesetas.

B2. This is an estimate based on the size of the stalls and the minimal equipment used.

B3. Costs D ÷ 2 = 17,271.04 pesetas.

C1. Annual loss of 10 percent comes to 3.6 calves produced per year × 20,250 pesetas = 72,900 pesetas.

C2. 1,250 pesetas × 4 = 5,000 pesetas.
D1. 4 × 2,324.77 = 9,299.08 pesetas.
D2. 146 pesetas × 4 = 584 pesetas.
D3. 4 × 4,000 pesetas = 16,000 pesetas.
D4. 250 pesetas × 4 = 1,000 pesetas.
D5. 5 percent × 153,180 pesetas = 7,659 pesetas.
 E. C − D = 43,357.92 pesetas.
 F. 6 percent × 186,451.04 = 11,187.06 pesetas.
 G. 5,625 per calf × 4 = 22,500 pesetas.
 H. E − (F + G) = 9,670.86 pesetas.

Table 5.10. *Case 4: garden production account (in pesetas)*

A. Land		1,596,050.00
B. Capital		
B1. Buildings and machinery	692,700.00	
B2. Circulating	267,150.00	
Total		959,850.00
C. Production		1,842,650.00
D. Costs		267,150.00
E. Gross profits		1,575,500.00
F. Interest	153,354.00	
G. Labor	306,100.00	
(F + G)		459,454.00
H. Net profits		1,116,046.00

$$\frac{\text{Profit}}{\text{Investment}} = \frac{1,116,046.00}{2,555,900.00} = 44\%$$

Key to Table 5.10:

 A. 6,850 m² × 233 pesetas per m² = 1,596,050 pesetas.
B1. This is an estimate made by subtracting the estimated values used in cattle raising from the total, or 922,830 − 230,130 = 692,700 pesetas.
B2. Enter costs D or 267,150 pesetas.
 C. 6,850 m² × 269 pesetas per m² = 1,842,650 pesetas.
 D. 6,850 m² × 39 pesetas per m² = 267,150 pesetas.
 E. C − D = 1,575,500 pesetas.
 F. 6 percent × (A + B) = 153,354 pesetas.
 G. This is again an estimate because in this case the laboring capacities of the individuals are enormous, and the actual wages to the laborers are unknown. Thus I took the total 351,100 pesetas labor value and subtracted the 45,000 pesetas employed in cattle raising to get this loose approximation, 306,100 pesetas.
 H. E − (F + G) = 116,046.00 pesetas.

The composite profit-investment ratio is as follows:

$$\frac{\text{Profit}}{\text{Investment}} = \frac{1{,}139{,}084.83}{2{,}900{,}857.37} = 39 \text{ percent}$$

These accounts show that the cows produce a fair profit and the calves a low profit; the garden produces high profits relative to investment. It is clear from the accounts that gardening alone could provide an excellent living for the family. Net profits plus payments to domestic group labor–discounting about 35,000 pesetas probably paid to wage laborers–result in an income of 1,455,184.83 pesetas or slightly over $20,000 a year. Clearly, on this scale, gardening is an amazingly profitable enterprise in Fuenterrabia. The hours are long and the work hard, but the profits are very high.

It is hard to see why all the labor is not dedicated to gardening, since land, labor, and capital are available for it. The farmer himself explained and provided a crucial key to understanding why cattle raising and gardening co-occur even when relative profits suggest cattle be dropped in favor of gardening. The problem is the organization of the wholesale and retail vegetable markets. The farmer's wife goes to the Irún retail market at 8:30 A.M. and sells there until about 1:00 P.M. The farmer makes the rounds of 32 stores, returning at least twice to the farm to reload the truck. They have the afternoon only to cut, clean, and prepare the next day's vegetables and to cultivate, plant, and transplant those for future sales. There is no other way to sell vegetables. The farmer would gladly give up selling if he could and garden to the fullest extent possible, but he cannot.

Others are in the same situation. That 0.70 ha. is the largest garden on any farm suggests that this affects all large gardens, in this situation of labor scarcity. They can easily produce more than they can sell. Therefore they keep cows and calves to employ the factors that cannot be used in gardening under present market conditions.

The most outstanding characteristic of the farm is the farmer himself. He is undoubtedly one of the most astute businessmen I have met. His talents are supported by his ideology that hard work is morally good and that God favors the hardworking man.

He is the youngest of three brothers and sisters, all of whom are farmers and universally known for the same talents as this man. The sisters all married onto good farms, and he advanced his brothers the money to help them with the farms onto which they married, in return for which he kept this farm intact. All the siblings support each other with mutual aid.

This was not easily done. I indicated that this farmer and the case 3 family are kinsmen. What I did not point out was that this farm was further divided into a third farm, given to his father's sister. As of 1963, the farm had only about 9,000 m² and the land was divided up into tiny parcels interspersed with those of the father's sister. She and her husband then died without issue and intestate. The farm was to be passed on to some of the father's sister's husband's kin, but this farmer offered them cash for it. He paid the taxes and got into a senseless feud with the people in case 3 who felt he had cheated them. As of 1963, this farm (case 4) first consolidated its lands into an exploitable single piece and the farmer was in debt. Six years later the high capitalization of the farm was a sign of just how profitable gardening could be.

This domestic group is unified and proud. Their main problem is that his economic zeal often turns to a petulance that has gained him enemies and cut him off from all other kinsmen beyond his siblings. He and his wife love farming and consider urban life to be immoral and unprofitable. He is developing a feed dealership in the eventuality that zoning laws ultimately do away with his farm. In addition he intends to educate his children as far as they wish, even to the university level. But he will demand that they learn how to farm, even if they do not choose to stay on the farm for life.

The complex history of this farm is similar to that of case 3, showing a decreasing involvement in cattle raising and constant increase of gardening. The main difference is that here all of the males in the last two generations have been deeply involved in successful contraband. Though it is impossible to get a line on their earnings, it probably helped them stay above water with a large family and a hopelessly divided farm.

They consider themselves traditionalists in their work ethic, although this is only partly true. The family is a moral unit, but the farm is treated entirely as a business. Of all the farmers in town, he was the only one who was actually interested in cost-profit accounting of the kind I did. In return for his help, he asked to be informed of the useful results of my study. For him and his wife, farming is a good, hard life, both of them are fully literate and could easily move to town and open a business.

The question of inheritance is far away yet, as he is one of the few young farmers in the area. At the moment his star is rising as he pushes ahead with a zeal approaching ferocity.

His success and charm have won him enemies in the area, but these enemies also watch him closely, hoping to learn new techniques of cattle raising and gardening.

Case 5

This large owner farm, producing cattle and vegetables, has 7.17 ha. of land divided almost equally between flat clay and flat sandy loams. It could support 14 milch cows or 3.50 ha. of garden if market organization and labor supply permitted such a large garden. At 84 pesetas per m², the farm land is worth 6,022,800 pesetas.

The farm building, valued at 450,000 pesetas, is medium size and in excellent condition. In addition they have a combination power tiller and reaper and a station wagon for a total of 598,574 pesetas in fixed capital.

This farm is labor poor. The elder couple, both aged 73, do a little work in the summer months. But because of the man's rheu-

Figure 5.6   Case 5: Production-possibility frontier

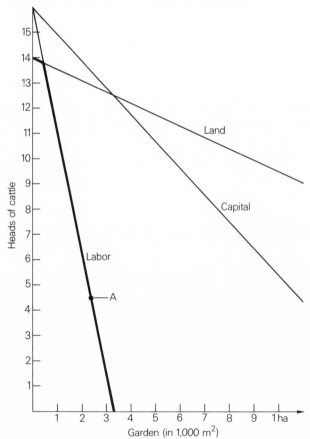

Heads of cattle

Garden (in 1,000 m²)

matism, they winter in Madrid with a married daughter, the dry climate easing his suffering. The younger couple is made up of the chief heir (43) and his wife (39), who is the sister of the farmer in case 4. After eight years of marriage they are childless. Two of the man's brothers (ages 36 and 33), live on the farm, but work in urban jobs full time. Everyone on the farm was born in Fuenterrabia. The total farm labor can be set at two full time laborers.

From the frontier (Figure 5.6), it can be seen that with plentiful labor, the farm could be exploited intensively and could produce as many as 14 cows or 1.50 ha. of garden. However, lack of labor and the barren marriage reduce the farm to a low overall production possibility. Production is set at four cows and two calves at level 2, and 0.24 ha. of garden at level 1. The farmers devote much of their labor to gardening in recognition of the high profits, but their reasons for keeping any cattle at all will have to be discussed after the accounts are presented (Tables 5.11, 5.12, and 5.13).

Table 5.11. *Case 5: milk production account (in pesetas)*

A. Land		1,680,000.00
B. Capital		
B1. Livestock	140,000.00	
B2. Buildings and machinery	199,325.14	
B3. Circulating	24,248.29	
Total		363,573.43
C. Production		
C1. Milk	103,680.00	
C2. Calves	12,800.00	
C3. Beef	7,502.00	
C4. Manure	13,000.00	
Total		136,982.00
D. Costs		
D1. Feed	15,536.80	
D2. Bedding	693.52	
D3. Replacement of cows	17,500.00	
D4. Miscellaneous	4,800.00	
D5. Upkeep	9,966.26	
Total		48,496.58
E. Gross profits		88,485.42
F. Interest	21,814.41	
G. Labor	45,000.00	
(F + G)		66,814.41
H. Net profits		21,671.01

$$\frac{\text{Profit}}{\text{Investment}} = \frac{21,671.01}{363,573.43} = 6\%$$

Key to Table 5.11:

 A. 4 cows at 5,000 m² each = 20,000 m² × 84 pesetas per m² = 1,680,000 pesetas.

B1. 35,000 pesetas × 4 = 140,000 pesetas.

B2. As new stalls were built in 1969 with sufficient room for about 14 head, I estimated the cattle related fixed capital as one-half the total or 598,574 pesetas ÷ 2 = 299,287. Then, because the cows are 2/3 of the cattle exploitation, I took 2/3 × 299,287 = 199,325.14 pesetas as an estimate.

B3. Costs D ÷ 2 = 24,248.29 pesetas.

C1. 80 percent producing × 4 cows = 3.2. 3.2 × 32,400 pesetas = 103,680 pesetas.

C2. Also 80 percent × 4 = 3.2. 3.2 × 4,000 pesetas = 12,800 pesetas.

C3. With 8 years' life, 0.5 cows' value is distributed over the years, giving 0.5 × 15,004 pesetas = 7,502 pesetas.

C4. 3,250 pesetas × 4 = 13,000 pesetas.

D1. 4 × 3,884.20 pesetas = 15,536.80 pesetas.

D2. 4 × 173.38 pesetas = 693.52 pesetas.

D3. As in C3. 0.5 cows' value must be replaced yearly or 0.5 × 35,000 = 17,500 pesetas.

D4. 4 × 1,200 = 4,800 pesetas.

D5. 5 percent × 199,325.14 = 9,966.26 pesetas.

 E. C − D = 88,485.42 pesetas.

 F. 6 percent × 363,573.43 = 21,814.41 pesetas.

 G. 4 × 11,250 = 45,000 pesetas.

 H. E − (F + G) = 21,671.01 pesetas.

Key to Table 5.12:

 A. Each calf requires 3,333 m², so 2 × 3,333 = 6,666 m² × 84 pesetas. per m² = 559,944 pesetas.

B1. 2 × 4,000 pesetas = 8,000 pesetas.

B2. 1/2 of the total fixed capital is devoted to cattle or 299,287 pesetas. 1/3 of cattle are calves, so roughly 1/3 × 299,287 = 99,662.57 pesetas.

B3. 18,424.67 divided by 2 = 9,212.33 pesetas.

C1. 90 percent survive to market or 90 percent × 2 = 1.8 × 20,250 = 36,450 pesetas.

C2. 1,250 × 2 = 2,500 pesetas.

D1. 2 × 2,324.77 = 4,649.54 pesetas.

D2. 2 × 146 = 292 pesetas.

D3. 2 × 4,000 = 8,000 pesetas.

D4. 2 × 250 = 500 pesetas.

D5. 5 percent × 99,662.57 = 4,983.13 pesetas.

 E. C − D = 20,525.33 pesetas.

 F. 6 percent × 116,874.91 = 7,012.50 pesetas.

 G. 2 × 5,625 = 11,250 pesetas.

 H. E − (F + G) = 2,262.84 pesetas.

Table 5.12. *Case 5: beef production account (in pesetas)*

A. Land		559,944.00
B. Capital		
B1. Livestock	8,000.00	
B2. Buildings and machinery	99,662.57	
B3. Circulating	9,212.34	
Total		116,874.91
C. Production		
C1. Beef	36,450.00	
C2. Manure	2,500.00	
Total		38,950.00
D. Costs		
D1. Feed	4,649.54	
D2. Bedding	292.00	
D3. Purchase of Calves	8,000.00	
D4. Miscellaneous	500.00	
D5. Upkeep	4,983.13	
Total		18,424.67
E. Gross profits		20,525.33
F. Interest	7,012.50	
G. Labor	11,250.00	
(F + G)		18,262.50
H. Net profits		2,262.83

$$\frac{\text{Profit}}{\text{Investment}} = \frac{2,262.83}{116,874.91} = 2\%$$

Table 5.13. *Case 5: garden production account (in pesetas)*

A. Land		197,400.00
B. Capital		
B1. Buildings and machinery	299,287.00	
B2. Circulating	91,650.00	
Total		390,937.00
C. Production		632,150.00
D. Costs		91,650.00
E. Gross profits		540,500.00
F. Interest	35,300.22	
G. Labor	127,800.00	
(F + G)		163,100.22
H. Net profits		377,399.78

$$\frac{\text{Profit}}{\text{Investment}} = \frac{377,399.78}{588,337.00} = 64\%$$

Key to Table 5.13:

A. 2,350 m² of garden × 84 pesetas per m² = 197,400 pesetas.

B1. 598,574 pesetas fixed capital divided by 2 (1/2 is used for gardening) = 299,287 pesetas.

B2. Enter costs D.

C. 269 pesetas per m² × 2,350 m² = 632,150 pesetas.

D. 39 pesetas per m² × 2,350 m² = 91,650 pesetas.

E. C − D = 540,500 pesetas.

F. 6 percent × 588,337.00 pesetas = 35,300.22 pesetas.

G. 2,350 m² requires the labor of 1.42 persons (1 person can do 1.650 m² and 2,350 is 1.42 percent of 1,650 m²). Thus 1.42 × 90,000 pesetas = 127,800 pesetas.

H. E − (F + G) = 377,399.78 pesetas.

The composite profit-investment ratio for this period is:

$$\frac{\text{Profit}}{\text{Investment}} = \frac{401,333.62}{1,068,785.34} = 38 \text{ percent}$$

Net profits and payments to labor total 585,383.63 pesetas or about $8,195, a low figure when compared with the farms in cases 3 and 4 which do not have such good or cheap land. Of this, the entire cattle exploitation contributes only about 80,000 pesetas or $1,125.

The garden profits are made particularly high because of the low cost of land compared with this cost in the other garden cases. Under these circumstances maximization of profit dictates that cattle raising be dropped entirely, even though it would leave a great deal of land idle. The scarce factor is labor and its productivity in gardening is much greater than in cattle raising. However, not only are cattle being kept, but the stable has just been renovated, showing an intention to continue cattle raising. This renovation is reflected in the high value of capital used in cattle raising and pushes profit-investment ratios even further down.

In part, this is plainly idiosyncratic, though social scientists do not like to accept such things. This farmer likes cattle; it pleases him to have them. The farmer had always had a lot of cattle, and though he now has few, he cares for them well. If the price of milk drops further, he will drop them, or at least, so he told me.

There is another dimension to this. The farmer has been a town councilman for 12 years, spending many hours off the farm at meetings. Before him, his father was for years, president of the local Brotherhood of Farmers. The excitement and external involvement in politics satisfy him, and fill the void left by the absence of children. Were they to devote full time to gardening, this life style would be impossible, the garden requiring continuous attention. The few cows can be cared for in short work periods during the day, and certain days can be set aside for plowing, haying, and the preparation of forage crops. He knows that the farm will not be passed on, and having no one to care for, he can afford the lower profits in order to occupy himself in something that gives him pleasure.

Previously this farm had been one of the most successful in Fuenterrabia. The father, a dynamic individual who embodies the ideals of spiritual strength and neighborliness, was among the first farmers from Fuenterrabia to begin selling milk in Irún and shipping it to San Sebastián in the late 1920s. Those clients then suggested that he bring in vegetables, too, giving rise to the development of gardening. He was, thus, at the forefront of these developments.

They always kept seven or eight cows, and had about 0.10 ha. of garden. The forced retirement of the elder male has brought about an increase in gardening and a decrease in cattle raising, a change stimulated partly by the heir and greatly by his wife, the sister of the farmer from case 4.

Both couples are committed to rural life and proud to be farmers. They view it as the occupation which, while tying them daily to the soil and animals, gives them the freedom of choice about what they will do, a freedom that the urban worker, ordered around by shop bosses, lacks.

The problem now facing a childless marriage is very serious in Fuenterrabia. Aside from the fact that these are very affectionate people who desperately desire children, there is an added problem. Once, such a couple easily could have adopted a child to be chief heir and thus ensured acceptable continuity for the farm. A child of a kinsman was generally chosen and all felt it to be a good arrangement. Recently it has become very difficult to adopt a child for this purpose. The couple has already tried to work out an adoption, with no success. Failing in this within the next few years, they are likely to abandon farming in the near future. Without continuity into the future, it makes no sense to them to go on keeping the farm.

This is one more way in which the chances of passing a farm on to the future generation have dwindled.

Case 6

The final farm provides a counterpoint to the previous cases, standing at the opposite end of the range of variation from the farm in case 1. This owner-operated farm is totally specialized in gardening, having no cattle at all.

The farm is one of the smallest in Fuenterrabia, having only 0.50 ha. of land. In addition its topography is abrupt with the garden located on a slope that at some points is as steep as 45 degrees. The soil was originally all clay, but the efforts of the farmer and his parents produced the 0.35 ha. of sandy loam it now has for gardening. Because of its slope it has a marvelous view of the bay, making the land worth 1,000 pesetas per m² in a few sections, with an average value of 364 pesetas per m². Note that, at this price, the land here is worth about $20,384 per acre. Yet it produces good profits.

Fixed capital is very limited. There is a small house, in good condition, worth 300,000 pesetas. The farmer's brother has a motorscooter worth 25,000 pesetas. Beyond this they have only hand tools. They cannot employ plows or power tillers because the slope causes the soil to tumble down the hillside. The total fixed capital value is 328,000 pesetas.

The labor force is made up of the farmer-owner (66), his wife (58), and his bachelor brother (56). All were born in Fuenterrabia, though the farmer and his wife were born on other farms close by. The brother was born on this farm. The marriage has produced no children and there is no heir. The brother is a reformed alcoholic and labors only at half capacity. He is a carpenter and worked, until 1967, in a wagon factory in Irún, supplementing the farm's income. Now he works on the farm when he is up to it. The wife markets all the vegetables in the Irún market. The value of the labor is thus 225,000 pesetas.

Figure 5.7   Case 6: Production-possibility frontier

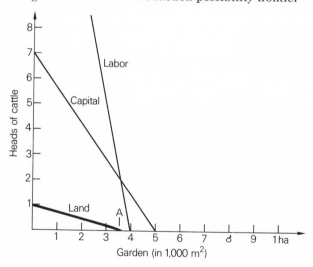

Garden (in 1,000 m²)

They produce 3,500 m² of garden at level 1 in the most intensive garden enterprise in the whole municipality.

The production-possibility frontier shows the land line to make up the entire frontier (Fig. 5.7). The choice is between having one cow or 3,500 m² of garden, and thus it is not a choice at all for no one could live on the profits from one cow. Either they must garden or move out. They garden at a high level of exploitation, and this provides them a very comfortable standard of living, as will be seen in the account (Table 5.14).

The profit-investment ratio is lower for this farm than for others because the land value is very high and increases overall investment and opportunity costs. Yet the fact remains that a tiny farm with miserable topography, located on a very high priced land, still makes an extremely good living from gardening with the gross profits coming to 805,000 pesetas. Net profits and payments to

Table 5.14. *Case 6: garden production account* (*in pesetas*)

A. Land		1,274,000.00
B. Capital		
B1. Buildings and machinery	328,000.00	
B2. Circulating	136,500.00	
Total		464,500.00
C. Production		941,500.00
D. Costs		136,500.00
E. Gross profits		805,000.00
F. Interest	104,310.00	
G. Labor	225,000.00	
(F + G)		329,310.00
H. Net profits		475,690.00

$$\frac{\text{Profit}}{\text{Investment}} = \frac{475,690.00}{1,738,500.00} = 27\%$$

Key to Table 5.14:

A. 3,500 m² garden × 364 pesetas per m² = 1,274,000 pesetas.
B1. Total value of fixed capital = 328,000 pesetas; entered as gardening is the only income source on the farm.
B2. Enter costs D = 136,500 pesetas.
 C. 269 pesetas per m² × 3,500 m² = 941,500 pesetas.
 D. 39 pesetas per m² × 3,500 m² = 136,500 pesetas.
 E. C − D = 805,000 pesetas.
 F. 6 percent × 1,738,500 (A + B) = 104,310 pesetas.
 G. 2.5 laborers × 90,000 pesetas = 225,000 pesetas.
 H. E − (F + G) = 475,690 pesetas.

labor come to about 700,000 pesetas, nearly $10,000. This income exceeds that of cases 1, 2, and 5, in spite of the much greater size of 1 and 5 and their high capital investments. The best cattle farm in Fuenterrabia cannot match the profits of this tiny farm. This is the significance of gardening in Fuenterrabia, especially for these small, marginal farms.

This domestic group has been sparked into this favorable position through the farmer's planning and impeccable execution of all farming tasks. Profoundly religious, he is considered a saintly man. He attends mass daily, and goes to the funerals of every person who passes away in Fuenterrabia, known or unknown to him personally. His ability has turned what could have been an abandoned farm into a profitable way of life. Interestingly, the farmer in case 4, famed for his entrepreneurial talents, is this man's sister's son.

The other two members of the family are moved along by him. The wife, though hard working, lacks intelligence, and his brother, having been undone by the things he witnessed in the army during the Civil War, lives in a state of constant depression.

The farmer's father bought this farm in the late 1920s, along with 0.80 ha. of river bottom lands. He also rented other river bottom land. They had been tenant farmers on an equally poor farm nearby. The farmer had three brothers, two older than he, plus the one living on the farm. All learned a trade and went to work off the farm. The elder brothers married and lived off the farm. He had two sisters who married, one onto the farm of case 4, and the other to a man in town. Thus he inherited the farm because the rest decided to move away and the younger brother decided not to marry.

His mother had died by the time he married in 1934 and his father died within a year of the marriage. Thus, he faced the inheritance settlement at the beginning of his marriage. The siblings inherited only the portion of the estate pertaining to the third of the legitimate offspring. Some got a little river bottom land as their part and the rest took payments in cash. At the end, the couple had about 2,000 m² of garden and seven cows which they supported through extensive rental of river bottom land.

It took eight years to pay off the inheritance settlement. During that difficult period, all of the topsoil on the upland part of the farm cascaded down the hillside one night, leaving only bedrock. The farmer brought it back up in wheelbarrows and put it in place again. Because the landslide had covered up a provincial road, the provincial government built a retaining wall at the bottom of the hill to hold it. But again in 1939 it fell away and was hauled up by hand. This time the farmer had a large cement retaining wall built halfway up the slope, an investment which took ten years to pay off. Since then the soil has not fallen again, though it requires constant attention to keep this from happening. They also rebuilt the house room by room, because it was in poor shape when they married.

So the first 15 years of marriage were very hard ones, with large debts and endless work. There were daily trips to the river bottom, to the mountainside and back, plus gardening, sale of vegetables, and other chores. The few cows they could raise provided them a very low income and they felt constantly pressured by economic need.

Although gardening became more profitable in the post-World War II period, he continued to devote most of his attention to cattle raising. However when a highway was cut through their river bottom land in 1963, the property was expropriated with a small indemnity. They had been long dissatisfied with cattle raising, but dared not drop it entirely. The loss of land forced a decision and they sold all their cows. To their own amazement, they immediately began to prosper, and they now have a large amount of savings.

They continue to exploit the farm, considering it to be insurance for them. They build up their savings yearly for the time when they cannot work. But they also work because they have come to prefer a life of work to one of leisure.

Being childless and owning a farm that will sell for a huge value, they are faced with an inheritance situation that makes life bitter for them. They are feuding with the sister's son from case 4. The only other close kin eligible for the inheritance is his other sister's son, a factory worker with 11 children and an unpleasant personality. He is openly courting their favor in view of their advancing years. They are not deluded by his play. They know he would never consider working the farm and would sell it immediately.

Though they must conform to the situation, they are bitter. They spent 36 years rebuilding the house and working the farm, but now the only prospect is of it being sold by an opportunist with slight feeling for it or for them. Here again is a case of people who value farming over urban living, but who will be the last to cultivate that farm.

They made a number of attempts, years ago, to adopt an heir. Once the matter had been settled when the fiancee of the heir-to-be suddenly refused to come to live on the farm. The couple finally gave up attempting to adopt an heir and resigned themselves to the fate of their farm. Thus a contingency that once could have been rectified by adoption now causes the abandonment of a farm.

The labors of this domestic group in their garden have a religious quality, recognized as such by other farmers. The farmer regards nature in a personal way; his garden is the testing ground on which he proves his worth as a human being. It is an old and well-known adversary and his domination of it, against very real physical odds, provides the core meaning of his life. In a sense, he conserves the relationship to the land that was characteristic of an earlier time here. He turns a profit, but it is a byproduct of his living out his own manhood by farming the land independently and with dignity.

Most people like him but think him strange. The young Basques are culturally so far removed from him that they have no idea how or why he lives, and yet his ideas would have been widely understood by young people no more than 20 years ago.

His attendance at funerals also merits comment. The enormous importance of funerary ritual has already been referred to (see Douglass, 1969). Not only was the farm thought of as a permanent part of a human landscape, but each farm was felt to have an identity that extended from the past to the future. The chief heir, as custodian of this identity, burned candles for those who lived on the farm before and expected subsequent generations of heirs to do the same. The farm, the chief heir, the dead and the living were tied into a single enterprise by which they also were born, lived, and ultimately could find salvation.

In the case of Fuenterrabia, this kind of funerary ritual is all but gone. Yet this man attends all funerals in Fuenterrabia because for him, Fuenterrabia is still a community of the living and the dead, and the living have an obligation to help the dead through Purgatory. His deepest concern is that with the farm gone and the young people living in the new urban world, no one will aid his soul in its passage into Heaven. He is a man conserving ideas now found only rarely among living Basques, ideas that help one to understand what farming once meant. His deep worry over the fate of his soul shows the price the survivors have paid for social change.

Conclusions

Most striking for me, as I developed the case histories of 20 farms, was how each farm appeared to be totally unique: a combination of different physical features, personalities, and problems. And yet, when the cases were reduced to their general results, the profit ratios, marketing problems, and process of farm abandonment were all there. While the reader can judge, I think there is a clear fit between my aggregate analysis and the case material presented.

Beyond this, the cases are most useful in bringing into focus the human proportions of the changes I have discussed. They make clearer the processes of reasoning and acting that led to the present condition of agriculture. They complete the analysis by bringing into it the behavioral focus washed out by the handling of aggregated data. It lends support to my argument for handling aggregated and domestic unit data from both the formal-economic and the cultural points of view.

I will briefly tie the analysis of these cases to the argument of the previous chapters. In five cases the production-possibility frontier is made up by the land and labor lines, and in one, by the land line alone, there being no case where the capital line forms part of the frontier. This is true of the 40 frontiers I constructed for cases not discussed. Though factors are scarce, lack of capital is not the cause of farm problems. This parallels the analysis of means of access in which capital is widely available.

The frontiers in cases 2, 3, 4, and 5, in which cattle raising and gardening are combined, show a tendency for the production point chosen to be toward more gardening. Given the higher profit ratio in gardening, where there is a choice, farmers tend to employ the factors in the speciality producing the highest profits on investment.

In cases 1 and 6 there is no choice of specialization. In both production is carried out at the highest possible volume, indicating that within the limits imposed by the farm, the factors are being employed to earn the highest possible return.

Differences in production-possibility frontiers thus impose different profit possibilities which must be achieved by different means. Thus the statistical homogenization of the rural economy can be a most risky endeavor, for the general economic trends, found in the aggregate data, are filtered through varying sets of production possibilities dictating different responses. That the frontiers emphasize this variation and allow a view of the operation of the general trends behind the diversity of the cases, is perhaps the greatest point in their favor as a technique of analysis.

By accounting individually for each specialization on each farm, I could test the profit-investment relationships seen in the general accounts, provide an idea of the magnitude of individual farms, and show something about concrete operations. A new piece of information was also gained. With one exception, beef production accounts show lower profits on investment than do milk production accounts. This serves to emphasize that the factors of production are employed in a way to allocate them to the specialization producing the highest profit on investment.

The accounts also support the aggregate accounts in that gardening, in every case, is much more profitable than any form of cattle exploitation. Most dramatic proof derives from the comparison of the best large cattle farm in Fuenterrabia with the best tiny garden farm, cases 1 and 6. This shows a much higher profit-investment ratio in the garden exploitation as well as a *higher absolute profit*. In the case of the various garden accounts, the strongest influence on profitability, beyond the level of exploitation, is the value of the land employed.

To the question why the cattle are maintained on the farms that could garden more, the cases provide some answers. Gardening and cattle raising are combined in four of the cases. In case 2 gardening is not expansible due to the land factor. There are many such cases. Cattle raising is thus carried on to add to income, even though it is known to be less profitable. In case 4, gardening can be expanded because there is enough of all the factors to permit expansion. However, expansion beyond 7,000 m² of garden is impossible because of the wholesale and retail vegetable markets. The farmer and his wife cannot market more than the produce of 7,000 m² in a year, and permanent labor cannot be hired for gardening. On other farms, with only two full-time laborers, this limits the size of gardens even more, for there are less man-hours available to distribute between producing vegetables and selling them.

Finally there are cases such as 3 and 5, in which the farmers' own preference to be somewhat self-sufficient in milk production for consumption and manure for fertilizer, or the preference for political and economic involvement in nonfarm activities result in the combination of cattle raising and gardening in spite of knowledge of the relative profits. These cases should not be shrugged off as unusual. As the aggregate analysis of the labor factor showed, outside involvement of labor is common, and may well account for a fair portion of the cattle raising that occurs, especially small-scale operations. A man may prefer to keep four cows and work full time at an urban job.

Keeping cattle also represents the farmers' general lack of confidence in the economic situation created by tourism and industrialization. It must be understood partly as the farmers' attempt to retain diversification in farming against the possibility of the collapse of either the markets for vegetables, milk, or beef. In terms of the experience of the last 50 years, this lack of confidence is certainly a good evaluation of the situation.

Although one can push such rationalizing explanations too far, it is clear that for a variety of reasons cattle raising and gardening will remain associated, in spite of the differences in their profitability. In concrete terms, 42 percent of the farms combine gardening and cattle raising, while 52 percent have only cattle, and 6 percent have only gardening. Of the cattle-only farms, 73 percent are restricted to cattle production by the lack of sandy loams on which to garden. This leaves 27 percent of the cattle-only farms that raise only cattle, when they could garden as well. This amounts to 14 percent of the total of farms in Fuenterrabia which do not follow the dictates of profit-making to the highest degree. Of the 6 percent of the farms having only gardening, all but one are too small to raise cattle profitably. In Fuenterrabia, no farm with sandy loam would be too small to provide an acceptable standard of living from gardening.

That the direct analysis of relative profitability of cattle raising and gardening does not adequately explain the activities of 14 percent of the farms, or alternatively, that profit ratios do explain the activities of 86 percent of the farms is for me an acceptable result. Given the wide variety of forces to which farms are subject, I find the 14 percent figure low and yet not so low as to cast doubt on the accuracy of the data gathered.

Other facts also emerged. Tenant farms have a very different relationship to the economy than do owner farms. In gardening, their profits are much higher because the large interest payments to the land employed in production do not have to be discounted. Their buildings tend to be in poor shape and investment in the stable area is low, raising profits in cattle raising also to relatively high levels. Thus, tenant farms, though being strongly pressured by landlords, are in a position to make considerable profits.

In case 2, a man working both as a bargeman and farmer can actually earn a better income than would be earned from urban moonlighting. This particular case is one in which the outside job was used to keep the farm going. This case should make one very cautious in interpreting the significance of outside involvement in urban jobs. Rather than being a necessary sign of agricultural collapse, it may indicate a strong commitment to agriculture on marginal farms.

Another point is that none of the six farmers has taken loans for purchase of equipment, livestock, or construction of buildings. These cases show that even very large amounts of capital, such as in case 4, are paid for with savings, making clear both the unwillingness to pay interest and the considerable availability of unused funds on the farms.

In the production histories of the farms, the general trend toward specialization and the increase of gardening at the expense of cattle raising is clear. In every case where there was a choice, gardening was expanded at the expense of cattle raising, with the most rapid expansion taking place since 1959. The factors are employed increasingly in the more profitable of the two specialities, although this has happened haltingly over the last 50 years. Beginning as a stop-gap measure to increase cash income, it has now become a major specialization with clear characteristics. As recently as 20 years ago, I think it would have been hard to identify this process even though it was in full swing.

The cases of farms 2, 3, 4, and 6 show gardening enabled them to survive. Had it not been for the appearance of highly profitable uses of small sections of land, these farms would have been abandoned long ago. Thus gardening has served, on small farms especially, as a temporary hedge against rural exodus.

Family histories themselves show the importance of the domestic cycle in this type of farming, especially in the present situation of labor scarcity. Though they are roughly comparable as gardeners, the activities of the families in cases 3 and 4 have very different purposes, ensuring economic security for old age as compared with educating and caring for many children. At critical junctures in the future these two farms and any others under similar conditions can be expected to make very different kinds of decisions, making broad generalizations risky.

The family histories also show the variety of ways in which farm abandonment occurs. Of the two cases in which there are young children, the tenants are soon going to leave farming, while the future of case 4 is in doubt. The two childless marriages will both end in farm abandonment since the adoption of an heir proved impossible. In cases 1 and 3, young but grown children all refuse to farm under any circumstances. This means that of six profitable farms, five will be abandoned and the best that can be said for case 4 is that the future is in doubt. There is no reason to consider this a quirk of my sample.

Every road leads to farm abandonment. Like so many small streams, inheritance squabbles, power plays by land developers, the decline of the prestige of agriculture, the failure to be able to adopt an heir, the lack of wage labor all feed into the same process, producing here, and apparently elsewhere, a torrent of rural depopulation. The human dimensions of the process need not be invoked here in novelistic fashion, but comprehension of the present age is not served by ignoring the sadness this has caused the older farmers. All the farms represent the results of the efforts and adjustments of a large number of people for whom these farms were the focus of all life's activity. As they carried on the efforts of their parents, whose old age they underwrote, they expected to receive the same treatment from their heir and to see the farm carried on.

And as the farmers are identified with the farm so intimately, their children's refusal to farm is much more than a mere change of occupation. The rejection of the farm is, in a real sense, the rejection of the parents themselves, a denial of the meaning of the way of life to which they are committed. The gulf between the young and the old is huge. The old wonder if all their efforts made any sense at all and the young assure them that they did not. This too is a cost of depopulation, not easily counted, but a cost nonetheless.

6

Conclusions

Having summarized the conclusions of each part of this study at the end of each chapter, I will not recapitulate them here. I prefer to present briefly the general implications of my findings.

In characterizing the commercialization of Basque agriculture over the last 50 years, I devoted much attention to the formal economic analysis of farming activities. My purpose was to demonstrate, rather than merely to assert, that in developing successful commercial specializations, the farmers showed ability to perceive avenues of economic gain and to exploit them successfully. The accounts, the census data, the problems in getting the factors of production together, and the case history material all show the farmers to have been responsive to their economic situation. One can only admire their abilities.

To demonstrate this responsiveness, not to assert it, was the point, because the economic acumen of the Basques does not derive here from a theoretical prejudgment that I have supplied. I collected this material, not to prove this point, but simply because I believe that all economic anthropologists should show clearly how, how much, and to what effect the subjects of their studies operate their particular modes of exploitation. Beyond my general assumption that most people are reasonably intelligent in their activities, I made no assumptions about the profitability of farming. However, the facts in Fuenterrabia are that farms are being steadily abandoned and that in a few years farming is likely to disappear. Because of the quantitative analysis I made, it is not possible to explain this rural depopulation by conventional means. A new explanation had to be elaborated.

The farms are being abandoned because the very same economic changes that helped make them profitable have brought farming, as a way of life, into conflict with long-held Basque ideas about man and about dignity in work. By migrating to the cities, they are sacrificing known economic rewards in service of these ideas. Further, commercialization has in itself increased old stresses within the domestic group and created life situations that are intolerable for most young Basques, while simultaneously opening up urban job opportunities.

What implications are to be drawn from this situation? Though I am fascinated by the suspension of the motive of pecuniary gain here, I see no point in romanticizing these people into a last outpost of morality in a capitalistic world. I firmly believe that other such unexpected results would be forthcoming if more studies were carried out in this vein. For this, the careful development of quantitative information, with all of the difficulties involved, is absolutely crucial. It is the lack of such evidence that makes it impossible at present to determine how representative the Basque situation is. This study shows that the process of commercialization is fraught with complexities often lost in our schematic models and generalized debates. I hope this work will stimulate closer scrutiny of other cases, with less theoretical prejudgment.

The complexity of this case shows that no simple behavioral assumptions or general models of agricultural commercialization can make sense of what these people are doing. They are neither "traditionalists" nor "modernists"; they are Basques who have worked out a complex adaptation to the world around them, one consistent with their history and the new elements forming part of their experience. The attempt to cut through this complexity with unidimensional models merely reduces Basque behavior to nonsense. A greater degree of complexity in the models we use to explain economic behavior is needed. The minimum acceptable level of complexity to explain behavior is higher than we often have been willing to admit.

When such a position was taken in the past, generally the cry has been raised that this is the defeat of social science. To hold that a specific case cannot be explained away by the laws of some general theory is taken as an attack on the theoretical edifice of social science. But surely our choice is not so stark; indeed to make it so is quite artificial. Unless one feels that the aim of social science is the articulation of a series of general laws of society of which all societies are merely examples, the question really comes down to the degree of complexity suited to a particular line of investigation. At present, I merely believe that more complexity is better in our search for understanding of economic change than less. In this, my approach is in the tradition of Firth (1966) and Salisbury (1962, 1970), who employ a judicious mix of general assumptions and attention to the specifics of each case.

The point is not so much the generalizability of the conclusions as it is the generalizability of the methods of analysis. While I have explained some of the special characteristics of the Basque situation, I have done so with methods easily transferrable to other cases. Analysis of variance in census data, formal accounting, the study of means of access to the factors of production, and production-possibility analysis all can be used in other cases to yield useful results. This is important because we must pursue the development of agreements about how to ask questions in a meaningful way before we can agree that answers have been provided in a particular case. I therefore do not wish to inflate the results of the Basque case into some universal explanation of rural depopulation.

However, this does not mean that the specific results of this study have no immediate and general implications. For peasant studies it should be clear that no simple or single model of "peasants" will suffice. There are many kinds of peasants in a variety of ecological situations and subject to different state organizations. They have unique cultural systems, mixing historical continuity with new elements. Whether convenient or not, all peasants must be understood in their particular historical, cultural, ecological, economic, and political setting. Nothing less will do.

In the pressing area of economic development policy, the implications are both clear and discouraging. There is no shortcut to the understanding of economic development. Macro-theories make no sense of Basques behavior. Each program of development must attend to the culture, history, and particularities of the people in question, or resign itself to accidental success or nearly certain failure.

In the particular case of the Basques in Fuenterrabia, the governmental planners are firmly committed to agriculture's disappearance. This is because they believe that agriculture is unprofitable. To them it is obvious. After all, no "modern" farms are small or operate on such poor terrain. That the people are leaving is "good," it shows how powerfully the industrial economy is attracting people into the cities. In fact everything is so obvious that nothing is being done. One cannot blame the planners for these judgments as they simply express their belief in theories current everywhere. But the long list of failed development efforts and the social costs of development programs, which have worsened rather than improved the distribution of wealth in many countries, is disturbing. It almost seems that no amount of failure can make planning more realistic, even in a country that has not succeeded with land reform after 150 years of effort.

Recent results in the development and extension of new varieties of wheat, corn, and rice show that the potential contributions of planning can be great, when the basic research is carried out in sufficient detail, that is, when the question is asked as to what is going on before the prescription for action is made out. The whole process of development is infinitely more complicated than we had ever dreamed. Perhaps the greatest challenge to economic anthropology is to find new ways to handle that complexity so that it can be made more immediately intelligible.

The problems in Basque agriculture have not been, on the whole, technical problems. The farmers have solved many of their technical problems and those that remain should not be difficult to surmount. It is the cultural context in which the development has taken place that turns high profits into rural depopulation. No amount of effort in basic research or government-sponsored technical aid programs would stop the farmers from leaving. The problem is not a technical one, in spite of what look to outsiders like inefficient agricultural practices.

Nor do the Basques need to be educated and made aware that they are leaving a good thing. To assume that because they are ignoring economic gains, they have made the wrong choice, and further, that it is our obligation to correct them, is to espouse the most crude form of ethnocentrism. They generally know what they are doing, and their choice of paths is one that will affect the future of the Basque country as a whole. Assignment of a judgment about the correctness of their actions will hardly help.

The most disquieting finding of all for me is that the market mechanism, which transmits the information to these people about supply and demand in the form of prices, did not determine their choice of activities. This is disturbing not because I think people should follow market incentives, but because, in most development planning, we rely on the assumption that the market mechanism can be depended on. It is this very assumption that blinds officials to the fact that Basque agriculture is more profitable, in this municipality, than the urban employment into which people are moving. Officials assume that people are following their own economic self-interest. In turn they limit their planning so that they manipulate people indirectly by intervening in the market rather than by more direct activity. This only works if people will respond properly.

In much of the thinking about agricultural development, the assumption is that existing forms of farming are not profitable. If a policy can make them profitable, there will be no trouble keeping people on the farms. In Fuenterrabia farming is becoming increasingly profitable, yet the people refuse to stay. These people are moving to the city when the market is signaling strongly for them to stay in farming. Thus the urban labor market is not pulling them in, and their presence in it is likely to drive low wages down even further.

On the agricultural side, the fact that profits do not keep them in farming means that the demand for food is strong but the producers do not care. At best a multiplication of this process can lead to a gross increase in food prices and at worst, an actual lack of food. Simultaneously, as noted above, urban wages may be declining. The stage is thus set for serious problems. Food prices rise as urban wages decline and all because the farmers are not obeying the demand signals emanating from the markets.

Perhaps this is an unduly bleak perspective, but it serves to dramatize the effects of the failure of the profit motive, when all governmental planning is based on the assumption that people will always strive to make the highest profits possible.

And perhaps the Basque case is merely unusual, the quirk of an odd people who speak a mysterious language. Given what is at stake, I do not think we can afford to guess about the answer. I hope to have provided a stimulus and some methods through which an adequate answer can be found.

Epilog

In 1969, Fuenterrabia was clearly undergoing drastic changes. Still I could not have imagined the rapidity with which the collapse of agriculture would come about.

I returned to Fuenterrabia for a few weeks in 1973 only to find out that the long-feared plan to rezone over half of the municipality had been approved. This legislative act converted most of the farming area into urban property which is subject to restrictions that virtually rule out agriculture. As a result, nearly 50 farms had already been sold and others were up for sale. The young Basques, who had rejected farming and its profits, were being joined in the cities by their parents who had never intended to be anything but farmers. What could have taken a generation occurred in four years.

On my last day there, I spoke with one of the most resourceful farmers. Though still hard at work on his farm, he told me of the measures he had taken to prepare his children for urban life. And he spoke uncertainly of his own future.

He was relaxed with me and I wondered why. With a smile, he confessed that my study of local economic life had worried him because he expected the government to use the information against the farmers. Asking about the fate of my book on Fuenterrabia, he suddenly said with an expression I shall never forget: "Go ahead and publish it. It doesn't matter anymore. It's all history now."

Notes

Chapter 1

1. By commercial farming, I mean only that almost all the produce, land, and capital are transacted through markets in terms of money prices.
2. The formalist school is generally considered to center on Raymond Firth, Richard Salisbury, and Harold Schneider. For a brief rendering of this view, see LeClair, 1962. The substantivist school centers on Karl Polanyi, George Dalton, Marshall Sahlins, and Paul Bohannan; the position is summarized in Dalton 1969. Recently Maurice Godelier has provided a review and trenchant critique of both positions in his *Rationalité et irrationalité en économie,* 1967. Whether or not these groups are sufficiently homogeneous to be called "schools" is a matter deserving detailed consideration in the future, but it would be out of place here. I do not align myself with either side.
3. A critical review of the peasant literature from this perspective is needed. I have undertaken part of it in Greenwood, 1974.
4. In Greenwood, 1974, a good deal of attention is devoted to the characteristics of the peasant-state as a system of adaptation.
5. In lectures given at the Department of Anthropology, University of Pittsburgh, during the year 1967–1968.
6. For a brief representation of the struggle that develops between those arguing for greater detail and complexity in planning and those who see this as the defeat of planning as a whole, see Mellor, 1969 and Eicher's comment, 1969.

Chapter 2

7. See the municipal map (p. 4) for its location.
8. The basis for classification was personal observation, in about half of the cases. The rest were classified by the local veterinarian.
9. For a brief and clear discussion of the concept of opportunity cost, see Dorfman, 1964:22–26.

Chapter 3

10. The sawdust and woodshavings are gaining popularity because they are simply trucked in and yet, mixed with manure, produce good results when used in the fields.
11. This one-third figure is a correction suggested by one of the anonymous readers of the manuscript. I lowered it slightly more because of the very rainy climate.
12. A few are buying garden tractors and experimenting with new seedbed techniques.

Chapter 4

13. There may be a semantic problem in my use of the term "substantive," because of the debate in economic anthropology. Most of the statements here are generalizations, and while they are derived partly from observation, the handling of them is in terms of my own formulation of the rules and conditions affecting behavior. It is more discursive and less statistical than the previous section, but it is not an attempt to render the "native" point of view in pure form. I call it "substantive" analysis, but it could be called "cultural" analysis. I am more attached to the analysis than to the terminology.

14. This distinction was made in lectures on the Cultures of the Middle East at the University of Pittsburgh, 1968.

15. Marriage contracts, duly notarized, which establish formally all conditions of this relationship and of the inheritance of land are not known in Fuenterrabia, though the practice is common in much of the Basque country. For more information, see Echegaray, 1950.

16. The only way a spouse could gain ownership at the death of the parents-in-law is if they chose to will to him part or all of their thirds of *libre elección* (see note 17).

17. In Spanish these are *el tercio de la legítma, el tercio de mejora,* and *el tercio de la libre elección.*

18. This third is divided into as many equal parts as there are legitimate offspring.

19. For a complete discussion of repudiations, see the *Código Civil,* Arts. 988–1,009.

20. Unless the heir is an unmarried, only child.

21. *Aparcería* will be discussed under reciprocal arrangements.

22. According to early maps lent to me by Don Julio Caro Baroja.

23. This information was supplied by the Caja de Ahorros Provincial de Guipúzcoa, Fuenterrabia branch, and was in effect as of May, 1969.

24. Payments may be for up to 30 years now. Until recently the limit for such loans was 20 years.

25. This insurance applies to a man's whole family and a man with aged parents often finds this the most economical way of providing health care for them.

26. This information was supplied by the Caja de Ahorros Provincial de Guipúzcoa, Fuenterrabia branch, and refers to May of 1969.

27. This figure is arrived at by calculating manure as a cost, as if it were purchased outside the farm.

Chapter 5

28. Throughout I indicate the farm plot sizes in rounded off hectare figures, but in the accounts, I use the exact square meter sizes as given to me by the cartographer.

29. The cattle possibilities are all treated as if the animals were milch cows, two of which can be supported by 10,000 m² of land. The number of beeves would be one-third larger, since three beeves can be raised on 10,000 m².

30. I am indebted to an anonymous reader of the manuscript for this clarification.

31. While the accounts and analyses of the six cases are as specific as I could make them, the reader should not interpret them as actual accounts in the sense of a day-by-day listing of expenditures made and profits earned. No farmer ever permitted me that kind of private information. What I did was to measure plots, observe the cattle, watch the care and feeding of the animals, and generally to keep track of farm operations. On this basis, I built up as specific a picture as

possible of the economic activities. House values, other investments, and labor should be quite accurate. In gardening and cattle raising, I had to rely on my categorizing of these farms according to exploitation levels, as described earlier. Thus the sets of data are approximations, rather than specific measurements of activities. These approximations are as accurate as I could make them, but are nothing more than approximations.

Of course, the profits the farmers made were checked in a variety of ways. I observed the kinds of items they purchased, the improvements made in their homes, and other disbursements of income in order to determine whether or not my accounts could fit with these consumption activities. I am satisfied that they do.

References

Adán de Yarza, Ramon (n.d.) "Descripción físico-geológica," in Francisco Carreras y Candi, ed., *Geografía general del País Vasco-Navarro*, Vol. 1, *País Vasco-Navarro*. Barcelona: Establecimiento Editorial de Alberto Martín, page reference lost.

Caro Baroja, Julio (1958) *Los Vascos*. 2nd edition, revised. Madrid: Ediciones Minotauro.

(1963) "The City and the Country: Reflexions on Some Ancient Commonplaces," in Julian Pitt-Rivers, ed., *Mediterranean Countrymen*. The Hague: Mouton & Co., pp. 27–40.

(1967) "Ensayo preliminar," *País Vasco*, Colección "Imágenes de España." Madrid: Editorial Clave, S.A., pp. 6–19.

(1971) *Etnografía histórica de Navarra*. 3 volumes. Pamplona: Editorial Aranzadi.

Chayanov, A. V. (1966) *The Theory of Peasant Economy*. Daniel Thorner, Basile Kerblay, and R. E. F. Smith, eds. Homewood, Ill.: Irwin.

Código Civil (1965) 12th edition, Colección popular de leyes y códigos, Vol. 1. Madrid: Editorial Góngora, S.A.

Dalton, George (1969) "Theoretical Issues in Economic Anthropology," *Current Anthropology* 10:63–101.

Dorfman, Robert (1964) *The Price System*. Englewood Cliffs, N.J.: Prentice-Hall.

Douglass, William A. (1969) *Death in Murélaga*. Monograph 49, American Ethnological Society. Seattle: University of Washington Press.

(1971) "Rural Exodus in Two Spanish Basque Villages: A Cultural Explanation," *American Anthropologist* 73:1100–14.

(1975) *Echalar and Murélaga: Opportunity and Rural Exodus in Two Spanish Basque Villages*. New York: St. Martin's Press.

Echegaray, Bonifacio de (1933) *La vecindad: relaciones que engendra en el País Vasco*. San Sebastián: Eusko-Ikaskuntza, Sociedad de Estudios Vascos.

(1950) *Derecho foral privado*. San Sebastián: Biblioteca Vascongada de los Amigos del País.

Eicher, Carl (1969) "Comment: The Subsistence Farmer in Traditional Economies," in Clifton Wharton, Jr., ed., *Subsistence Agriculture and Economic Development*. Chicago: Aldine, pp. 227–8.

Firth, Raymond (1966) *Malay Fishermen: Their Peasant Economy.* 2nd edition, revised. Hamden, Conn.: Archon Books, (originally published in 1944).

Godelier, Maurice (1967) *Racionalidad e irracionalidad en la economía.* Nicole Blanc, trans. Siglo Veintiuno Editores, S.A., México (originally published as *Rationalité et irrationalité en économie.* Paris: Librairie François Maspero; English edition, *Rationality and Irrationality in Economics.* New Left Books, London, 1973).

Greenwood, Davydd (1972) "Tourism as an Agent of Change: A Spanish Basque Case," *Ethnology* 11(1):80–91.

(1974) "Political Economy and Adaptive Processes: A Framework for the Study of Peasant-States," *Peasant Studies Newsletter* 3(3):1–10.

Hill, Polly (1970) *Studies in Rural Capitalism in West Africa.* Cambridge: Cambridge University Press.

Laffitte, Vicente (n.d.) "La industria sidrícola y la ganadería de Guipúz coa," in *Album gráfico del País Vascongado: Guipúzcoa.* Title page missing, 82–4.

Larramendi, Manuel de. S.J. (1969) *Corografía o descripción general de la Muy Noble y Muy Leal Provincia de Guipúzcoa.* J. Ignacio Tellechea Idígoras, ed. San Sebastián; Sociedad Guipuzcoana de Ediciones y Publicaciones, S. A., (manuscript composed about 1754).

LeClair, Edward, Jr. (1962) "Economic Theory and Economic Anthropology," *American Anthropologist* 64:1179–203.

Mellor, John (1969) "The Subsistence Farmer in Traditional Economies," in Clifton Wharton, Jr., ed., *Subsistence Agriculture and Economic Development.* Chicago: Aldine, pp. 209–27.

Polanyi, Karl (1944) *The Great Transformation.* New York: Holt, Rinehart and Winston.

Pospisil, Leopold (1963) *Kapauku Papuan Economy.* Yale University Publications in Anthropology, No. 67. New Haven, Conn.: Yale University Press.

Potter, Jack, May Diaz and George Foster, eds. (1967) *Peasant Society: A Reader.* Boston, Mass.: Little, Brown.

Primer censo agrario de España: Octubre de 1962, Guipúzcoa, No. 20. (1964) Instituto Nacional de Estadística, in conjunction with the Ministerio de Agricultura and the Organización Sindical, Madrid.

Salisbury, Richard (1962) *From Stone to Steel.* London: Melbourne University Press and Cambridge University Press.

(1970) *Vunamami.* Berkeley: University of California Press.

Samuelson Paul (1967) *Economics: An Introductory Analysis.* 7th edition. Tokyo: McGraw-Hill, International Student Edition, Kogakusha Company.

Sokal, Robert R. and F. James Rohlf (1969) *Biometry: The Principles and Practice of Statistics in Biological Research.* San Francisco: W. H. Freeman.

Tax, Sol (1953) *Penny Capitalism.* Chicago: University of Chicago Press.

Wolf, Eric (1966) *Peasants.* Englewood Cliffs, N.J.: Prentice-Hall.

Conversion table of weights and measures

Unit of measurement	U.S. equivalent
1 céntimo	$.0014 (1969 exchange rate)
1 peseta (100 céntimos)	$.014 (1969 exchange rate)
1 square meter	1,550 square inches
1 hectare (10,000 square meters)	2.471 acres
1 square kilometer (10 hectares)	.3861 square miles
1 lineal kilometer	.62137 miles
1 kilogram (1,000 grams)	2.2046 pounds
1 liter	1.0567 quarts

Index